PEOPLE AND SOCIETY
IN SCOTLAND

PEOPLE AND SOCIETY IN SCOTLAND

III
1914–1990

Edited by
TONY DICKSON
and
JAMES H. TREBLE

A Social History of Modern Scotland
in Three Volumes

JOHN DONALD PUBLISHERS LTD
IN ASSOCIATION WITH
THE ECONOMIC AND SOCIAL HISTORY
SOCIETY OF SCOTLAND

ISBN 0 85976 212 2

Reprinted 1994
Reprinted 1998

Acknowledgements

We would like to thank the People's Palace, Glasgow, the Springburn
Museum Trust, and the Picture Library of the Communist Party of
Great Britain for their permission to reproduce the relevant photographs
in this collection.

T.D.
J.H.T.

Also in this series:

People and Society in Scotland, I: 1760–1830
edited by T. M. Devine and Rosalind Mitchison

People and Society in Scotland II: 1830–1914
edited by W. Hamish Fraser and R. J. Morris

British Library Cataloguing in Publication Data
A catalogue record for this book is available from the British Library.

Phototypeset by The Midlands Book Typesetting Company, Loughborough
Printed and bound in Great Britain by J. W. Arrowsmith Ltd., Bristol

General Introduction

Modern Scottish historical studies have experienced a vigorous phase of unprecedented growth over the last quarter of a century. Scholars are addressing a novel range of issues and themes, fresh perspectives on established topics are common and innovative methods are helping to transform the nature of research investigation. The subject has, in consequence, a new intellectual vitality. Of course, much remains to be done. Indeed, one of the fascinations for the professional historian is that so many key areas still remain unexplored. This contributes both to the challenge and the excitement of ongoing research in the archives and libraries. But substantial advances have already been made in the serious study of Scottish society since the eighteenth century and have produced results which warrant exposure to a wider audience than the readership of learned journals and scholarly monographs.

In 1985 the Economic and Social History Society of Scotland and John Donald Publishers agreed to publish a three-volume social history of Scotland from the middle decades of the eighteenth century to the present day. It is intended that the series should appear over a cycle of three years from 1988. Each volume has two editors and all contributors are recognised authorities in their respective fields. The project as a whole was supervised by an editorial committee appointed by the Society, consisting of T. M. Devine, Chairman (Strathclyde University), Anne Crowther (Glasgow University), T. Dickson (Glasgow College of Technology), W Hamish Fraser (Strathclyde University), Rosalind Mitchison (Edinburgh University), R. J. Morris (Edinburgh University) and J. H. Treble (Strathclyde University).

The series is intended to appeal to undergraduate and postgraduate students, lecturers, teachers, archivists, museum staff, local historians and others with an interest in the social history of modern Scotland. Each author attempts to convey the results of recent published research while at the same time introducing insights, interpretations and evidence from their own personal investigations. None of the various themes are analysed in an exhaustive fashion but contributors provide in the notes at the end of each chapter references to the most important published work in the relevant field as a guide to further reading. Individual chapters convey something of the vitality of the subject at its present stage of development. Historical analysis inevitably produces variations in opinion, method and conclusion and these are honestly revealed in the different approaches adopted by different contributors. The editors made no attempt to iron out contrasting interpretations of key issues. The resulting volumes are therefore not so much bland textbooks as studies which reveal the 'state of the art' in modern Scottish history.

T. M. Devine
Chairman
Editorial Advisory Committee

The Economic and Social History Society of Scotland

Over the last few years there has been a remarkable increase in both popular interest and serious research in Scottish historical studies. A series of major books have appeared; local history societies are flourishing: museums continue to improve in both quality and quantity; in television and press there is a new fascination with Scotland's history.

The subject is now taught in seven of the eight Scottish universities and curricular changes in school examinations ensure that more attention is devoted than ever before to the study of Scottish historical development. The Economic and Social History Society of Scotland was formed in 1983 to provide a national focus for much of the current research which is being undertaken in this expanding field. Its current membership of around 500 includes professional historians from universities and colleges, schoolteachers, undergraduate and postgraduate students, representatives from local history societies and museums, and members of the public with an interest in Scottish history. Most come from the United Kingdom but there are several also from Australasia, Canada, Europe, Ireland, Japan and the U.S.A. Members automatically receive a copy of the Society's journal, *Scottish Economic and Social History*. The first issue was published in 1981 and annual volumes of approximately 150 pages in length have appeared since then. The journal always includes the following items.

★ Three to four main articles. These are based on original research or contain critical evaluations of recent work on major themes. In the last four years essays have been published on the Highland Clearances; the Union of 1707; Early Modern Towns; Urban Elites; the Clyde Tobacco Fleet; the Twentieth-Century Economy; Literacy and Education in Scotland

★ A comprehensive book review section with essays on new publications of general interest and specialised reviews of recent work.

★ An annual *Register of Research* which lists the interest of individuals engaged in serious research in this field.

★ A list of annual publications of both books and articles.

The Society also publishes an annual *Newsletter* with a diary of forthcoming events, conferences and seminars of interest to members. The *Newsletter* in addition provides a focus for correspondence relating to the Society's activities and development.

Among ESHSS's most successful activities are its conferences which are normally held twice a year in different centres throughout Scotland. At each meeting a particular topic is explored in depth with formal lectures combining with panel discussions and workshop sessions. Recent conferences have focused on Women in Scottish Society, Business Elites, Urban History and Unemployment in the Twentieth Century.

In September 1987, the Society organised its first Residential Conference at the University of Aberdeen on the Society and Economy of the North of Scotland, 1700 to the Present, with sessions on Government and Crofting; Famine; Migration and Emigration; Landlords.

If you are interested in Scottish history or economic and social history and want to keep abreast of developments in the field your modest membership fee will be a worthwhile investment. Applications for membership and further information should be addressed to ESHSS, Department of History, University of Strathclyde, McCance Building, 16 Richmond Street, Glasgow G1 1XQ, Scotland.

Contributors

Michael Anderson
Professor of Economic History, University of Edinburgh

Callum G. Brown *
Senior Lecturer in History, University of Strathclyde

Tony Dickson
Professor and Assistant Director (Resources), Newcastle Polytechnic

John Foster
Professor of Applied Social Studies, Paisley College of Technology

Christopher Harvie
Professor in British Studies, University of Tubingen

William Knox
Lecturer in Scottish History, University of St Andrews

David McCrone
Reader in Sociology, University of Edinburgh

Arthur J. McIvor
Lecturer in Economic and Social History, University of Strathclyde

Andrew McPherson
Professor and director, Centre for Educational Sociology, University of Edinburgh

T. C. Smout
Professor of Scottish History, University of St Andrews

James H. Treble
Visiting Fellow in Social History, University of Strathclyde

Illustrations

Contents

Scotland, 1914-1990

Tony Dickson and Jim Treble

The story of Scotland in the twentieth century reflects the curious duality of its development since the Act of Union in 1707–locked into its involvement with the general processes affecting British society yet retaining quite distinctive features that give an enduring base for the assertion of a unique Scottish identity. Thus, many of the major changes in Scotland since 1914 reflected the wider transformation of the economic and social structure of Britain. At the same time, the precise trajectory and impact of these changes was often different when expressed in the particular context of Scottish experience. The development of the Scottish economy illustrates this especially clearly.

In 1914 the Scottish economy was still dominated by iron and steel, coalmining, shipbuilding, heavy engineering and textiles. To some extent, of course, each of these industries was a self contained economic entity, subject to the rhythms and logic of its own market. In the case of coalmining and textile production the prosperity or otherwise of individual firms owed little directly to the prevailing fortunes of other sectors of the staple trades. The same verdict, however, could not be applied to shipbuilding, steel and important segments of the engineering industries. For, to emphasise the exclusive aspects of their markets without highlighting the strength of the linkages which existed between them, provides at best only a partial insight into the dynamics of these major sectors of Scotland's industrial base. In a few instances these linkages were legally formalised. This was true of Beardmore's, iron and steel producers in the east end of Glasgow, who guaranteed a secure outlet for their castings and steel plates by taking over the Napier Shipyard in 1900. Six years later they were to extend their stake in the shipbuilding industry when they laid down new berths at Dalmuir.

However, in the majority of cases the ties which bound together these three different layers of heavy industry derived their sanction not from the process of vertical integration but from shared economic interests. Thus, any prolonged period of bad trade in shipbuilding –such as that, for example, which occurred during 1908-1909–speedily affected employment prospects and profitability among suppliers and sub-contractors in the two remaining elements of the metallic trades.

1

Equally important for the health of the Scottish economy, any downturn in the general level of economic activity in the staples was quickly transmitted, via the mechanism of the multiplier, to other areas of the labour market. Expressed in another form, the economic vitality of the country had by 1914 became unduly dependent upon the performance of the staples (including textiles and coal) in increasingly competitive British and international markets.

That competition had already left its imprint upon significant components of the textile industry. From the 1870s onwards the Scottish cotton industry had experienced an almost unbroken process of contraction, unable to respond to the challenge of more efficient producers in Lancashire and India. Similarly Dundee's jute barons had been compelled, by the mid-1880s, to cede ground to Indian companies in the market for coarse sacking,although they were to show much greater flexibility than the majority of their counterparts in cotton by concentrating thereafter upon retaining their hold on a still buoyant world market for more specialised lines. Elsewhere the high cost structure of the Scottish steel industry made it vulnerable to external threat and helped to reinforce the dependence of some firms upon the price discounting arrangements for their steel plates which they had concluded with Clydeside shipyards. Finally, swathes of the engineering industry, largely tied to labour intensive methods of production and product differentiation, failed to perceive the nature of the threat to their traditional markets which was presented by foreign rivals who had invested heavily in plant and who were prepared to exploit the greater growth potential of standardised capital goods and standardised spare parts.

The outbreak of conflict, however, in 1914 meant that many of these challenges were temporarily forgotten as manufacturing industry was compelled to respond to the distinctive demands of the war economy. Scarcely surprisingly, because of their pivotal role in meeting the material requirements of the war effort, Scotland's metallic trades experienced boom conditions throughout the years 1914-1918. Yet, in the light of the pattern of events that followed, it is also clear that the First World War represented a watershed in the fortunes of Scottish heavy industry since, notwithstanding the short-lived boom of 1919-1920, the inter-war era witnessed the emergence of deep-seated structural problems that owed something to the legacy of the war itself but which owed much more to changing conditions of the world and domestic markets. Among the range of adverse factors that were to pressurise entrepreneurs operating in this sector of the economy, were the rise of foreign competition, the return to the Gold Standard in 1925 at the pre-war pound sterling/dollar exchange rate, the growth of protectionism and the threat posed by product substitution.

The social sequel to these deleterious trends was a contraction in the size of the textiles, shipbuilding, coalmining and iron and steel industries and the emergence of mass unemployment which cast baleful shadows across the strongholds of heavy industry in the West-Central belt. Those shadows appeared in their most menacing form during the profound slump of 1929-1933. But they were never simply a cyclical phenomenon. For, after 1920, they were to disfigure Scotland's industrial landscape throughout the remainder of the inter-war period. While, therefore, the rearmament programme of the late 1930s provided some stimulus to these depressed areas of the Scottish economy, it was never sufficient by itself to undo the damage to the social fabric that had been inflicted by long-term structural unemployment. Indeed, the depressed state of the labour market was itself a major factor in retarding the pace and direction of change in Scotland's industrial structure.

Once more it was to require the outbreak of war in 1939 to revitalise the country's traditional manufacturing base and the prospects of its working population. The advent of peace in 1945 did not, however, bring in its wake the widespread economic dislocation which had characterised the inter-war era. Between 1945 and 1960 unemployment remained relatively low; regional policy, promoted initially by the 1945-1951 Labour government, yielded new growth points in the Scottish economy; the staple industries, in the first flush of peace, seemed to have escaped from the difficulties which had beset them in the 1920s and 1930s; and, what was a new phenomenon, foreign firms emerged as major investors in manufacturing. Nevertheless these gains, real as they were, have to be kept in perspective. Unemployment during the 1950s remained consistently higher in Scotland than in Britain as a whole, while the size of the occupied population in the West-Central belt recorded only the most modest growth between the 1951 and 1961 Censuses. In short, by 1960 economic diversification had not proceeded far enough to offset the fact that heavy industry, even in this relatively propitious climate, could no longer act as a powerful generator of economic growth.

When, from this point in time onwards, the country's engineering, shipbuilding, steel and coalmining industries, confronted by vigorous foreign competitors and shift in the demand for their goods, resumed their downward slide, the vulnerability of the Scottish economy was fully exposed. That vulnerability meant that the radical restructuring of the domestic economy which was to occupy the next three decades but whose origins can be traced back to the 1930s and 1940s, imposed considerable burdens upon groups of workers whose livelihoods had been inextricably linked with the fortunes of heavy industry. During the 1960s and 1970s there was a steady decline in the number of jobs in manufacturing. During the 1980s the shedding of blue collar workers continued at an accelerating rate. Inevitably much of this loss was concentrated in the staple trades, although the chronology of this process varied not merely from industry to industry but also, even within a single industry, from location to location. None the less all was not gloom since alongside the decline of heavy industry has to be placed the creation of new employment outlets in light engineering, the service industries and white collar occupations. The net result of these kaleidoscopic changes was that by 1991 the industrial classification of the occupied population differed radically from what it had been at the start of our period of study, a conclusion that is underlined by the declining importance of blue collar jobs in the national labour market[1].

This fundamental restructuring of the Scottish economy forms the backdrop against which must be set a complex series of changes in the experiences of individuals and groups in Scotland since 1914. Pre-eminent among those experiences which can be causally related to the undynamic nature of the job market was the continuing loss of a substantial part of the natural rate of increase of the country's population through out-migration, as men and women, drawn overwhelmingly from the economically active age groups, moved to England and abroad in search of employment.[2] Between 1901 and 1961 the scale of this outflow was equivalent to more than 65% of the natural rate of increase, although within these six decades there were substantial differences in the timing and dimensions of that movement. Net migration reached its peak in the depressed conditions of the 1920s. But it was also to reach high levels during the more benign economic climate of the 1950s and harsher environment of the 1960s. In fact, surveying the post-1911 decades as a whole, it was only during the 1930s when job opportunities outside Scotland were adversely affected by a depression which afflicted all the advanced industrial countries of the capitalist world and during the 1940s when they were influenced by the demands of total war, that net migration was reduced to more modest proportions. Nevertheless, notwithstanding the unevenness of this pattern, the important point which must be stressed is that throughout every decade with which this volume is concerned, it never ceased–tangible evidence that there was a marked divergence between the growth rate of the labour market and the rate of natural increase of Scotland's population which made out-migration an economic necessity.

The question which remains to be answered is how those who stayed, responded, in their working lives, to the course of economic change that we have outlined. Such changes, when judged with hindsight within a wider comparative framework, may of course seem inevitable. But that was not how they were viewed by those affected by them. The shifts away from manufacturing, the decline of the craft unions which dominated Scottish trade unionism from 1914 to the 1960s, the waves of job losses in the 1920s and from the 1960s onwards–all of these were contested by the participants. From the conflicts that created the imagery of Red Clydeside in the First World War and the Rent Strikes which influenced the 1919 Housing Act; through the General Strike of 1926 and the 'Little Moscows' that sprang up as centres of radical local political action in the inter-war period; to the UCS Work-In that forced the Conservative Government of the time into its famous "U-Turn"; to the various locally based work-ins that accompanied the job losses of the 1980s–the history of occupational and economic changes in Scotland has been one of popular resistance to those features of this process which were seen to be eroding employment opportunities and established patterns of working[3].

It would be a mistake, however, to view these changes solely in terms of industrial relations conflicts and work-based resistance. For many people they had much more positive connotations. For example, it is worth remembering that until 1939 the largest single employment outlet for women was domestic service, usually in conditions of extreme drudgery and exploitation. The experience of both World Wars was to give many women a positive insight into the world of collective employment, even if post-war reassertions of the status quo were designed to force females out of those sectors of work traditionally dominated by men. Nevertheless, the full employment conditions of the 1950s, together with the shift towards such occupations as teaching, nursing, the professions, office work and the retail trade ensured a consistent demand for women's labour. At the same time, changing social conditions such as the reduction in the number of children per family, have been reflected in important alterations in patterns of female employment. For example, in 1921 only 6.3% of employed women were married; by 1981 this figure had risen to 62%. The female participation rate in the economy has risen from 32% in 1921 to 42% in 1981[4].

But, if some of the conditions of female employment have improved and expanded, many aspects of discrimination against women in the labour market remain. For instance female employees are often employed only on a part-time basis. Between 1951 and 1981 the proportion of female jobs that were part-time rose from 5% to 41%. Furthermore, even within these sectors of the economy where women are well represented, few females are to be found in the senior managerial ranks. Scarcely surprisingly both low pay and low status are the usual characteristics of women's jobs in contemporary Scotland. Equality of opportunity in employment for women is still a distant goal.

At the same time, the changing experiences of women in Scotland cannot be divorced from the dramatic improvements in social conditions during the century. For at least half of this century many Scots were exposed to appalling housing, diet and working conditions. In 1911 12.8% of dwellings in Scotland consisted of one room. Even by 1951 31.7% of all Scottish houses had only one or two rooms. In the same year 43% of households did not have access to a fixed bath and more than a third shared a WC. Only from the late 1950s did the housing boom initiated by local authorities begin to have an ameliorative impact on housing conditions. Again, in the 1930s infant mortality in Scotland was the worst in Western Europe apart from Spain and Portugal. In these circumstances the impact of improved nutrition could be dramatic. During the Second World War when the food market was controlled by rationing rather than the price mechanism, the average height of Glasgow children aged 13 increased by just under 2 inches, while the number of children dying in their first year fell by 27%–the largest fall anywhere in Europe[5].

The watershed for these major improvements in the living conditions of Scots was the Second World War. After 1945 a series of changes combined to enhance the quality of most people's lives–better housing, rising wages, more employment, better diet and medical care, the easy availability of contraception as an aid to limiting family size. From the 1960s onwards there was a second wave of relative affluence reflected in the consumer boom that had such an impact on the nature of domestic life. These long term improvements illustrate the dangers of analysing changes in the economy and in occupational structure in isolation from the wider social and cultural processes in which they are enmeshed. Since 1914 there have clearly been profound shifts in the everyday lives of the Scots.

Religious affiliations have altered and loosened. Secularisation, measured in terms of church attendance and membership, has affected Scotland as it has most Western European countries. However, the declining influence of the churches in Scotland has to be qualified in various ways. First, the higher birth rates of Catholics meant that over time they claimed an increasing share in the total number of church adherents in Scotland as a whole, although after 1970 the Catholic Church seems to have begun to suffer from the same decline in church attendance that their Protestant counterparts had experienced somewhat earlier. Second, the decline in religious affiliation amongst Protestants has been an uneven process, with periods of revival that seem to have been associated with times of economic recession. Nevertheless, the process of religious disaffiliation accelerated in the 1960s as the impact of mass leisure pursuits drew people away from the Churches, especially among the young who were affected by the youth oriented consumerism of the 1960s and 1970s. Third, secularisation has been a geographically uneven process, having least effect in those outlying regions of Scotland where the circumstances of community life are more supportive of a close-knit religious collectivism. Thus, the Hebrides and the Western Highlands in the 1980s demonstrated a higher level of church attendance than any other part of mainland Britain[6].

The process of secularisation since 1914 should not disguise the very real sectarian antagonisms that have often characterised social life in Scotland in this century. Discrimination on religious grounds was commonplace in certain sectors of the job market, where Catholics were markedly under-represented in some of the skilled trades–particularly in shipbuilding and engineering–and correspondingly over-represented in many of the strongholds of unskilled labour. The slump in the 1920s and 1930s provided a base for stridently anti-Catholic groups to win seats at local elections. The process of Catholic assimilation in Scotland has therefore been a protracted one, mediated through the close association since the 1920s between the Labour Party and the Catholic vote. Perhaps a good symbolic guide to how slow and uneven that process has been is the decision in the late 1980s by Glasgow Rangers to sign a Catholic player for the first time in their history. The fierce reaction against the decision by many of their supporters is a reminder of the underlying tensions that still remain.

Intertwined with the secularisation process in Scotland has been the transformation in the social and cultural life of most Scots. In common with the rest of Britain, the general rise in living standards has been reflected in the consumer and leisure revolution. From the 1950s domestic life has changed radically as the acquisition of washing machines, vacuum cleaners, cars, telephones, televisions, video recorders has pointed towards a concern with family centred home life that has been described by many commentators as 'privatised', that is, concerned with the immediate interests of individuals and those with whom they share their house, rather than with the neighbourhood and wider community. At the same time cultural life has been increasingly focussed at the national or international level, as the products of national newspapers and national television networks have been beamed to homes throughout Britain. Reinforcing this trend has been the revolution in holiday making as Scots, in common with the rest of Britain, have developed a liking for holidays abroad.

The impact of these changes is in two areas. First, Scots have become part of a much wider British and international community as a result of the mass impact of alterations in their cultural and leisure pursuits. Second, the sharply defined class differences that characterised the first half of this century have become more blurred. For example, the absolute divide between the gentry with their predeliction for grouse shooting and salmon fishing, and the day trips 'doon the watter' by the working class of glasgow has been eroded. Whilst income differentials are still clearly an important determinant of leisure opportunities the effect of mass communications and the consumerism of the last thirty years has been to impart more homogeneity to people's social activities. Even the male dominated character of Scottish pubs has been removed by the development of facilities aimed at providing a comfortable environment for all customers to enjoy the consumption of alcohol[7].

On the basis of these kinds of changes it might be tempting to conclude that the history of Scotland in the twentieth century is little more than that of a region of Britain adjusting to the same processes of economic and social restructuring that have affected the rest of the British Isles. Yet, there are good grounds for arguing that this would be an extremely limited and flawed assumption. Despite the relevance of these general changes, much of Scottish life and social development points to the continuing distinctiveness of Scottish experience and identity. For one thing, its educational system remains quite separate from that of England and Wales. The structure and content of qualifications are different both at school and higher education levels, with the Scottish ordinary degree and four year honours degree being more similar to European systems than to that which prevails in England. Comprehensivisation of schools in Scotland took hold earlier and was more complete. In more general terms it has been an important factor in reducing class differences in educational attainment as well as ensuring that a far higher proportion of the population gain access to a higher education than is the case in England[8].

Other institutions of Scottish civil society exhibit these differences.

The Church of Scotland, albeit with a declining flock, continues to see itself as speaking with a national voice, drawing on the legacy of collectivism and democracy in its internal organisation to attack the policies of the Thatcher administrations after 1979 as alien to and inappropriate for Scotland. The Scottish legal system has its origins in European traditions quite different from those that underpin the English system, and operates in distinctive ways, such as through Children's Panels and the office of the Procurator Fiscal. Thus, there is a long established and continuing basis on which the social institutions of Scotland provide a distinctive Scottish identity.

In addition, as already indicated above, there is also a long history in Scotland of popular resistance, whether to landlords (as in the Clearances, the Crofters War, and Rent Strikes) or to employers (as in the dilution struggles of the First World War and the UCS Work-In). This history developed, as the Labour Party emerged, a political expression increasingly associated with that party though not without significant periods in which support was fragmented between the ILP, the Liberal Party, and nationalist movements. Nevertheless, by the end of the Second World War, the main division in Scottish politics seemed not dissimilar to that in England–a conflict between the Labour Party and the Conservative (Unionist) Party with some support depending on the circumstances for Liberalism and nationalism[9].

However, from the 1960s onwards, Scottish political life began increasingly to diverge from the English pattern. A long term decline of the Conservative vote set in. The 1987 General Election saw the Conservative Party reduced to 24% of the vote in Scotland (lower than in any other region of Britain) at an election in which it gained an overall majority of more than 100 seats in England. In Scotland the Conservative Party won only 10 of the 71 parliamentary seats. This situation was the most obvious manifestation of the very different nature of Scottish development.

It reflected the way in which the distinctiveness of Scottish identity, together with the tradition of popular resistance to control had become focused on Conservative stewardship in Scotland. As control of the economy after the War became to depend more and more upon either the British State (mediated through a Westminster Parliament) or upon firms owned externally, so popular sentiment crystallised around the resentment of external control of Scottish life. Mobilised successfully in the 1970s by the Scottish National Party (around the slogan 'It's Our Oil') this perception of Scottishness revolves around the recognition of the country's dependence on forces not within its control. Thus, the one

party in the 1987 election that campaigned in Scotland on a platform
that explicitly embraced the union with England and rejected any idea
of devolution or independence was humiliated by the electorate[10].

It appears that, as the end of the twentieth century beckons,
Scotland's development has impelled it along a path whose destination
is far from certain. Government by the Conservative Party through
a Westminster based Parliament has thrown into sharp focus the
constitutional questions raised by the fact of political control based
on a small minority of the votes cast in Scotland. The wider context is
a federal Europe in which the fragmentation of Eastern European States
is likely to give further weight to the SNP's aim for 'Independence in
Europe'. In this situation, the future path of Scottish development may
begin to diverge even more obviously from that of England.

NOTES

1. See Chapter 7
2. See Chapter 1
3. See Chapter 4 and Chapter 7
4. See Chapter 5
5. See Chapter 7
6. See Chapter 2
7. See Chapter 9
8. See Chapter 3
9. See Chapter 8
10. See Chapter 6, Chapter 7 and Chapter 8

Population and Family Life

M. Anderson

Population Growth and Structure

On census night in 1911, just over 4.76 million people lived in Scotland, almost three times as many as at the first census of 1801. Between 1871 and 1911, the population had grown by 1.4 million, but after 1911 rapid increase came to an end and in the 1920s the national total fell by almost one per cent. The 1971 peak, at 5.23 million, showed a rise of less than half a million since 1911. In the 1970s the number of people in the country declined by nearly two per cent and by 1988 the total was down to 5.09 million, an increase of only 7.3 per cent since 1911.[1]

These trends in Scotland were in marked contrast to those of the other constituent countries of the United Kingdom: for example, the population of England and Wales rose by almost forty per cent between 1911 and 1988. Between 1961 and 1987 the population of Scotland fell by 1.4 per cent, while England's population rose by 8.8 per cent. The population of Wales increased by 7.6 per cent, and that of Northern Ireland by 10.4 per cent. Even more significantly, in no national State of the EEC did population fall over this period; the lowest growth, in Belgium, was 7.7 per cent.[2]

Figure 1, using modern regional boundaries, shows that the pattern of change within Scotland was also very uneven. The populations of Dumfries and Galloway and of Tayside were almost constant over the whole of the twentieth century. By contrast, between 1911 and 1971, the numbers living in the Borders, in Highland Region and the Western Isles, and in the Northern Isles fell markedly (the total for these regions was down by about 70,000 over the period and in the Western Isles the population fell by more than half between 1911 and 1971). Up to 1971, there was also a small fall in Grampian though here, as in Highland Region, growth in tourism and the impact of oil development produced a significant recovery by 1981 and this continued during the 1980s. In Shetland, the population rose by almost 60 per cent between 1971 and 1981, but the end of the initial oil boom led to a recession in population in the 1980s (though population at the end of the decade was still significantly higher than at any time since the 1920s).[3]

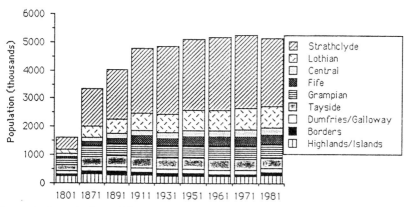

Figure 1. Population of Scotland by regions, 1801–1981 (*Source: Census 1981 Scotland* (Historic Tables 1801–1981) Table 2).

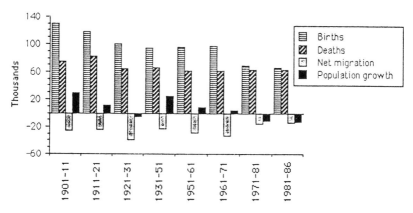

Figure 2. Components of population change, 1901–1986 (annual averages) (*Source: Scottish Abstract of Statistics* (1987) Table 1.3).

At a regional level, significant long term growth was almost entirely confined to Central Region (up a third between 1911 and 1981), to Fife, and to the Lothians (both up a fifth but in the former case largely before World War Two). Until about 1961 population also grew in Strathclyde, but from then through to the 1980s there was a fall of over a quarter of a million people, reducing the population almost to the 1911 level.

Some of the changes that lay behind the national trends can be seen in Figure 2. Births fell from an annual average of around 131,000 in the 1910s to around 90,000 in the 1930s. This occurred in spite of a roughly ten per cent increase in the number of women in the principal child-bearing age groups over the period. As we shall see later, the birth rate fluctuated dramatically during and immediately after the War, but there was then a steady rise through the 1950s and into the 1960s (to a peak of 104,355 births in 1964). Thereafter, fertility fell back rapidly until a low point of 62,342 births was reached in 1977, followed by fluctuations at a depressed level throughout the 1980s.[4]

By contrast, the total number of civilian deaths, having fallen until about 1920, stabilised at between 62,000 and 65,000 per annum right through to the 1980s. As the birth rate fell back in the 1970s, the natural increase of the population (which had averaged about 35,000 per annum in the 1920s and again in the 1960s) was markedly reduced; in 1976 and 1978 there were actually more deaths than births. When account is taken of the significant net emigration of Scots in the 1970s and 1980s (it reached 23,100 in 1981 and averaged almost 15,000 per year between 1972 and 1986), it is not surprising that, after 1971, Scotland suffered a fall in population in every year except 1973 and 1974. Before the 1970s there had been heavy net emigration in every decade except the 1930s and the 1940s. At its peak, in the 1920s, 390,000 more people left the country than entered it. Emigration was also heavy in the 1950s and 1960s, with a total net outflow of over half a million people, roughly equally balanced between those who moved overseas and those who went to the rest of the United Kingdom.

However, while emigration was significantly in excess of immigration in almost every year, there was some inward flow and, at every census, between eight and ten per cent of those living in Scotland were born outside the country. About three quarters were born elsewhere in the British Isles, with the proportion from Ireland falling somewhat over time and the English share rising (from 3.4 per cent of the population in 1911 to 4.4 per cent in 1951 and 5.9 per cent in 1981). Immigrants from Commonwealth countries made up just 0.6 per cent of the population in 1951 and 1.1 per cent in 1981, with Canada and the Indian subcontinent providing the largest share throughout the period. Immigrants of all kinds were markedly concentrated in the urban areas of the Central Belt (particularly those with new technology industries and services attractive to the young adults who comprised a large part of the the inflow); as might be expected, there was also significant local cross-border migration from the northernmost counties of England.[5]

Within the country, a number of striking local changes are revealed by Map 1. Over most of rural Scotland population decline was endemic and often profound, as generations of younger men and women left to

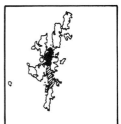

Growth of 15% or More

Growth of less than 15%, loss less than 15%

Loss of 15% or more

Map 1. Percentage population change, 1911–1981.

seek greater opportunities and better living standards in the Cities and
the Central Belt or outside the country. The only major exceptions were
in the prosperous small farming areas of the far north-east and east and
in some of the major tourist areas, notably along the line of the A9
south of Inverness and in the Spey valley. Here, as in some of the
remoter areas from the 1970s, incomers, some from outside Scotland,
replaced many of those who left. Particularly striking is the tendency for
population outside the Central Belt and the cities to show any dynamic
growth outside the towns. As the Map shows, even quite small places
like Kirkwall, Forres, Kelso and Annan saw significant growth, and
some of the unexpected apparently rural increase turns out on close
observation to involve expansion of single towns (notably Thurso, Oban
and Fort William) within large parishes spatially dominated by rural
depopulation. Clusters of population increase can also be observed in
(but especially, with spreading suburbanisation, around) the cities, and
in some of the major mining areas of the Central Belt and Ayrshire
and in seaside resorts. The impact of relative prosperity in the Borders

1. Mobility within Scotland: The pull of urban labour markets. The
Manderston family, photographed in 1913, before moving from Moulin,
Pitlochry, Perthshire to Galashiels, Selkirkshire and wider employment
opportunities. Back row: Jessie, Alec, Lizzie, Hamish, Maggie. Front row:
James (father), John, Jessie (mother), Adam. (Courtesy of Mrs E. Treble –
nee Manderston).

textile areas and the new industrial centres like Glenrothes are also apparent.[6]

More detail of the impact of these changes on the structure of Scotland's population is revealed by Figure 3. This compares the number of males and females alive at each single year of age in 1911, 1951, and 1987. The 1911 plots show a pattern typical of a society in the midst of a transition from a regime of high fertility and high mortality to one of low fertility and low mortality. The reduction in numbers alive at each successive age is relatively smooth, reflecting relatively high mortality at all ages and little annual variation in numbers born; where marked variations appear they result partly from inaccuracies in the ages that people declared on their census returns and, quite significantly for young men at this time, from the pre-War surge in emigration. In earlier decades, numbers at very young ages would have been relatively higher, but by 1911 there had been a significant reduction in infant and child mortality and in marital fertility, and this had begun to produce a flattening of the curve at younger ages.

By 1951, a very different pattern had appeared. Widespread adoption of family limitation, combined with low child and young adult mortality, produced a situation where, on average, the population contained only marginally more children than middle aged adults. However, even after the temporary absence overseas of men on National Service has been taken into account, there were marked fluctuations in numbers alive at different ages. Note, particularly, the consequences of the restrained fertility of the later years of World War One and of the 1930s. By contrast, the sudden surges of fertility at the end of the two World Wars is clearly reflected in substantial peaks at around the ages of 4 and 30.

The consequences of this volatility in fertility are even more obvious in the 1987 data. The birth surges of 1921 and 1947 are still clearly visible. Even more notable is the rise in fertility of the mid-1960s and the subsequent rapid fall, sometimes referred to as 'the demographic decline', which bottomed out in the later 1970s as the small birth cohort of the early 1950s reduced the numbers reaching child-bearing age. One important consequence of all these changes is that, in 1987, there were fewer children alive than there had been at any period since the 1840s. The implications for the provision of a wide range of social and educational services for children and, in the longer term, for support of the 1980s middle-aged in their old age, should be noted. So, too, should the widening gap between the numbers of older women and older men, the result of a marked improvement in women's survival chances

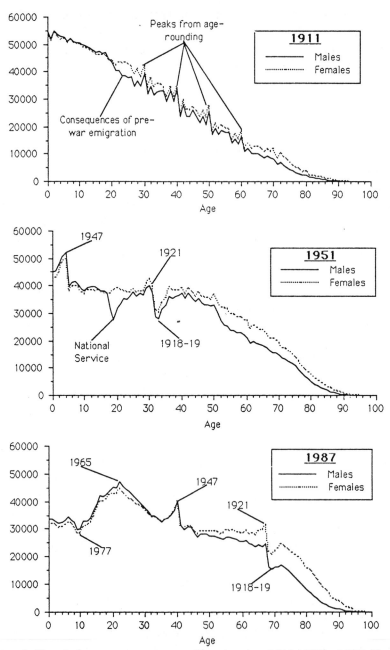

Figure 3. Population age structure profiles, by sex, 1911, 1951, 1987 (*Source: Census of Scotland 1911* (Vol 2) Table XXIII; *Census 1951 Scotland* (Vol 3) Table 21; *Annual Report of the Registrar General for Scotland* (1987) Table A2.1).

compared with those of men. By contrast, in the 1970s and 1980s, falling child mortality and emigration, for the first time, produced a situation where there were significantly more men than women in the principal marrying age groups. The longer term consequences of these trends are not yet clear.

Mortality

As we have already seen, among the major factors changing the structure of Scotland's population since 1911 have been changes in patterns of mortality. The national death rate per thousand of the population fell from 15.3 in 1911–14 to 13.3 in 1935–38. The rate for 1946–50 was 12.6 per thousand. Thereafter, there was no significant further fall in the overall national rate, because reductions in mortality at all ages (in some cases of dramatic proportions) were largely offset by a steadily aging population.[7]

It would be a mistake to see the trends and variations in mortality simply as a result of the interaction between the biological actions of disease and the developing technique of doctors and medical scientists. Throughout the period, death chances varied according to where one lived and the social and economic conditions under which one lived. In the mid-nineteenth century, these differences had been very substantial indeed; for example, the death rate in Glasgow in 1861 was 73 per cent higher than in the islands districts of Scotland. Much of this variation had declined by the First World War, but even in 1920–22 the death rate in Glasgow was still 25 per cent above that in the rural areas. Similarly, in the 1920s, the chances that a child which had survived the first six months of life would die in the next six were more than double in burghs with populations over 20,000 compared with those of under 5,000. Even in the mid-1980s, the death rate in the eastern area of Glasgow (15.6 per 1000 in 1986) was still, *after controlling for differences in the age and sex composition of the population*, 29 per cent above the rate for the Western Isles. Even more significantly, it was 71 per cent above Bearsden and Milngavie (9.1 per 1000).[8]

At all periods, some of this variation was associated with dense concentration of population (in particular, the cities and some larger towns had significantly higher rates of mortality from diseases linked to contaminated food and water supplies). However, much of the variation was due to working and living conditions, and, throughout the period, to variations in standards of living. For example, it says much about the appalling social conditions of much of Scotland's urban population in the 1920s that, while workers in coal mines in the age group 25–44 had mortality only eight per cent above the average for all males at that age, general labourers were 24 per cent above the mean. Similarly, while fishermen had mortality just one per cent above the average, the death chances of iron and steel foundry labourers were 52 per cent in excess of the mean. At the other extreme, solicitors' death chances in the 1920s were only 41 per cent of the average and ministers and clergymen were 38 per cent below the mean. Moving forward to 1959–63, mortality among men aged 25–44 in Social Class 5 was 78 per cent above the average but in Social Class 1 it was 27 per cent below it. The extent to which this was a reflection of home and economic circumstance rather than work environment can be gauged when we note that the wives of men in Social Class 5 had a death rate 78 per cent above the mean, while for wives of men in Social Class 1 it was 29 per cent below.[9]

Nevertheless, there had clearly been major improvements over time. In 1946–8 the chances that a baby would die in its first year of life were more than three times as high if it was born into a Social Class 5 home than if its father was in Social Class 1. In 1978–80 the probability of death for a Social Class 5 infant was only 75 per cent above that of a baby from Social Class 1. However, one side effect of the declining role of disease in mortality among younger adults (to be discussed shortly) was that, by the early 1960s, relative death chances were extremely accentuated in certain dangerous occupations. For example, in the 20–44 age group, the mortality of fishermen was now 125 per cent above the mean, and

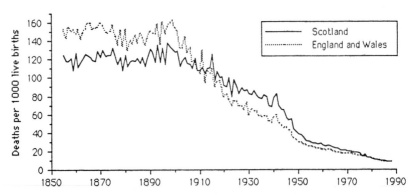

Figure 4. Infant mortality, Scotland and England and Wales, 1855–1988 (*Source:* B. R. Mitchell, *British Historical Statistics* (Cambridge 1988), Population and Vital Statistics, Table 13; *Annual Report of the Registrar General for Scotland* 1988 Table A1.2; Population Trends No. 59 (1990) Table 19).

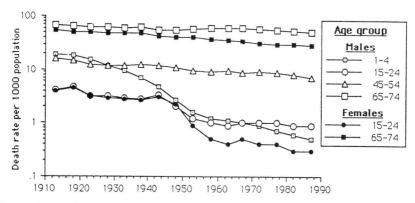

Figure 5. Death rates per 1,000 population, 1911–1988 (Annual averages, selected age groups) (*Source*: B. R. Mitchell, *British Historical Statistics* (Cambridge 1988), Population and Vital Statistics, Table 15; *Annual Report of the Registrar General for Scotland* (1988) Table B1.1).

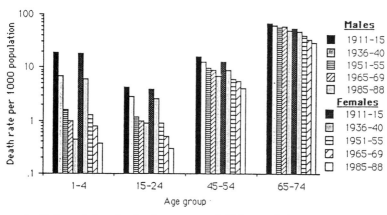

Figure 6. Male and female death rates per 1,000 population, 1911–1988 (Annual averages for selected age groups and years) (*Source*: B. R. Mitchell, *British Historical Statistics* (Cambridge 1988), Population and Vital Statistics, Table 15; *Annual Report of the Registrar General for Scotland* (1988) Table B1.1).

deck and engine room ratings, barge and boatmen were 130 per cent above the average. At the other extreme, it is perhaps not insignificant that the lowest mortality of any group for which data were published in the 45–64 age group was for 'Ministers of the crown, MPs and senior civil servants' (with a death rate almost exactly half of the average for their age group).[10]

More detail of the general pattern of mortality decline by age is shown in Figures 4, 5 and 6. Figure 4 compares a century of infant mortality in Scotland and England.

In both countries, a gradual but erratic decline set in around 1900, though there was considerable regional diversity within both countries. Overall, the fall was initially much more rapid in England, though the reasons for this difference are still not properly understood. Scotland also experienced much more significant leaps in mortality at the start of both the World Wars. From the mid-1940s there was a decade of more rapid reduction in infant deaths, coinciding with the widespread introduction of antibiotics. Then, from the mid-1950s, the trend continued slowly downwards to the end of the 1980s, by which time Scottish infant mortality had fallen to around the English and Welsh level. As would be expected if improved living conditions were particularly important, the initial decline was largely confined to infants over six months old; between 1922–25 and 1936–40 the fall for males aged six months to one year was 46.3 per cent, compared with 2.6 per cent for babies under one month. Subsequently, except for the first seven days of life (where much death is associated with congenital abnormalities, prematurity or accidents during birth) the fall was almost as large at all ages, reflecting a combination of social and medical factors.[11]

In parallel with these trends there was a steady reduction in the stillbirth rate. Precise figures are not available before 1939, when the rate was 42.2 per 1000 births. By 1951–55 it was down to 25.5 and in 1987–88 averaged just 5.3, producing a situation where well under one woman in one hundred would experience a stillbirth, compared with almost one in ten fifty years earlier.[12]

Figure 5 shows changes in death rates at older ages. Note particularly the rapid and accelerating fall in deaths among young children, which only slowed once very low levels were reached in the 1960s. Only well after World War Two could most couples reasonably expect that they would rear all their children to adulthood. Only then could it become a very special tragedy for one of one's classmates to die while still at school. Among young adult women, the downward trend in mortality was more gentle over the period than for small children, except for a sharp downward step in the later 1940s and 1950s; again antibiotics must be a major factor, especially through their impact on what had been the most significant killer of young adults, tuberculosis. Finally, though there was quite significant improvement in the long term for those over 35, it was much less rapid. This was particularly the case at the oldest age groups, as is clear from Figure 6.

Figure 6 also shows how, while the death rate for boys aged 1–4 fell almost as rapidly as it did for girls, at older age groups improvement in mortality for males was markedly slower than for females. As a result, expectation of life for women at all adult age groups improved much more rapidly than it did for men. In fact, death rates in the later 1930s were actually slightly higher among men in their late seventies and early eighties than they had been between 1911 and 1915. Even by 1985–88, they had fallen to only 76 per cent of their pre-First World War level (the figure for women was 57 per cent). And, while mortality among women aged 15–24 continued to fall right through to the 1980s, among men of this age the reduction brought about after 1950 by medical and environmental improvements was almost entirely offset by rising accidental deaths, especially on the roads. In 1921–25 the female death rate in this age group had been the same as that for men; by the 1980s three times as many young men as women were dying.

These changes in age-specific mortality had significant impact on life-cycle patterns of survivorship and on expectation of life (the average number of additional years that a person of any age could expect to live). In 1910–12, expectation of life at birth for baby boys was 50.1 years, compared with 53.2 for baby girls. At this time, the very high infant death rates meant that, for those that survived, life expectancy actually improved between birth and a child's first birthday (to 55.8 for boys and 57.8 for girls). As Figure 7 shows, thereafter, improvements in life expectancy at birth were steady for both sexes between the 1910s and the 1980s, and at all ages women moved further ahead of of men. The contrast is clearest at older age groups. For men of 65, life expectancy

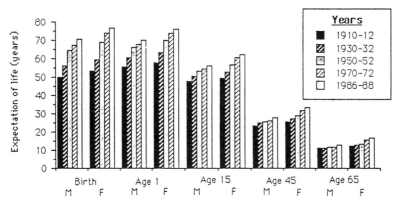

Figure 7. Expectation for life at birth, 1910–12 to 1986–88, by sex and age group (*Source: Annual Report of the Registrar General for Scotland* (1988) Table J1.1).

was 10.9 in 1910–12 and was still only 13.0 in 1988. For women, the improvement was from 12.2 to 16.7 years. Life expectancy at birth rose over the same period from 50.1 to 70.5 for males, and from 53.2 to 76.7 for females.

Table 1 elaborates some of these trends, showing the percentage of males and females who died by various ages, and also the proportions who died between certain ages.

The major importance of infant and child deaths in survival chances becomes very clear from this table, as does the marked difference between male and female patterns in later middle age. This is in marked contrast to the very similar mortality of men and women in the 25–34 age group. In modern populations, male death rates are significantly in excess of women's at all ages and even in pre-industrial populations the enhanced risk of mortality resulting from childbirth is seldom high enough to override this (except perhaps for a very few years). Thus, where female mortality exceeds that of men, there are likely to be significant social factors involved, though these are often difficult to identify. In mid-nineteenth century Scotland, excess female mortality occurred quite widely at ages from young childhood through to the mid-thirties and was particularly high in some mining and manufacturing areas; in Dundee in 1861, for example, female death rates exceeded male at ages one and two as well as in the age groups 10–14, 20–29, 30–39 and even 40–49. With excess female deaths occurring at such a wide range of age groups, we cannot simply attribute the heightened mortality to childbirth but must look at patterns of distribution of

Table 1. Mortality Changes Between Different Ages, 1921, 1951 and 1988
(Percent Dying of Those Alive at the Earlier Age)

	1921		1951		1988	
	Males	Females	Males	Females	Males	Females
Percent dying between ages:						
0 and 5	15.6	13.1	4.8	3.8	1.2	0.8
0 and 25	20.5	18.1	6.7	5.5	2.4	1.2
0 and 35	24.4	22.1	8.6	7.3	3.6	1.7
0 and 65	53.5	47.7	39.1	27.9	27.9	16.7
5 and 25	5.9	5.8	2.0	1.7	1.2	0.4
25 and 35	4.8	4.9	1.9	1.9	1.2	0.5
35 and 65	38.5	32.8	33.4	22.2	25.2	15.0

Source: J.C. Dunlop, *Transactions of the Faculty of Actuaries* Vol X (1925); *Life Tables Supplement to the 99th AR* (1954); *AR* (1988) Table J2.1.

food within households, at energy requirements associated with female work activities and at accentuated risks of exposure both to injurious substances at work and to disease at home. Several of these circumstances would help to explain the very much higher mortality of young women from tuberculosis throughout our period; in 1921–30, for example, the death rate for pulmonary tuberculosis for women aged 15–24 was more than a third higher than for men, and the disease led to more than a third of all female deaths in this age group.[13]

However, by the 1920s, falling tuberculosis deaths meant that this disease had already become less important at older ages and maternal mortality became the most important source of excess female deaths in Scotland in the inter-war period. In 1920, the maternal mortality rate, at 6.2 per 1000 live births was actually above the pre-War level, and it reached 7.0 per 1000 in 1928 and again in 1930. While some of the subsequent reduction comes from reclassification of causes of death, it is seems that mortality began to fall in the early 1930s as improved knowledge of the transmission of puerperal sepsis led to better patient care. From about 1935, case fatality fell with the introduction of early antibiotics. By the late 1930s, improvements in the management of pregnancy and childbirth began to reduce deaths from other causes of maternal mortality, and the fall was also helped by improved nutrition among working class women. As a result, by 1945, maternal mortality was down to 2.8 per 1000 live births; in 1951 it was 1.1 per thousand and in 1988 it was just 0.12 (in 1949, it had already temporarily fallen as low as 0.2 per 1000 births in Edinburgh). Within a period of seventy years, Scotland had moved from a position where one mother died for every 143 births and more than one married women in forty could expect to die at some time in her life from a childbirth-related condition, to a situation, aided by reduced fertility, where the chances that a woman would die through childbearing had fallen below one in 4000.[14]

More detail on trends in some of the other major causes of death is shown in Figures 8, 9 and 10. Before the First World War, significant numbers of children were still dying each year from a range of 'childhood diseases': measles, scarlatina, whooping cough, diphtheria and croup. These conditions accounted for over six per cent of all deaths, but were the cause of over a third of deaths in the 1–4 age group and more than a quarter of deaths in the age group 5–9. Diarrhoeal diseases were also significant causes of mortality, especially for infants and very young children. As has already been noted, lung tuberculosis was also still a major killer disease (seven per cent of all deaths in 1912–14, but almost a third of all deaths in the 25–34 age group, where it killed

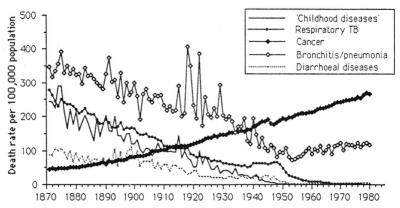

Figure 8. Death rates by selected causes, 1871–1980 (*Source: Annual Reports of the Registrar General for Scotland* for 1920 (Table 39), 1959 (Table 40) and 1958, 1968, 1973, 1980 and 1988 (Table C1.2). For a comment on the reliability of the figures see Note 16).

one person in every 600 each year). In the inter-war period it was becoming concentrated in the Highlands and Islands rather than the great Cities where it had been commonest at earlier dates. Other major fatal conditions at the start of the period were non-pulmonary tubercular conditions (about four per cent of all deaths) and bronchitis and pneumonia (the cause of 14 per cent of deaths in 1912–14). By comparison with the second half of the twentieth century, cancers (about seven per cent of deaths) and heart disease (about nine per cent) were less important, though there is certainly some under-recording of these conditions in the published figures, which also fail to distinguish adequately the many deaths from the range of circulatory conditions which today are popularly referred to as 'strokes'.[15]

Figure 8 shows the trends in some of these conditions from 1910 to 1980. By the outbreak of the Second World War, only whooping cough and diphtheria remained major threats to the lives of young children and in both cases there had been a marked improvement over the previous thirty years. All kinds of tuberculosis mortality had also fallen to less than half their pre-First World War levels. With the probable exception of diphtheria, little if any of any of this improvement can be attributed to major advances in medical treatment or in clinically-based preventive measures. Where they were important at all, these advances only became significant during and after the Second World War, when mortality from all these conditions rapidly declined to trivial levels. The balance of factors responsible for the earlier as well as for some element of the more recent changes is still a major subject of debate. There can, however, be little doubt that a growing popular awareness of the ways in which disease was transmitted, an increasing concern with the welfare of children in all social classes, a wide range of measures to improve the quality of water, food, sewerage and nuisance removal, and improved living standards all played some part. The impact of support given to these developments by the widening influence of nurses, midwives and health visitors, as well as advice from medical practitioners, must not be under-estimated.[16]

By contrast, as Figure 8 also shows, trends in mortality from other major conditions were less encouraging. Bronchitis and pneumonia mortality fell until about 1950, and years of epidemic crises largely disappeared, as the worst forms of industrial and smoke pollution were controlled and new methods of treatment were introduced. Over the second half of the century, however, little further improvement occurred and this was more than offset by the rising share of the population who survived to the older and more susceptible age groups. The experience with cancer and heart disease was, overall, even worse, though there is some under-recording in earlier periods. In 1912–14 the overall death rates were 111 per 100,000 population for cancers and 140 for heart disease, and these figures changed only a little by the early 1920s. Thereafter, however, mortality steadily climbed in all social groups. The overall cancer death rate for men rose from 110 per 100,000 in

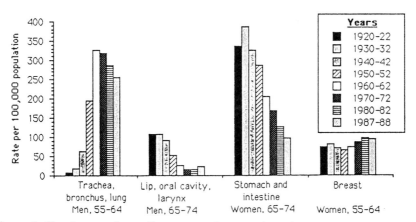

Figure 9. Death rates for malignant neoplasms, selected age groups, 1920–22 to 1987–88 (*Source: Annual Reports of the Registrar General for Scotland* for 1961 (Table 6.5) and for 1988 (Table C1.4). For a comment on the reliability of the figures see Note 16.

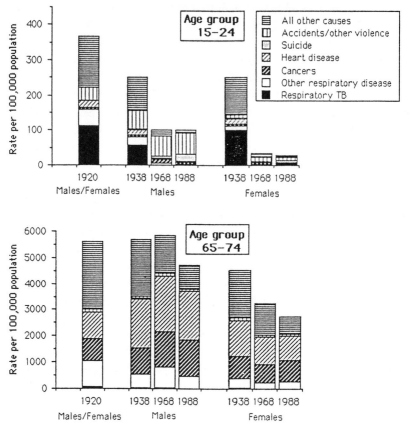

Figure 10. Death rates by selected causes, 1871–1980 (*Source: Annual Reports of the Registrar General for Scotland* for 1920, 1938, 1968 and 1988. For a comment on the reliability of the figures see Note 16).

1920–22 to 206 in 1950–52 and 305 in 1987–88. Male heart disease rates rose from 136 in 1920–22 to 425 in 1950–52 and 480 in 1978–79. They then fell back to 434 in 1987–88, probably largely as a result of dietary and behavioural change.[17]

Within the cancer group, however, there were major differences between different conditions, and some of these are shown, controlling for age, in Figure 9. The trends in lung and in lip, mouth and throat cancer are substantially attributable to changes in patterns of tobacco smoking. The less publicised changes in stomach and intestinal cancers (also occurring among men and at all ages) start so early and are so continuous that they clearly reflect dietary changes (especially increased consumption of fruit and vegetables and reduced use of some older preservatives) rather than medical and surgical advances. The reasons for the persistence of significantly high levels of breast cancer among women, in spite of improved diagnosis and treatment, remains a mystery, though it seems likely that both dietary and behavioral factors are involved. Perhaps significantly, given its probable association with various aspects of a more affluent lifestyle, breast cancer mortality in England and Wales approached or even exceeded the Scottish rate throughout the period. In deaths from most other major cancers and also in heart disease, the Scottish rates tended to exceed the English by between ten and twenty-five per cent, clearly reflecting some combination of poorer diet and higher exposure to the effects of alcohol and tobacco. The fact that bronchitis rates, though high, were in general lower than for England and Wales suggests that working environment and industrial pollution were less disproportionately significant.

Figure 10 summarises some of these trends for two specific age groups (the graph for the 15–24 age group is drawn on a scale fifteen times that for the 65–74 group). For the 65–74 age group, the significance of changing mortality from heart disease and cancers is clear. Among young adults, the early importance and subsequent near disappearance of respiratory tuberculosis is well shown, as is the importance of 'violent death' (accidents, suicide and homicide and assault), particularly among males. In 1912–14 the violent death rate for Scotland as a whole was 65 per 100,000 population (about four per cent of all deaths, though almost one in ten at the 15–24 age group). After the First World War, the rate fell slightly and by 1946–50 it was down to 52 per 100,000 population. In 1988 it was 58 per 100,000. Throughout the period the male rate has been roughly double the female, but with this excess much higher among young adults. In 1988, for the 15–24 age group, the male violent death rate was 101 per 100,000 while the female rate was 29. A third of all male deaths in this age group, and a quarter of female, were from road accidents, a fifth of male and a sixth of female deaths were recorded as suicide, and one male death in six was from accidents at work, at home or in leisure activities. The death rate for homicide and other violence was somewhat inflated in 1988 by the Lockerbie terrorist attack, but in general the overall death rate from physical violence has been remarkably stable over long period of time except for a near doubling which occurred quite rapidly in the early 1960s.[18]

Fertility and Nuptiality

Figure 11 shows births in Scotland between 1900 and 1988. The upper line shows legitimate births, while the lower gives births to unmarried parents. The graph clearly shows the depressed fertility of the inter-war period, the boom in births in the 1960s, and the marked subsequent decline, particularly focused on births within marriage. This fall in legitimate births has been matched by a steady rise in the numbers of illegitimate births since the early 1980s. In most years in the inter-war period, between six and eight per cent of births were illegitimate. There was some rise during the Second World War, but thereafter the figures fell back until, by the late 1950s, only around four per cent of births occurred out of wedlock. A slow rise in numbers of illegitimate births began in the 1960s and, as the numbers of legitimate births fell from the end of that decade, the share of births to unmarried parents rose steadily. By 1976–80, one birth in ten was illegitimate and in 1988 the figure had reached 24.5 per cent.

Changes in the patterns of legitimate fertility result from changes in proportions of the population marrying and in patterns of childbearing within marriage. For a century before 1961, Scotland passed through a major transition, from a demography in which the number of legitimate births was principally determined by the numbers of women who were married, to one where the main determinant was fertility *within* marriage. This transition began in the 1860s but even in 1911 the country was a long way away from a modern fertility regime, particularly in the Highland counties and in some of the principal mining and manufacturing areas of the Central Belt. Following a pattern which stretched back at least until the mid-nineteenth century, Scottish marital

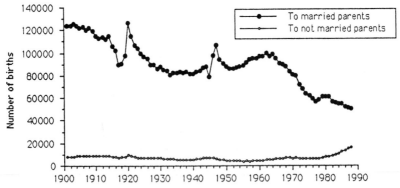

Figure 11. Number of births, 1900–1988, by legitimacy (*Source*: B. R. Mitchell, *British Historical Statistics* (Cambridge 1988) Population and Vital Statistics, Table 10; *Annual Report of the Registrar General for Scotland* (1988) Table A1.2).

fertility was significantly higher than that of England, while women's marriage chances were markedly lower.[19]

We can use the indicators developed in the Princeton European Fertility Project to explore these interactions; a plot of two of the indicators is shown in Figure 12. The first (plotted on the horizontal axis) is a measure of nuptiality (more precisely, an estimate of the proportion of women's potential fertility that is available for exploitation within marriage — clearly variations in both ages at marriage and proportions ever marrying have some influence here). The second indicator (plotted on the vertical axis) is a measure of marital fertility (more precisely, the proportion of the potential marital fertility of married women that is actually achieved through live births). Were there to be no illegitimate fertility, a combination of these two variables would show the proportion of all potential fertility that any group of women actually achieved. The curves that cross Figure 12 from top left to bottom right join points where similar overall levels of fertility are achieved by different combinations of nuptiality and fertility within marriage.

The results are of considerable importance and show the constrained nature of Scottish fertility throughout the period. The plots when set against the diagonal lines show that, in both 1911 and 1961, in most counties of Scotland and England, women were only bearing within marriage between one sixth and one quarter of the number of children

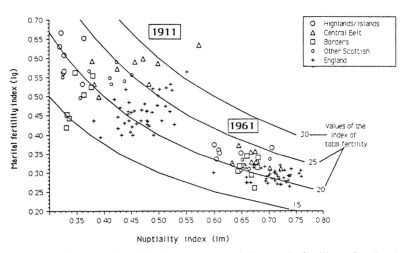

Figure 12. The relationship between nuptiality and fertility, Scotland and England, 1911 and 1961 (*Source*: Calculated from data in A. J. Coale and S. C. Watkins, *The Decline of Fertility in Europe* (Princeton 1986) Chapter 2).

that they could have had if they had achieved 'maximum' fertility. Moreover, in both periods, almost every Scottish county had lower nuptiality and higher fertility than the majority of English counties. Over time, in both countries but particularly in Scotland, a much higher proportion of women's fertile lives began to be spent within marriage (note how the nuptiality index rose), but marital fertility fell markedly. When the plots are read against the marital fertility axis, it is clear that, while the total group of married Scotswomen in 1911 bore about 57 per cent of the children of which they were in theory capable, by 1961 this figure had fallen to 34 per cent.

After 1961, fertility at first stayed low and then fell further. From the early 1970s, nuptiality also fell, amid much popular discussion of a general 'flight from marriage'. Between 1961 and 1988, the nuptiality index fell from .656 to .547, but even in 1988 nuptiality was everywhere at a level very well above any pre-War year (even in the Western Isles, the 1981 figure was .621). Meanwhile, however, the marital fertility index fell from .341 in 1961 to .199 in 1988. This depressed level (at which married women were only having a fifth of the number of children of which they were 'capable') was far below that achieved at any earlier period of Scottish history, though lower levels had occurred in parts of England in the 1930s. However, when this low fertility is combined with nuptiality, the proportion of overall potential fertility that women achieved within marriage in the 1980s was well below even the lowest parts of the Borders in 1911. Even when the high

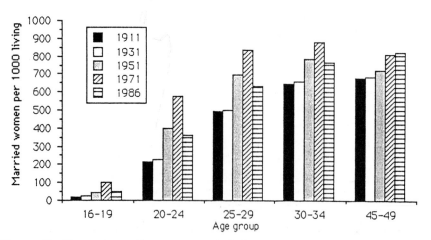

Figure 13. Proportions of women married, by age group, 1911–1986 (*Source: Annual Report of the Registrar General for Scotland* (1988) Table Q1.4).

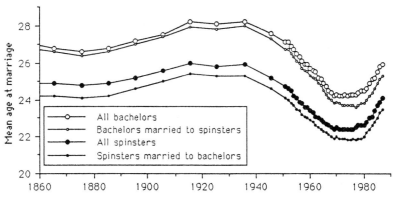

Figure 14. Mean ages at first marriage, 1860–1987 (*Source: Annual Report of the Registrar General for Scotland* (1988 and earlier years) Table Q1.5).

rates of illegitimate fertility are taken into account, only some 14.4 per cent of Scots women's potential fertility was being realised by 1988, compared with 19.2 per cent in 1931 and 26 per cent in 1911. In the past in Scotland, only Selkirk and Bute had ever (in the 1930s) had overall fertility below the modern national levels. In 1981, the last year for which it is possible to calculate regional differences, the marital fertility index still showed traces of earlier patterns, being highest in the Western Isles and Highland region and lowest in Lothian, Tayside and Borders.[20]

Changes in the proportions of women married and in the average ages at marriage are shown in Figures 13 and 14. In 1911, only 22 per cent of women aged 20–24 were married, and only 68 per cent of women aged 45–49. There were, however, major regional differences across the country: in the Highland counties, just 10.7 per cent of women aged 20–24 were married, while in the counties of Renfrew, Lanark and Ayr the figure was 24.5 per cent. In these latter counties, 84.6 per cent of women aged 50–54 were married, compared with only 71.0 per cent in the Highlands. Broadly similar patterns applied to men. No major changes occurred before the Second World War, but thereafter changes were rapid. Nationally, by 1971, 10 per cent of women in the 16–19 age group were married, and in the early 1970s the mean age of first marriage for women fell to an all-time low of 22.4. In 1971, 58 per cent of women aged 20–24 and 81 per cent of those aged 45–49 were married, in spite of rising divorce rates. Thereafter, however, average marriage ages rose steadily and, by 1988, only three per cent of women aged 16–19 and 33 per cent of those aged 20–25 were married. A new trend, however, developed, with a marked increase in cohabitation in all sections of the population. Unfortunately, there is little direct evidence on the emergence of new patterns of couples living together outside marriage in Scotland but in Great Britain as a whole only about seven per cent of women marrying for the first time in the early 1970s cohabited before marriage, compared with 26 per cent of those marrying in the early 1980s. Over time, moreover, the length of time spent in cohabitation tended to increase.[21]

In the inter-war period, not only was cohabitation at a low level but very few women indeed bore children in stable non-marital unions. The 1970s and especially the 1980s saw a marked change in this respect. Some insight into these trends can be seen from Figure 15, which shows age-specific birth rates among unmarried women. From this graph it is clear that a general tendency to bear children outside marriage developed from the 1950s, but it was partly concealed, initially, by the falling proportion of women who were unmarried; from the late 1960s, it was further checked, temporarily, by the increased availability of the contraceptive pill to unmarried women. From the later 1970s, however, as marriage rates fell steeply, all the younger age groups increased their propensity to bear children outside marriage. In the past, cohabitation and illegitimate births were much more common in second and subsequent partnerships, but the illegitimacy rise of

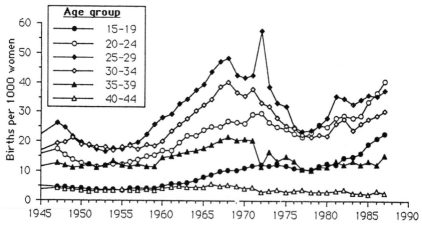

Figure 15. Illegitimate births per 1,000 unmarried women, 1947–1987, by age group (*Source: Annual Report of the Registrar General for Scotland* (1988) Table S1.8).

the 1970s and 1980s in part reflected a new tendency for such births to occur to couples in first partnerships. Since the numbers of these younger unmarried women far exceeded the numbers in the older age group, the falling marriage rates produced an illegitimacy explosion; similar trends are apparent elsewhere in the British Isles.

From the time that Registration data were first published for 1855 through until the Second World War, Scotland had marked regional patterns of illegitimacy, with, unusually in an international comparative perspective, high levels of illegitimate births in some rural areas (notably the north-east and south-west); even in the 1930s, for example, the proportion of births that were illegitimate was three times higher in Wigtown than in Glasgow. By the 1950s, however, these regional patterns were already becoming less marked, as illegitimacy increased in working class areas of the cities and manufacturing towns. The rapid rise in illegitimate births since the early 1970s further accentuated the urban excess, though parts of the north-east continued with high levels of extra-marital births. The highest published figure in 1988 was in the northern health district of Glasgow where 49 per cent of births were to unmarried parents. In all, by 1988, 40 per cent of all births to unmarried parents occurred in the four City districts, compared with only 28 per cent of births to married parents. More than a quarter of all births were illegitimate in Clackmannan, Kirkcaldy, Nairn, Edinburgh, Dumbarton, Glasgow, Inverclyde, and Dundee districts. The lowest figures were in the middle class suburbs of the Glasgow conurbation,

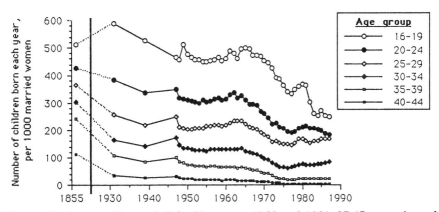

Figure 16. Age-specific marital fertility rates, 1855 and 1931–87 (*Source: Annual Report of the Registrar General for Scotland* (1938) p lxii; *Annual Report of the Registrar General for Scotland* (1988) Table S1.8).

in North East Fife and in Kincardine and Deeside. The traditionally low areas of the Western Highlands and Islands all recorded figures of between fifteen per cent and twenty six per cent of all births.[22]

Figure 16 shows changes in the pattern of childbearing across the life course of married women; no detailed birth data by age of mother are available before 1938 with the exception of what can be inferred from the 1911 and 1931 Fertility Censuses; there are also some tabulations from the detailed information which was collected only in the first year of Civil Registration in 1855. Figure 16 shows the extent to which by 1931 fertility had come under control at all age groups. From a low point in the 1930s there was some slight increase in almost all age groups after the War but, thereafter, child-bearing became progressively rarer at the older age groups as women not only married younger but also concentrated their children increasingly into the early years of marriage. From the later 1960s, there was a further substantial fall in fertility at all ages; this was particularly marked among married teenage women, who, nevertheless, continued to conceive three quarters of their first births out of wedlock. The national data published in 1911 showed that women married between ages 22 and 26 and living with their husbands for at least fifteen years had on average almost six children. More than one fifth had nine or more. By contrast, by 1951, women marrying in the mid-1920s, at between ages 20 and 24, had on average just under three children; only 7 per cent had seven or more, 42 per cent had one or two. The most recent detailed Scottish data available are from the 1971 census where, taking women married at ages 20–24 in the mid-1940s, we find a mean family size of around 2.5 children; only 3 per cent had seven or more while 51 per cent had one or two. Only 3 per cent of women in this cohort were childless, less than half the figure for those marrying the inter-war period. Subsequent data for England and Wales would suggest that women marrying in the 1960s and 1970s continued the downward trend in very large families and the concentration of families onto two children in particular, but that there was some significant increase in the proportions of married women who remained childless (though the figures will probably not reach those of the interwar period even for the cohorts marrying in the 1980s).

The reasons for these fluctuations in family size are complex and not fully understood, though they are broadly parallelled across most of the Western world. In part, we clearly see, in the early years of the period, the working through to the mass of the population of the factors which induced the onset of the fertility decline in the second half of the nineteenth century. By the 1930s, the idea that family size should be controlled was coming to be accepted almost right across the social spectrum, though there were still some groups who were unable through ignorance, repugnance, or failures in marital communication to achieve their ambitions and some for whom the whole notion of planned parenthood remained obnoxious. In general, however, 'responsible parenthood' was encouraged not only by social pressures from peers and authority figures (particularly doctors) but also by economic pressures and by new patterns of leisure activity: Victorian families would not have fitted into small family cars and to take them on holiday to the seaside even for the day would have been prohibitively expensive for most of the working classes. Lengthening child dependency was a further factor. For the increasingly child-centred middle classes, the aspiration for each child to have his or her own bedroom and to own special and increasingly expensive toys was equally challenging. The economic and political uncertainties of the inter-war period simply made prudence even more attractive.[23]

After the war, the prospects of expanding opportunities seem to have removed some of the inhibitions to marriage and child-bearing, though the economic and social disadvantages of very large families became ever more apparent. Scotland, like the rest of Britain, increasingly became a home-centred society with many women right through to the late 1960s giving up work on marriage to concentrate on child-rearing and home-making. The reduction in child-bearing of the 1970s and 1980s remains difficult to explain. In part the expanding opportunities for female employment (discussed in the next section) and the high costs for women of leaving or remaining for long outside the labour force are important. The economic uncertainties of the 1980s clearly also played a part in checking both marriage and child-bearing. But it is difficult to explain such rapid shifts simply in economic terms. Both the employment aspirations and the leisure interests of many women in the later 1970s and the 1980s were inimical to a child-centred existence and, for the first time, they had available to them the means almost to guarantee that they could avoid pregnancy if they wished. The whole culture of family life was beginning to change.

Wider Changes in Family Life

The changes in fertility and mortality described in earlier sections had other major impacts on family experience, particularly for women. The fall in family size and the reduction in infant and child mortality meant that most women who grew up after the Second World War did so in families of no more than three children, all close to their own age. Compared with their parents and grandparents, few of those born after the early 1950s would have endured in childhood or even in young adulthood the death of a sibling or even of a close friend or relative of their own age.[24] Most of their friends' families were of roughly the same size, so that they would have had little experience of the major variations of living standards according to family size which were such a marked feature of the years before the Second World War. Once the post-war generations married (at a rather younger age than their parents), personal inclination, aided from the mid 1960s by markedly improved contraceptive technology, concentrated child-bearing for most couples into just a few years. By their mid-thirties at the latest, most women could have the confidence to contemplate a long period of life without the encumbrance of small children. The rising demand for part-time labour encouraged increasing numbers of women, right across the social spectrum, to return to paid work, totally transforming the life-course pattern of female employment (see Figure 17). At the other end of the life cycle, the much more rapid fall in mortality among older women compared with men meant that women could contemplate a period of widowhood which had grown on average from about six to about ten years over the course of two generations, and which would take them well into their eighties before they died.[25]

However, while a falling proportion of marriages were dissolved in their early years by death, increasing numbers were broken by separation and divorce. Figure 18 shows the rapid growth of divorces in Scotland; this began in the mid-1960s, well before the 1976 Divorce Act affected the figures. This growth was spread across all durations of marriage. It thus probably reflected a rise in tensions within marriages as expectations of men and women about family and work life changed, together with an increasing willingness to resolve these tensions by terminating marriages that had become unsatisfactory to one or both of the partners. Changes in women's employment were another factor which allowed increasing numbers to contemplate marital dissolution. Changing attitudes to the position of women in society, legal aid in divorce proceedings, and a more supportive social welfare system for the single mother in particular are almost certainly secondary factors in these changes.[26]

The rise in marital dissolution, combined with increased levels of illegitimate births, produced a rapid growth in the number of lone parent families in the 1970s and 1980s. By 1981, 13.7 per cent of families with dependent children were not headed by a married couple and 12.5 per cent of all dependent children were in families headed by a lone

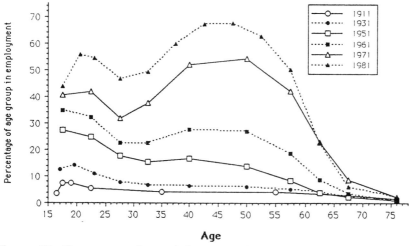

Figure 17. Percentage of married women in employment, by age group, 1911–1981 (*Source: Censuses of Population* 1911–1981).

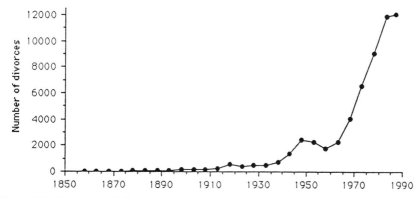

Figure 18. Number of divorces, 1855–1987 Annual averages over five years and 1987) (*Source: Annual Report of the Registrar General for Scotland* (1988) Tables R1.1 and R1.22).

parent. Over the course of the 1980s these figures grew significantly. For earlier periods, the available information is less precise. In Great Britain as a whole in 1979–81, 12 per cent of families with dependent children had a lone parent; this compared with eight per cent in 1971–3. By contrast, in the inter-war period, falling mortality had produced a drop in the number of children living with just a single parent. No precise and reliable estimates of the numbers of families or of children affected are available for Scotland but, in the Report of the 1921 Census, the Registrar General for Scotland jointly published figures with his counterpart for England and Wales. These showed that just under six per cent of all children aged 0–9 had lost their fathers, and that 11.3 per cent of 0–14 year olds had lost one or other parent. The most precise later comparisons come from the two National Child Development Studies. 4.3 per cent of the fathers of the sample of British children born in 1944, and 2.6 per cent of the mothers had died by the time the children reached the age of 15. Of the sample born in 1958, by age 16, 3.4 per cent had lost fathers and 1.4 per cent mothers. Comparable figures for later birth cohorts would be even lower.[27]

The rapid rise in single parenthood in the 1970s and 1980s has sometimes been seen as evidence of a collapse in 'traditional' family life. However, in a Scottish context it is important to remember the high rates of illegitimate births in some parts of the country in the early twentieth century, as well as the high levels of young widowhood. Moreover, while remarriage rates after divorce fell in the 1980s, the majority of lone parents eventually remarried. Even more significantly, while only 40.8 per cent of all households in 1981 contained a married couple with children, 83.2 per cent of male household heads aged 35–44 headed households in this category, a figure almost unchanged from 1971.[28]

In other ways, the conditions of family existence for the majority of the population underwent dramatic improvement in Scotland over the period under review. In 1911, 12.8 per cent of dwellings in Scotland consisted of only a single room and a further 40.5 per cent had only two. Almost half of the population (49.5 per cent) lived in houses with only one or two rooms. The consequent lack of privacy can be seen from the fact that, in 1911, 45 per cent of the population lived at a density of more than two persons per room. In some areas the situation was even worse. In Kilsyth, Wishaw and Armadale, more than one fifth of the population lived in single roomed dwellings, in Coatbridge more than 70 per cent lived at a density of more than two to a room, and in Wishaw over a third lived at a density in excess of four persons per room.[29]

Over the next forty years slow progress was made. In 1951 31.7 per cent of all Scottish dwellings had only one or two rooms. These houses were heavily concentrated in Glasgow, where more than half of all households were still in this type of accommodation, but they were well distributed also in the other cities. Between them, one and two roomed houses in 1951 still contained more than a quarter of the population.

This was the period when residents of Leith described to social investigators the need for the men and boys to go out on a Friday night so that the women and girls could bath in a tub placed in front of the fire in the single living room (in 1951 43.1 per cent of all Scottish households did not have access to a fixed bath — 50 per cent in Glasgow, 32 per cent in Edinburgh, 58 per cent in Dundee, 51 per cent in Aberdeen, 70 per cent in Orkney, 64 per cent in Ross and Cromarty and 72 per cent in Shetland). There was an equal problem with other amenities. More than one housewife in twenty-five (almost all in rural areas) had to make do without any piped water in their homes and/or had no kitchen sink and/or had no access to a kitchen range or cooker. More than a third of Scottish households shared a WC in 1951, but in Dundee the figure was 42 per cent; it was 46 per cent in Motherwell and Wishaw, 43 per cent in Falkirk, and 49 per cent in Paisley.[30]

By 1961 mass demolition of older housing and the construction of huge housing schemes on the fringes of the cities had reduced the numbers of one and two roomed houses by a third but six per cent of the population of Glasgow still lived in a single room. The general amenity of the housing was also slowly improving but more than one housewife in five still had to make do without hot water from a tap (it was one in four in the Clydeside Conurbation); more than a quarter of households still had no fixed bath (40 per cent in Dundee, 41 per cent in Glasgow, 72 per cent on Barra and 75 per cent on North Uist) and one in seven still shared a WC (two in five in Aberdeen and a quarter in Dundee and Glasgow).[31]

Under these circumstances, for most of our period, working class married women's lives remained a constant grind. Keeping homes and husbands and children clean, carrying and heating water, preparing meals with few convenience foods and almost no domestic appliances, systematically starving themselves to allow their husbands and young children an adequate diet, last to bed and first to rise: it is hardly surprising that photographs of working class women right into the 1950s so often show them worn out and old before their time, easy to see why so many succumbed to the strains of pregnancy and to disease. And yet, in part because of the continual battles that were their lives, these mothers have a special place in the memories of their children. Indeed, before their communities were fragmented by the mass rehousing of the post-War period, they often formed mutually supportive networks in a joint struggle to do the best for their children and their families.[32]

However, even in the inter-war period, some labour-saving domestic technology began to appear in middle class households, initially in compensation for the declining availability of domestic servants. After the war, rising living standards brought electricity and new easily controlled cooking and heating systems; it also encouraged the spread of labour saving domestic machinery such as washing machines and vacuum cleaners. Developments in chemistry brought easily cleanable surfaces, synthetic fibres that could readily be washed and ironed and, in detergents, much more powerful cleaning aids. The chemical engineering industry and market demand brought a widening range of foods which could be prepared without a major labour input. For an increasing proportion of families, and especially those who lived on the new estates which flourished everywhere after the Second World War, comfortable living standards in more conveniently sub-divided space could be maintained without the need for housework to be an almost full-time occupation for one or more women in every household. Moreover, by now, a larger (though still usually quite small) share of domestic tasks was being performed by husbands.[33]

Conclusions

The rapid changes in marriage and family life discussed in the previous section have close parallels in most of the rest of the Western world. Almost everywhere, nuptiality and fertility were depressed in the inter-war period and boomed in the 1950s and 1960s. From the 1970s both went into reverse, accompanied by rising divorce and cohabitation and an increase in the proportion of births that occurred outside marriage. As family size fell, aided by improved contraceptive technology, and fewer and fewer women had children after their early thirties, there was an increasing trend for women to return to work while their children were still at school, and a growing minority worked throughout their whole adult lives. These trends were aided by shorter working hours and by developments in domestic technology and in the availability of food and other household commodities in forms which required a much lower labour input before they could be consumed.

Everywhere in the West in this period, there was widespread media and political concern about an actual or potential crisis in family life. In part, as will be clear from what has been written above, this sense of crisis was the result of a failure to set current developments in a longer term historical perspective. In Scotland, for example, low nuptiality and high illegitimate fertility, as well as large numbers of lone parent families (though mainly due to death rather than parental separation), were only new if seen from the perspective of the early post-war years. Some of the trends, in married women's employment and in the relationships between older people and their married children, were almost inevitable side-effects of highly beneficial demographic changes which for the first time allowed women to control their fertility effectively and allowed males and females of all but the very oldest ages significant improvement in their expectation of life.[34]

Nor did this period see a mass rejection of all underlying principles of family life as it had been known for centuries before. In spite of the rise in cohabitation, most young men and women not only expected to marry but eventually did so. Most young women still expected to have children and hoped that they were marrying for life. Most of those who divorced eventually remarried. Most women, even among the professional middle classes, still treated their own employment career as secondary to their partner's.

The changes that did occur involved more subtle shifts of emphasis within family life. Firstly, right up to the Second World War (and for many women in particular for much longer) the claims of the family took precedence over individual aspirations and desires. For example, children worked to maintain family living standards, women sacrificed even their own health to keep the breadwinner fit and well-fed. By the 1980s, and reflecting a much wider shift in social attitudes, personal satisfaction and happiness came to take primacy of place. Not only did these offer a less stable basis for long term relationships, but they were also, in a rapidly changing world, more susceptible to variation over the course of people's lives, at the very time when achieving a high level of satisfaction in interpersonal relationships became increasingly important.[35]

Secondly, the post-war world increasingly offered to individuals both a greater sense of freedom and a rising ability to exploit freedoms. Individual opportunities were increased by growing confidence in the ability to control one's fertility inside or outside marriage and by rising material living standards (even at the end of the 1980s there was a much more supportive Welfare State than was available before the War). Increasing employment opportunities for women and an expanding housing market (even if at rising costs) further reduced earlier constraints.

One crucial consequence of these two sets of shifts was a growing diversity of life styles *within* social class and occupational groups. In earlier generations there had been major differences *between* social groups but occupational and community pressure, marked differences in the availablity of free time and in housing provision, and clearly banded male income levels, had in general structured family life into relatively homogeneous patterns within social groups. In the post-War world, life styles even of those in similar occupations increasingly diverged. After-tax household income differentials (particularly when women's earnings are taken into account) were reduced between classes and increased within them. Older working class and particularly occupational communities were broken up. Reduced working hours and longer holidays, with many new leisure opportunities, became available through improved transportation and higher incomes. At the same time, the dissemination by the media of alternative ways of thinking about family life was yet one more factor encouraging people to make their own lives as they wanted them.[36]

The result was an unprecedented diversity of family life styles and, as a consequence, an increasing uncertainty and insecurity. It would be wrong to imply that all rules and guidelines were thrown away. However, the debates that raged from the 1960s, even in religious circles, on such topics as sex before marriage and remarriage of divorced clergy showed a society in which breaking the old rules no longer produced the same deleterious consequences as in the past, while often it was not at all clear what the new rules ought to be. Even at the very end of the 1980s, while most commentators agreed that a return to a single dominant family morality (such as was arguably widespread in Scotland in the interwar period) was unlikely, it was still unclear whether a more stable family system could re-emerge on the basis of the acceptance of a plurality of rules.

NOTES

Abbreviation: *AR*: Annual Report of the Registrar General for Scotland

1. Calculated from *Scottish Abstract of Statistics* (1987) Table 1.3. and *AR* (1988), Table A1.1.
2. B. R. Mitchell, *British Historical Statistics* (Cambridge 1988) Population and Vital Statistics, Table 2; *Population Trends*, No 23 (1981) and No 59 (1990), Table 1.
3. Census 1981 *Scotland* (Historic Tables 1801–1981) Table 2; *AR* (1988) Table A2.2.
4. A useful summary of the trends in births, deaths and emigration is in *Scottish Abstract of Statistics* (1987) Table 1.3. The detailed annual figures cited in this and the next paragraph are from *ARs*.
5. *Census 1951 Scotland* (Volume 3) Tables 32, 38 and 39; *Census* 1981 *Scotland* (Country of Birth Report).
6. I am indebted to Donald J Morse for most of the work involved in producing this map. For a similar map covering the years 1831 to 1911, see M. Anderson and

D. J. Morse, 'The People' in W. H. Fraser and R. J. Morris (eds) *People and Society in Scotland, Volume II, 1830–1914* (Edinburgh 1990), p. 10. For a summary review on counter-urbanisation see H. Jones 'Evolution of Scottish migration patterns' *Scottish Geographical Magazine* CII (1986) pp. 151–64. For an insightful discussion of an extreme example of the effects on the viability of community by selective outmigration of young men see T. Steel *The Life and Death of St Kilda* (London 1975).

7. Mitchell, Population and Vital Statistics, Table 13; *AR* (1988), Table A1.2.

8. *Detailed AR* (1861) Tables XXII and XXVI; *Supplement to the 78th AR* (Part II) Table Q; *AR* (1988) Table A2.2.

9. *Supplement to the 78th AR* (Part II) Table R; *Second Supplement to the 104th AR*, Tables 3 and 5.

10. *AR* (1986) Table D1.6; *Second Supplement to the 104th AR*, Table 3.

11. *AR* (1946) Table 0(1); *AR* (1988) Table D1.4.

12. *AR* (1939) Appendix VI; *AR* (1988) Table A1.2.

13. *Detailed AR* (1861) Table XXVIII; *Supplement to the 78th AR* (Part II) Table 20; M. Anderson 'The social implications of demographic change' in F. M. L. Thompson (ed) *The Cambridge Social History of Britain* (Cambridge 1990), vol 2. Study of working class diets right through the inter-war period, suggests strongly that the still not uncommon practice of giving larger portions of meat to males than females is the successor to a situation where women, who had most need for red meat, frequently obtained none at all.

14. Figures from *ARs*. There is a useful survey of trends in maternal mortality in *AR* (1945), App X. For a valuable general review see I. S. L. Loudon 'Deaths in childbed from the eighteenth century to 1935' *Medical History* XXX (1986) pp. 1–41.

15. M. Flinn *et al. Scottish Population History from the 17th Century to the 1930s* (Cambridge 1977), Part 5 Sections 5 and 6; R. M. Mitchison, *British Population Change since 1860* (London 1977), Chap 3; M. A. Heasman and I. Lipworth *Accuracy of Certification of Causes of Death* (GRO Studies on Medical and Population Subjects 1966).

16. Note that over a period as long as that covered by Figures 8, 9 and 10, there were significant improvements in diagnosis and also some major reclassifications of causes of death (see Heasman and Lipworth, and Mitchison, Chap 3). As a result, the trends should be seen only as indicators of the general pattern of long run change. Where possible later figures which attempt to take retrospective account of changes in classifications have been used. In the debate over the causes of the long term changes in mortality, Scottish material has not been used as much as it might usefully have been (though note Mitchison, esp Chap 3). For important recent contributions to a debate initiated by T. McKeown (summarised in his *The Modern Rise of Population* (London 1976)), see S. R. S. Szreter 'The importance of social intervention in Britain's mortality decline, c1850–1914: a re-interpretation of the role of public health', *Social History of Medicine*, I (1988), pp. 1–38; R. I. Woods *et al.* The causes of rapid infant mortality decline in England and Wales, 1861–1921', Parts 1 and 2, *Population Studies*, XLII (1988), pp. 343–66 and XLIII (1989) pp. 113–32.

17. For important cautions on the reliability of the data referred to here (especially on heart disease) see footnote 16 and the useful discussion in Mitchison, pp. 54–6. The data on heart disease are from *ARs* (1961, Table 6.6; 1988, Table C1.7).

18. The detailed figures in this paragraph are from the *ARs* for the respective years. 94 of the Lockerbie deaths were registered in 1988, including the deaths of 23 males and

5 females in the 15–24 age group. If these are excluded, ten per cent of male deaths and eight per cent of female deaths were from homicide and other violence. A significant source of mortality not included in these figures is deaths on military service overseas. In addition to smaller numbers in almost every year, about 74,000 Scots servicemen were killed outside Scotland in World War One and 34,000 in World War Two (*Census 1951 Scotland* (Volume 3) p. vi).

19. A summary of trends in this period can be found in Anderson and Morse, pp. 32–42.

20. Calculated from data in *Census 1981 Scotland* (Scottish Summary) Table 6 and *AR* (1981) Table S2.1.

21. *AR* (1988) Table Q1.4. On trends in cohabitation, see J. Haskey and D. Coleman 'Cohabitation before marriage: a comparison of information from marriage registration and the GHS' *Population Trends* No. 43 (1986) and the useful short summary in K. E. Kiernan, 'The family: formation and fission', in H. Joshi (ed), *The Changing Population of Britain* (Oxford 1988), pp. 27–41.

22. A. J. Coale and S. C. Watkins, *The Decline of Fertility in Europe*, (Princeton 1986), Chap 2; more recent data on districts are from *AR* 1988 Table S2.1; for a more general discussion of trends up to the 1980s see also W. Brass, 'Is Britain facing the twilight of parenthood?' in Joshi *Changing Population* . . .

23. For a more detailed discussion of some of the points raised in this and the following paragraph see Anderson and Morse, pp. 32–42; Mitchison, chap 2; W. Seccombe 'Starting to stop: working class fertility decline in Britain', *Past and Present* No. 126 (1990) pp 151–88; K. E. Kiernan 'The structure of families today: continuity or change', in Office of Population Censuses and Surveys, *Occasional paper 31* (London 1983).

24. For siblings of those born in the early 1950s the figure was only about one in fifteen by the age of 25.

25. For a broader discussion of these trends, see M. Anderson 'What is new about the modern family: an historical perspective', in Office of Population Censuses and Surveys, *Occasional paper 31* (London 1983); M. Anderson 'The social implications of demographic change . . .'. In the 1980s, a tendency emerged among a minority of women to delay children until well established in their careers. The extent to which this will lead to a significant reversal of a twentieth century trend towards the clustering of childrn into the earlier years of marriage is unclear (and many will as a result probably remain childless).

26. *AR* (1988) Table R1.4. For further discussion of the causes of these shifts see below. The role of employment of married women is usefully reviewed in J. Ermisch 'Divorce: economic antecedents and aftermath', in Joshi *Changing Population* . . .

27. Calculated from *Census 1981 Scotland* (Household and Family Composition), Tables 12 and 17; *Census of England and Wales 1921* (General Report); *Census 1951 Scotland* (Volume 3); K. Fogelman (ed) *Growing up in Great Britain: Papers from the National Child Development Study* (London 1963) p. 93. A sign of things to come was already apparent in the fact that 16.4 per cent of the 16 year olds in the 1958 cohort were not living with both their natural parents.

28. Calculated from *Census 1971 Scotland* (Household Composition Tables) Table 14 and *Census of Scotland 1981* (Household and Family Composition) Table 6.

29. Data in this and the next paragraph are from *Census of Scotland 1911* (Part II); *Census 1951 Scotland* (Volume 3) Introduction and Tables 42, 47 and 48; *Census 1961 Scotland* (Volume 4 Part 1) Introduction and Table 9.

30. M. Harrington, 'Resettlement and self-image', *Human Relations*, XVIII (1965), 115–37; *Census 1951 Scotland* (Volume 3) Table 58.

31. *Census 1961 Scotland* (Glasgow Report) Table 13; *Census 1961 Scotland* (Housing and Households Volume 1) Table 26.

32. M. Harrington, 'Co-operation and collusion in a group of young housewives', *Sociological Review* New Series XII (1964), pp 255–82; L. Jamieson 'Limiting resources and limiting conventions: working-class mothers and daughters in urban Scotland c1890–1935' in J. Lewis (ed) *Labour and Love: Women's Experience of Home and Family 1850–1940* (London 1986); L. Jamieson 'Theories of family development and the experience of being brought up' *Sociology* XXI (1987) pp. 591–607.

33. C. Davidson, *A Woman's Work is Never Done: a History of Housework in the British Isles 1650–1950*; C. Hardyment *From Mangle to Microwave The Mechanisation of the Household* (Cambridge 1987); G. Hutton, *Social Environment in Suburban Edinburgh* (Joseph Rowntree Memorial Trust 1975); F. R. Elliott *The Family: Change and Continuity* (London 1986) chap 4. The post-War housing estates erected around the cities have justifiably been much criticised as communities in which to live, and they lacked the close sense of mutual assistance which characterised many older urban areas. There can, however, be little doubt doubt that, whatever their drawbacks, even the worst equipped houses were easier to run than most of the urban working class housing erected in Scotland in the previous hundred years.

34. By far the most stimulating of the recent reviews of changes in family life in the West since World War Two is L. Roussel, *La Famille Incertaine* (Paris 1989). I have explored a number of aspects of this topic as it relates to Britain in M. Anderson 'What is new about the modern family . . .'; and in M. Anderson, 'The relevance of family history' in C. C. Harris (ed) *The Sociology of the Family: New Directions for Britain*, Sociological Review Monograph No 28 (1979). See also D. Gittins, *The Family in Question* (London 1985).

35. Some of these shifts were brilliantly summed up by P. L. Berger and H. when they wrote that 'Typically, individuals in our society do not divorce because marriage has become unimportant to them, but because it has become so important that they have no tolerance for the less than completely successful marital arrangement they have contracted with the particular individual in question' ('Marriage and the construction of reality', *Diogenes* (1964), reproduced in M. Anderson (ed) *The Sociology of the Family: Selected Readings* (Second edition, London 1980), p. 321)). Uncertainty over how to handle children in this new world was neatly discussed by C. C. Harris in 'Changing conceptions of the relation between family and societal form in Western society' in R. Scase (ed) *Industrial Society: Class, Cleavage and Control* (London 1977).

36. On diversity see Jamieson 'Theories . . .'. In addition to the sources cited in footnote 34 above, much of the material which underlies the interpretations offered in this paragraph comes from oral history and other semi-structured interviews conducted in Kirkcaldy by Jim Smyth, Dorothy Sinfield and Pat Straw under the ESRC Social Change and Economic Life Initiative. Elizabeth Roberts of the University of Lancaster has been doing important parallel work on Lancashire towns, also supported by an ESRC grant. An illustration of the uncertainty which characterised family life in the 1980s was the continued widespread uncertainty over how to treat cohabiting partners not only in law but also in everday conversation (How should one, in conversation with a third party, refer to one's daughter's 'partner', or the children of one's daughter's partner's first marriage?).

CHAPTER 2

Religion and Secularisation

Callum G. Brown

I

The fortunes of religion have changed more radically since 1914 than in any previous century. The decline of church adherence and attendance, the withdrawal of religious issues from the political arena, and the secularisation of habits and of popular thought constitute a widespread phenomenon within western civilisation. But though the twentieth century is taken by many to be 'the secular century'[1], there has been comparatively little detailed research and analysis on either Scotland or Britain.

Various factors compel consideration of religion's social history this century. Firstly, the decline of the churches has taken place almost entirely within the last ninety years, not earlier as many assume; this means that the declining social significance of religion — 'secularisation' — has been and remains an important element in contemporary cultural development. Secondly, decline has not prevailed continuously throughout the century, but has been reversed by significant church growth in some decades; this means, amongst other things, that secularisation has not been inevitable nor linear. And thirdly, the decline has not been simultaneous, nor identical in form, in every country and region.

II

Statistics of church adherence and churchgoing are an obvious starting point in examining religious change, but they have been little used by historians of British religion in the twentieth century.[2] Declining church connection — in Scotland especially — has been taken too readily for granted. But, as this section demonstrates, when available statistics of church adherence are assembled and analysed, some very surprising conclusions emerge.

Graph 1 (*see also* Appendix) shows the changing level of church adherence in Scotland from 1914 to 1986, 'Church adherence' is defined as those who have a connection with a church through membership

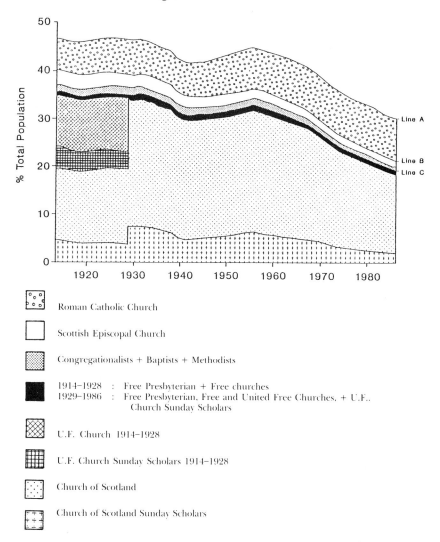

Graph 1. Church adherence in Scotland, 1914–1986.

or equivalent of either a church or a Sunday school. (The peculiar position of Catholic data is discussed below.) The figures for each denomination and denominational Sunday school have been expressed as percentages of total Scottish population, and the figures have then been 'stacked' for each year. Thus, Line C shows the total presbyterian adherence *per capita*, Line B total Protestant adherence *per capita*, and Line A (the top line) shows an estimate of total church adherence *per capita*. It must be emphasised that the figures are incomplete: excluded categories include Bible Class membership, Sunday-school membership of non-presbyterian churches, and adherents of some minor churches (like the Brethren) and 'church-like' organisations (such as the Salvation Army and the Faith Mission). Consequently, the graph is a *minimum* figure for church adherence, with the real figure being perhaps ten per cent higher in the 1910s and 1920s, and perhaps five per cent higher in the 1980s.

The value of the graph comes, not through showing *absolute* figures of church adherence, but through showing *trends* over the course of the seventy years. In general, the fortunes of the Protestant and Catholic churches can be separately analysed. The Catholic Church has no category of 'membership', and the graph instead displays a notional figure for mass attenders. (This is assumed to be 57 per cent of estimated Catholic population (E.C.P.), derived from a formula which postulates that E.C.P. is equivalent to mass attenders multiplied by a factor of 1.75.) In this respect, the Catholic data in the graph — unlike all the other data — do not indicate year-to-year changes in church connection, but merely provide an indication of relative changes in the number of Catholics to a scale roughly equivalent to Protestant church adherence. As a result, what the figures indicate is a steady rise in the Catholic share of total population during the century as Catholic birth rate exceeded the national average (Catholic births accounting for 16 per cent of the Scottish total in 1916–20, and for a peak of 24 per cent in 1970–75). This has in some measure been due to children of 'mixed' (Catholic-Protestant) marriages being baptised and brought up in the Church. Scottish Catholic adherence reached its peak share of Scots population in 1976, and its *absolute* peak in 1980. It has only been in the 1980s that general levels of Catholic adherence have started to show signs of 'leakage'.

The long-term rise in the Catholic community from the early nineteenth to late twentieth centuries contrasts with the fluctuating fortunes of the Protestant churches. A graph covering the period 1840–1914 appeared in volume 2 of this series, showing how Protestant (and total) church adherence grew until 1905 when the peak of church connection in Scotland was attained. A very slight but still significant downward trend set in between 1905 and 1914, with the decline coming entirely from presbyterian membership and Sunday-school enrolment. The present graph shows that this trend continued during the First World War, with the decline being sharpest in Sunday-school and United Free Church membership. But what is most significant is the resurgence in church connection in 1918–25, and the high plateau from 1925 until 1931. This resurgence was felt by most categories (especially the Roman Catholic population and Church of Scotland membership), though not Sunday-school enrolment (which was affected by a fall in the birth rate), and is all the more remarkable for the high level of adult emigration during the early 1920s. But from 1931 until 1941, Line A indicates a fall in connection of almost 5 per cent. However, the vast bulk (63 per cent) of this fall was accounted for by a steepening decline in Sunday-school enrolment (especially during war-time child evacuation in 1939–41).

The interesting conclusion to be derived from this is that despite the economic dislocation and high unemployment of both the 1920s and 1930s, adult Protestant church connection only fell very slightly overall. This is confirmed by analysis of the proportion of Church of Scotland members who communicated at least once a year. In contrast to the measurement of 'passive' church connection by membership given in Graph 1, taking communion at least one a year is one measure of 'active' presbyterian church adherence. An analysis of 'active' Church

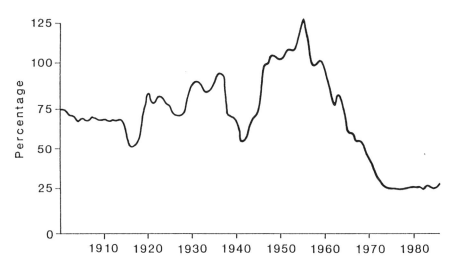

Graph 2. Church of Scotland: Success in recruitment, 1900–1986. New communicants in year n expressed as percentage of baptisms in year n-18. Data on 'admissions by profession' and on baptisms are from R. Currie *et al.*, *Churches and Churchgoers: Patterns of Church Growth in the British Isles since 1700* (Oxford, 1977), pp. 169–170; and *The Church of Scotland Yearbook*, 1971–88.

of Scotland communicants as a proportion of total members indicates a *rise* during each year of the economic recession of the early 1920s (from 63 to 72 per cent in 1918–25). Though the data are unavailable for the period of the Slump (1929–31), the economic downturn of 1937–8 also indicates a rise, whilst the periods of better economic performance (1927–8 and 1934–36) indicate falls in active connection.[3]

Further evidence of this comes from Graph 2 which provides a measure of the Church of Scotland's success in recruitment. It shows that new communicants (admitted mostly in their late teens), expressed as a percentage of those baptised (overwhelmingly in infancy) eighteen years before, rose significantly during the inter-war years — almost entirely in years of relative economic hardship (1920–23, 1929–32, and 1937). Despite falling success in some years of relative prosperity (1924–28, and 1934), the Church's recruitment achievements as measured by the size of its own baptised 'constituency' were higher in every year from 1919 to 1937 than in any year between 1900 and 1914.

Such evidence suggests that church connection was not adversely affected by general economic circumstances in the inter-war period. Indeed, economic depression and the coal strike in 1921–2 produced quite widespread religious revivals. However, it is noteworthy that the largest single fall in presbyterian communion in the inter-war period occurred in 1926, the year of the second coal strike and the General Strike — events marked by many clergy (both Protestant and Catholic) preaching opposition to industrial action and by divided congregations in mining communities.[4]

Perhaps the most remarkable feature of Graph 1 is the very significant growth in church connection between 1941 and 1956. The scale of this church growth has been singularly underestimated by observers. Church of Scotland membership rose 4.7 per cent, reaching its all-time *absolute* membership peak in 1956. This was the largest church growth in Scotland since the 1880s, marked by a number of significant religious events: religious revivals in Hebridean communities, the Church of Scotland's 'Christian Commandoes', the reformed churches' 'Tell Scotland' campaign, and the Billy Graham crusade of March and April 1955 which used BBC radio, the popular press, and closed-circuit relay television to extend the outreach of mass meetings held at Hampden Park and Tynecastle football stadia.

However, it is clear that the Billy Graham campaign had little effect on church connection, coming at the end, not the beginning, of this last period of Protestant church growth in Scotland in 1941–56; nearly 70 per cent of Church of Scotland ministers reported that it had little or no effect, and very few adults came forward for conversion. It was children who were most affected.[5] During 1941–56, the greatest growth in religious adherence was amongst children with Church of Scotland Sunday-school enrolment rising 41 per cent. This growth fed through in an enormous growth in the number of new communicants between 1946 and 1955, reaching 45,832 in the latter year — the highest figure this century. The religiosity of presbyterian eighteen-year-olds in the late 1940s and early 1950s becomes all the more impressive when it is set against the number of baptisms eighteen years earlier. As Graph 2 shows, this figure rarely went above 90 per cent in the 1920s and fell to under 70 per cent in 1938, but rose to well over 100 per cent between 1947 and 1956, falling back thereafter.

In short, the Church of Scotland around mid-century was recruiting well in excess of those baptised 18 years before: amongst those non-baptised, and amongst other age groups. These nine years were a period of phenomenal recruiting success unmatched this century or, probably, since the middle decades of the preceding century. The level of church adherence per capita in 1956 was only marginally lower (1.7 per cent less) than in 1914, and only 3.3 per cent less than the all-time peak of 1905. Indeed, a greater proportion of Scots were formal church adherents in the mid 1950s than between 1840 and 1883.

It was thus in 1956 that the first sustained decline in church adherence commenced in Scotland. And the scale and rapidity of decline were staggering, mostly due to the worsening condition of the Church of Scotland. By 1963, the level had fallen to the lowest this century. However, many indicators point to a watershed in 1963–65. In those three years, the proportion of marriages being religiously solemnised in Scotland took its first major peace-time drop (from 80 to 77 per cent, falling thereafter by more than 1 per cent per annum every year).[6] Most importantly, those three years saw the rate of Church of Scotland recruitment (Graph 2) take a cataclysmic fall from 82 to 60 per cent of baptised persons, well below the level at which the Church could replace members. It then fell by another 16 points in 5 years, and halved in just over a decade. By the early 1980s, recruitment had stabilised at a haemorrhaging rate of around a mere 28 per cent of the baptised 'constituency'.

The period 1963 to 1975 was a membership catastrophe for the Church of Scotland. Church reports of the period show some awareness of the problems, but failure to appreciate sophisticated statistical analysis left the Church then (as arguably now) ill-informed as to the order of magnitude of its own declension.[7] It did not suffer alone. The

Congregationalists, the Baptists and the Methodists — the evangelical 'wing' of Scottish Protestantism — saw a major decline after 1963, but it 'bottomed out' in the 1980s. Only in the Church of Scotland — one of the least puritanical and the least evangelical of denominations — has the rate of decline been sustained right up to the present.

None the less, the Protestant share of total church adherents has fallen since 1914 whilst only the Catholic share has risen appreciably (from 13.9 per cent in 1914 to 21.9 per cent in 1970). But the divergences between Protestant and Catholic fortunes are even wider than that. Whilst *membership* data show that serious decline only set in after the mid 1950s, the more scant data on church*going*, shown in Table 1, point to falling Protestant fortunes much earlier. Comparing dates with similar measures shows the scale of decline between 1851 and 1984 (columns A and C in rows 2 and 7), church attendance virtually halved in Scotland as a whole from 35.9 to 17.2 per cent of population, and fell by a third in Glasgow from 31.1 to 19.5 per cent of population. The loss is even more marked if presbyterian attendances per head of non-Catholic population are isolated (columns B and D, rows 2 and 7), showing a decline of over two-thirds in Glasgow and almost four-fifths in Scotland as a whole during 1851–1984. Most interestingly, other figures (columns B and D, rows 4 and 5) show that the vast bulk of this decline had already occurred long before the peak of twentieth-century presbyterian membership in the mid 1950s. Presbyterian church membership by then allowed great laxity in active attendance. Catholic attendance was much higher, accounting for 43 per cent of the total in 1984 — making the Catholic Church the largest in terms of attendance in Scotland. Falling Catholic attendances only became significant in the 1970s: by the early 1980s, Catholic congregations were reporting an annual drop of 0.76 per cent.[8]

Therefore, secularisation as measured by church connection has been characterised by an early fading of Protestant enthusiasm for church worship (probably at the turn of the century), but must be set against a high level of church membership until the early 1960s sustained by periods of vigorous recruitment in the inter-war period and, especially, during 1946–56. At the same time, Catholic adherence has grown by natural increase and by a late development of — thus far — relatively-mild religious alienation amongst Catholics. Secularisation as a widespread breach of popular church connection (membership, religious marriage and baptism[9]) occurred only from about 1963–65. From then until the present, the slide in all indices has been very severe for most Protestant churches.

Table 1. Sunday Church Attendance Rates in Glasgow and Scotland, 1851–1984

| | Glasgow | | Scotland | |
	A Attendance per capita %	B Presbyterian attendance per capita of non- RC population %	C Attendance per capita %	D Presbyterian attendance per cap, of non-RC population %
1851				
1. Morning adults +child.	20.7	16.7	25.6	29.0
2. All diets adults +child.[1]	31.1	25.7	35.9	40.2
1876				
3. Morning? adults +child.	19.3	18.6		
1954				
4. Morning[2] adults	14.2	6.3		
1959				
5. All diets[2] adults			17.7	10.8
1984				
6. All diets[2] adults	15.3	6.2	13.1	6.3
7. All diets[2] adults +child.	19.5	8.1	17.2	9.0

[1]This figure for attenders calculated on the 'Mann formula' of all morning plus half afternoon plus a third of evening attendances.

[2]By the 1950s, the terms 'morning' and 'all diets' became virtually interchangeable because of the decline of afternoon and evening services.

Sources: Figures calculated from attendance data in Census of Religious Worship and Education, Scotland, 1851, *P.P* 1854; R. Howie, *The Churches and Churchless in Scotland* (1893, Paisley), p. 98; J. Highet, 'The Churches', in J. Cunnison and J.B.S. Gilfillan (eds), *The Third Statistical Account of Scotland* (1958, Glasglow), Appendix p. 956; J. Highet, *The Scottish Churches* (1960, London), p. 60; P. Brierley and F. Macdonald (eds); *Prospects for Scotland: Report of the 1984 Census of the Churches* (1985, Edinburgh and Bromley), pp. 60, 90. Additional estimates of Catholic Population taken from R. Currie *et al.* (eds.), *Churches and Churchgoers.* (1977, Oxford).

III

These national trends conceal important differences in regional and social experience of church connection. For Scotland contains considerable diversity both in scale of religious adherence and in the distribution of denominations.[10]

By the 1980s, the Hebrides and the western Highlands[11] had by far the highest turnout for Sunday church services not only in Scotland but in mainland Britain as a whole. In the Western Isles (the Outer Hebrides) and Lochalsh District (the Isle of Skye and adjacent mainland) in 1984, 53 per cent of the total population were estimated as attending Sunday worship or Sunday school, compared to the Scottish average of 17 per cent. Distinctive economy, culture and language survived in the Highlands and Hebrides to sustain strong qualities of 'peasant religion'. Against a nineteenth-century background of the 'Clearances', repression of Gaelic, and subsistence crises, the victory of tenurial security under the 1886 Crofters Act not only 'froze' the economic and social structures of the region, but secured the religious character against some at least of the forces for religious change being felt elsewhere in Scotland and mainland Britain.

In some places along a west-to-east band, Catholicism survived three centuries of the Protestant Church virtually unscathed: Hebridean islands like Barra and South Uist, mainland peninsulas at Morar, Moydart and Knoydart, and in some inland glens and estates stretching from the Great Glen to Aberdeenshire. The culture of the Catholic islands has retained a flavour unique in Scotland with popular culture dominated by the Church. Here alone in Scotland, wayside shrines are evidence of the weakness of presbyterian hostility. By the early 1950s, the traditional home ceilidh was displaced by the public ceilidh where the priest presided as 'M.C.', and the Canon owned the island's cinema projector and selected the films. Everyone went to the Church for some purpose at least twice a week, and many of the elderly went once a day. In this way, secular Gaelic culture and religious culture remained closely intertwined.

Despite a similar economy and language, the rest of the Hebrides had a very different religious environment. The strict presbyterianism which had arisen in the late eighteenth and nineteenth centuries had created a near monopoly for the Free Church in the crofting counties and a considerable strength in the farming economy of the eastern and southern Highlands. But the Highland Free Church was split by two secessions: the first in 1893 when some 8,000 adherents who disapproved of weakening presbyterian standards formed the Free Presbyterian Church; and the second in 1900 when about half of the Highland Free Church joined the new United Free Church. The split of 1900 caused severe ruction in many congregations in the Highlands. At Ness on the Isle of Lewis, the majority Free Church congregation occupied the Church while their former minister obtained an interim interdict upon it in the name of the new United Frees. The Secretary of State arranged the despatch of a gunboat with eighty police aboard to make a night-time landing to dislodge the squatters, whilst soldiers were ready at Fort George if events became more serious. Confrontation was only averted when the Free Church Assembly Clerk intercepted the police and convinced them of the peaceful end to the occupation.[12]

Thus, the Highland Church of Scotland of today derives mostly from the Free Church element that joined the United Free Church in 1900 and which then joined the Church of Scotland in 1929. This has given it a religious ambience rarely found in Lowland congregations of the Church of Scotland. A religious revival in west Lewis in 1949–53 was focused on the Church of Scotland parish church at Barvas. A young woman convert recalled:[13]

> I had been converted about the end of March 1949, and a few young people became Christians at that time. And I suppose there was quite a *hunger* in the congregation and a liveliness among the Lord's people. And a new minister came to our congregation in April, and that again is new life, new interest. And there was fantastic *urgency* in prayer among the whole congregation really — in the prayer meetings — and there was always prayer for revival.

In total contrast to the adjacent Catholic islands, presbyterianism in Lewis clashed with the secular Gaelic culture of the dance hall. A

2. Reunion gathering of the Scottish Churches (Church of Scotland and the United Free Church of Scotland), October 1929. J Buchan and G. A. Smith *The Kirk in Scotland 1560–1929* (1930).

local man and his mother recalled a confrontation at Carloway during the revival:

Son: I was the MC at the dance that night, and one of the girls that were with us — they were singing a Gaelic song. And she had just finished and we were all sitting down in a kind of circle when the back door of the hall opened and in walked this minister and his wife. Of course, this had never happened before in anyone's experience — a minister coming to a dance in Lewis. I'd had a bit to drink that night, and I immediately got up and was very angry — more or less tried to get rid of him. In fact, I ordered him out of the dance hall. And I asked him point-blank: 'Have you got a ticket to come in here?'

Mother: Mr MacLennan answered 'No, I've got a ticket which would take me anywhere.' And my son said: 'Well, you should have paid your way in, and not come in the back door.' . . . My son called for a dance, and nobody moved. [The minister asked the girl to sing a psalm, and then offered prayer and spoke to the revellers.] Before Mr MacLennan had spoken a lot, my son got up and I thought the same thing was going to happen again. I said: 'Be quiet for a minute . . .' 'It's alright, Mummy', he said in quite a different voice to what he had. So he went and apologised to Mr MacLennan. That was his conversion.

Young people — many from that dance — were drawn 'in buses, lorries and those who had cars' to the parish church at Barvas, where a visiting minister, Duncan Campbell, became a key preacher in the revival. He recalled:

Of course the church couldn't accommodate them now. They're standing outside, the place is packed: the pulpit steps, the pulpit itself. And when I managed to get in the pulpit, there was a young woman lying on the floor — a schoolteacher who had been at the dance when God swept in. She's now under deep conviction of sin.

The Barvas revival lasted three years, and like an earlier revival in the 1920s occurred during a period of economic adjustment in the Hebrides. The more measured pace of Highland religious life has been represented by the annual summer 'Communion season'. The 'season' starts with a Thursday Fast Day which the poet Alasdair Maclean recalled at Sanna on the Ardnamurchan peninsula during his childhood as 'a sort of buckshee Sunday' in which 'I would have to Sunday it from dawn to dusk and not be able to hammer nails or saw wood or whistle or scuff my feet or any of the other things forbidden out of doors on a Highland Sabbath, where one's neighbours might see and hear'.[14] Church services continue through to Sunday when the communion table is 'fenced' by the minister's warning to the 'unworthy' and only a small number of usually elderly people come forward from the congregation. This characteristic presbyterianism of the Gaels has been in geographical retreat since the 1880s. The decline of Gaelic church services has swept northwards and westwards from the Highlands to the point in the 1980s when English services are now more popular than Gaelic services in many parts of the West Highlands. In the train of this anglicisation has come the demise of presbyterian dissent itself. Only in isolated mainland communities and in the Western Isles does the traditional puritanism survive in the Free Church, Free Presbyterian Church and within some congregations of the Church of Scotland.

Revivalism has this century tended to be most apparent amongst isolated crofting communities, but it has also occurred in fishing and mining villages which have been noted throughout Britain as centres of evangelical religion.[15] Occupational and community unity have tended to create an environment in which organised religion — often split between varied evangelical congregations and temperance lodges — dominate local culture. Fishing and mining (like crofting) were industries in which crises of family and community survival became sparks to religious fervour after the 1880s. Slumps in fishing and in coal in the early 1920s, together with coal strikes in 1921 and 1926, instigated the growth of revivalist and teetotal movements encompassing different evangelical sects and temperance organisations. At Inverallochy on the Moray Firth in 1921, the fishing depression brought 200 men to bible readings at the harbour; a journalist reported that 'after each parable had been explained they knelt down wringing their hands and swaying their bodies to and fro.'[16] In these communities, smaller evangelical denomination were strong: the Brethren (both the more liberal Open Brethren and the very strict Close Brethren of mining and fishing villages), the Methodists (strong in the fishing and fish-curing communities of Shetland), the Congregationalists (in east-coast and Morayshire fishing villages), the Churches of Christ (fishing villages) and Baptists (on the crofter-fishing island of Tiree and in mainland villages). In addition, a plethora of independent evangelical organisations flourished: the Salvation Army, the Faith Mission (which enjoyed considerable success both in the Highlands and elsewhere for the prominent role it gave to women), county Christian Unions (which sent evangelists touring their communities), and teetotal friendly-societies like the Rechabites (in fishing villages) and the Good Templars (which had enormous popularity in Lanarkshire pit villages and in small-towns throughout Lowland Scotland).

The puritanism and evangelical quality of fishing and crofting communities in the early twentieth century had been presaged in the nineteenth century in textile-mill villages, agricultural districts and large cities. This was still evident in the inter-war period. Molly Weir remembered in Glasgow that as well as attending 'the big Church, where we went to Sunday School and Bible Class, and had our church parades of Girl Guides and Boys' Brigade, we had the excitement in summertime of tent missions coming to Springburn to convert us' where 'we often stood up to be saved several times during the week'. She and her friends attended Church of Scotland, Salvation Army, Methodist and even Catholic meetings for nothing 'but the sheer enjoyment' and 'just because one gave tattie scones, the next sausage rolls and the other gave pies'.[17] A woman born in 1913 recalled a similar milieu for religion in interwar Stirling:

> . . . we went to an awful lot of religious meetings in those days. Not I think for any religious feelings, but the fact — material gain, you know. We got a wee bag with maybe different things in it — cookies and things in it, and that was a sort of draw. Not that we were hungry; we werenae as bad as all that, but just it was something different . . . There was a wee Railway Mission at the end of the street . . . a lovely wee Mission Hall. . . . And then y'see we went to the different Sunday schools — I went to the South Church Sunday school. I chummed with the same wee girl. . . . And then I was in the Salvation Army . . . the Salvation Army people were always wanting to convert you and they used to say: 'Now put up your hand anybody that wants to be saved.' So you would look along the line to see who wanted to be saved, and if you thought you were safe you'd put your hand up. . . . Oh yes, it was all religion. And another thing. Another friend, another pal of mine, her father was a caretaker of the Baptist Church. Now we went to the Baptist Church meetings. I don't know why we didnae sprout wings![18]

But the puritanical and revivalist ambience of Lowland religion was starting to change in the 1920s and 1930s. In country districts[19] increasing farm ownership in place of tenancy reduced the social schism which had helped fuel evangelical dissent amongst farm tenants, whilst mechanisation, improved transport and rural depopulation undermined plebeian religious solidarity. This culminated in 1925 with the removal of landowners' rights to own, allocate and rent-out parish-church pews, ending the last of the dissenters' grievances. Rural presbyterian congregations started to collapse in the 1930s and 1940s after the church union of 1929. Depopulation and growing disinterest accelerated amalgamations of congregations and parishes in the 1960s, 1970s and 1980s. Even in fertile and relatively-populous Lowland areas, the falling number of parish churches has been diminishing the role of religion as a community focus.

Urban areas have presented different types of problem for religion. The Scottish city in the twentieth century has been changed more radically and more rapidly than virtually any in the non-communist world. In 1911, 98.2 per cent of householders in Glasgow rented their homes from private landlords — usually one- or two-bedroomed tenement flats. By 1980, 73 per cent of Glasgow homes were rented from state agencies — dominated by the large peripheral council housing 'schemes' constructed in the 1950s and 1960s with up to 50,000 people in each.[20] The scale of state-engineered rehousing and 'overspill', notably between 1945 and 1965, fractured congregations, causing turmoil in church attempts to maintain contact with their flocks. The Church of Scotland[21] found difficulty in raising enthusiasm and funds for church extension, especially after the union of 1929 and the declining rolls of the 1960s left a burden of excess church buildings in the wrong, inner-city areas. In the 1940s, state restrictions on the construction industry slowed down the churches' ability to follow their migrating population — both during and after the war. In practical terms in the 1950s, the Protestant churches looked upon the housing schemes as missionary 'fields' where teams of evangelists, youth leaders and Sunday-school teachers were 'sent in'.

By comparison, other churches seemed more flexible and adept in their response to population movement. The Catholic Church was by far the most adventurous with its work in the schemes, having left the bulk of its church-building programmes to the 1945–65 period.

3. The Bible Societies' kiosk at the Empire Exhibition, Glasgow, 1938. W. C. Somerville *From Iona to Dunblane* (1948).

In Glasgow, Paisley, Dunbartonshire, Lanarkshire and Ayrshire, 96 parishes had been founded by 1914, all but nine after 1845 (a rate of more than one per year). But between 1914 and 1939, this average fell with only 13 new parishes being added, mostly to small towns. Despite the growth in Catholic population between the Wars, there was relatively little movement to areas served inadequately by existing chapels. But from 1941 to 1972, 116 new parishes were added (a rate of almost 4 per year) with the vast majority in housing schemes and new towns of the Glasgow conurbation.[22] Catholics — relatively poorer than the majority of the Protestant working class — seem to have only become council tenants in large numbers with the mass slum-clearance and overspill policies of the post-war decades. By the 1970s, the Catholic population of Scotland probably had the highest proportion of council tenants amongst all church adherents. One of the few studies of its kind, conducted in Alloa in that decade, showed that whilst 68 per cent of all families lived in council houses, this figure rose to 82 per cent for Catholics.[23] In this large-scale movement, the Church utilised the opportunity to open Catholic state schools beside new churches, church halls and presbyteries, creating vital community centres which combined devotional, educational and leisure functions. Whilst residential segregation of Catholics in the new schemes varied, it appears that this unique opening played a major part in sustaining the community and cultural functions for the Catholic Church, and thus church adherence as a whole.

Smaller Protestant denominations also were relatively more responsive to the 'migrations' than the Church of Scotland. A good example is the Baptist Union of Scotland which, despite being the least centralised of the major Protestant denominations, yet had probably the most effective policy of church planting and evangelism. For much of the century, the central Baptist Union paid four-fifths or two-thirds of the cost of the erection of new churches, resulting in quick responses to rising new communities: in the 'garden city' of Rosyth (1923), and Glasgow housing schemes at Cathcart (1923), Mosspark (1924) and Knightswood (1929) — helping the Baptist Union to its peak of membership in 1935. This continued in the post-war period with new churches at Drumchapel, Easterhouse and Castlemilk in Glasgow, Craigmiller and Wester Hailes in Edinburgh, and in the new towns. The Baptists combined church building with an active evangelistic policy; during the Slump in 1933, an evangelism campaign produced 150 conversions at Irvine and 110 in Wishaw. Whilst Baptist membership has fallen 29 per cent between 1935 and 1986 (compared to 32 per cent in the Church of Scotland), its membership downturn in the years after 1956 was reversed from 1982. Though it is too early to tell whether this signals the start of significant growth, it does show how small evangelistic churches may find a 'bottoming-out' of decline. Those churches which remain 'firm in the faith', or resistant to compromise with secular influences, may well experience limits to seculariston not felt by larger churches.[24]

Taking the Lowlands as a whole, it is becoming clear that the highest rates of church attendance are to be found in the western industrial counties. This reversed the general trend found in the 1851 Religious Census. Aberdeen had a significantly high rate of attendance in 1851, but by 1984 had the lowest rate (9.9 per cent of population) in Scotland. It was in the Glasgow conurbation that the highest Sunday turnouts — between 21 and 27 per cent — were to be found in 1984. This raises important questions about the effects of social class and community-type upon religion.[25] Most research on class and religion in Scotland took place in the 1960s and early 1970s when the prevailing orthodoxy in sociology, social anthroplogy and history was that the secularisation of religion had been due to the religious alienation of the working classes. Research by Robertson in a small district of Edinburgh (Prestonfield) appeared to show that the religiosity of the working classes was very much less than that of the middle classes. However, larger-scale research by Sissons on Falkirk (Table 2) showed that in the late 1960s

Table 2. Religion and Social Class in Falkirk, 1968–70

	Professional	Intermediate	Skilled	Partly-skilled	Unskilled
	%	%	%	%	%
Social structure of Falkirk	3	10	51	19	13
Social structure of churches adherents:					
C of S	11	29	52	7	1
R.C.	0	20	60	16	4
Other Protestant	7	23	66	3	2
Church members claiming attendance every Sunday	61	55	59	76	83

Source: P. Sissons, *The Social Significance of Church Membership in the Burgh of Falkirk* (1973, Edinburgh), pp. 60, 71

working-class religiosity was considerable. Amongst church members, the skilled working class predominated in all churches, and in fact had a representation in each church higher than in the burgh as a whole. Whilst the professional and lower-middle ('intermediate') classes had a significantly high representation in all the Protestant churches (and none in the Catholic Church), the partly skilled and unskilled were less likely to be church members. Moreover, in response to questionnaires amongst church members alone, middle-class claims to church attendance every Sunday were lower than working-class claims.

Further evidence of working-class religiosity came from Panton's work on Alloa. In an analysis of church membership according to type of housing, he showed that 66 per cent of owner-occupiers were church members but that this figure fell only slightly to 58 per cent for council tenants. The lowest figure, 47 per cent, came with those in privately-rented property, perhaps suggesting that the most mobile sections in the community were the least likely to have established connections with a local congregation. In a sophisticated statistical projection, he conjectured that level of church membership rose from a very low level amongst the lower working class to a very high level with the upper working class, falling back to about average for the intermediate social group to rise marginally with the lower middle class, and then to fall off to a very low level with the upper middle class. Though this research is inconclusive, it provides a very plausible account.

In short, the evidence of working-class alienation from religion during this century is no greater than the evidence of middle-class alienation. Indeed, the social forces unleashed in the crucial era of church-membership decline in the 1960s and 1970s point to a greater growth of bourgeois irreligion. Though this may well have started at the turn of the century, the major breach occurred during the 'swinging sixties' when the children and the young of suburban Scotland lost religious faith. The alienation of youth had started slowly after the mid-1890s when Sunday-school membership per capita of children peaked (at over 50 per cent) and when religious organisations had a dominance of the organised leisure pursuits of the young. Despite the sustained growth of church-affiliated uniformed organisations like the Boys Brigade and Scouting organisations, the decline of the much larger Sunday schools was crucial; in the fifty years to 1981, Church of Scotland Sunday-school pupils as a proportion of 5–15 year old fell from 38 to 11 per cent. The bulk of this fall occurred during the 1960s and 1970s. The 'moral metamorphosis' amongst the middle-class young displaced church values and traditional concepts of 'respectability' with a secular transatlantic youth culture. From youth to adulthood, new lifestyle values emerged, producing novel demographic changes — increases in divorces, civil marriages, cohabitation and single-parent families — creating new constituencies for which the churches are failing to cater.

IV

Though the decline of popular religious adherence occurred relatively late in the century, profound changes in the *institutional* role of religion started in earlier decades.[26] Between the 1870s and the 1920s, the churches had played a significant part in creating and controlling local civil government. Ostensibly 'secular' institutions were created to develop local democracy — in large part at the behest of presbyterian dissenters seeking the break-up of the Established Church's monopoly control of civil institutions like the parish-school system and the poor-relief system. In the late nineteenth century, a succession of new popularly-elected authorities came into being: school boards (replaced by elected county education authorities in 1920–30), parish councils (1895), town councils for small burghs, and county councils. In addition, the Temperance (Scotland) Act 1913 instituted local veto plebiscites from June 1920 in which the electorate in local-authority wards could vote their districts free from public houses and off-licenses. Avenues opened up for churchmen to create a state-run 'Godly Commonwealth' using the vote as 'a sacred trust'.

Church dominance of civil institutions varied. Greatest success came in the school boards and county education authorities in which, with the exception of Labour candidates and a few others, the elected members were almost entirely church candidates representing their denominations. In both large cities like Glasgow and Edinburgh, and in rural parishes, the school board sustained the traditional aims of church schooling, retaining the same financial structure of school management and employing teachers wholly trained at denominational teacher-training colleges. Despite the increased secular content of the syllabus, with religious instruction timetabled separate from other subjects, the Protestant churches were perfectly happy with state schooling. However, the traditional evangelical philosophy of education was gradually undermined from the 1890s onwards by the growth of Christian socialism, the social-welfare functions of the schools, and by the state takeover of presbyterian teacher-training colleges in 1908. None the less, church influence did not diminish, even in urban areas. The majority of members remained church-nominated, the 'secular' curriculum acquired new subjects like 'Temperance' and 'Civics', and Catholic schools were preserved within an enlarged state system after 1918.

Parish councils also retained strong religious control. Even in large cities like Glasgow, there were ministers on the councils. The parish councils were direct descendants of the kirk-sessions, and they tended to operate in much the same way. In a Borders parish, claimants for relief were checked for their drinking habits, and even the Medical Officer of Health was threatened with the sack unless he 'freed himself from the scandal' of adultery. On the Catholic island of Barra, it was observed that the parish council 'must look like a Holy Synod'.[27] The advent of increased local democracy introduced in the Hebridean islands an era of ministers and priests acting as county and district councillors and, since 1975, as Western Isles Authority councillors. More controversially, the local-veto plebiscites of the 1920s produced large-scale church campaigning throughout Scotland for the temperance vote. Church influence in civil affairs appeared to be growing.

However, the 1920s proved to be cathartic for democratic religious administration. Open sectarian division between Protestants and Catholics at the triennial education elections was probably the final straw for the government, which brought Scotland into line with England and Wales by passing control of state schools to the county councils in 1929. In the same year, parish councils were abolished as part of the wider British reorganisation of welfare administration. And the local-veto plebiscites, successful in making around 30 of Scotland's over 500 wards 'dry' in the early 1920s, became by the late 1920s much less successful as the brewers and distillers helped to swing public opinion, and especially the Labour vote, to 'wet' policies. Not only was direct church influence in local democracy diminishing, but evangelical social policy was in retreat as the state took greater control of public life.

The decline of religious control over social policy by the early 1930s had a great bearing on public perception of the role of religion. The churches — predominantly the presbyterian churches — no longer held the answers to social questions, no longer provided the ideology of social improvement. Social salvation was being divorced from religious salvation in an unprecedented way. In a direct sense, parishioners no longer approached ministers and elders as agents of the poor-relief, and no longer had to answer to them as school-board members for the truancy of their children. Indirectly, the churches were no longer accepted as the arbiters of social policy. The evangelical concepts of self-reliance and self-help, as embodied in parental payment for child education and in poor-relief for the non-able-bodied, were falling into desuetude as items of public policy in the face of prolonged and large-scale unemployment in the inter-war years. The old certainties of religious influence, which had survived industrialisation and urbanisation in the nineteenth century, were in the twentieth being swept away.

However, whilst social policy has witnessed the erosion of such institutional religious influence, it has also witnessed a diversification — and even radicalisation — of the social-policy options being promoted by the churches. This has been most evident within the Church of Scotland and the Roman Catholic Church in the the later decades of the century. Whilst Christian socialism was marginalised by the political environment of the inter-war period, a strain of committed socialism survived — exemplified within the Church of Scotland after 1938 by the work of the Rev. George Macleod (later Lord Macleod of Fuinary) with the Iona Community amongst the young and unemployed of Govan in Glasgow, and within the Catholic community since the early 1920s by the Labour Party's reliance on the Catholic working-class vote. Whilst Macleod remained a controversial figure in both doctrinal matters (over second baptisms, for instance) and wider issues (such as his pacifist stance), the ideological and cultural hiatus of the young in the 1960s introduced anti-colonialist and pacifist sentiments to young clergy — resulting in small-scale church campaigns over issues such as the Campaign for Nuclear Disarmament, the Vietnam war, and the Biafran War. For Catholics, the Labour Party came to be seen, as Tom Gallagher has put it, 'not for the material gains it brought them — which were pitiably few till the 1940s — but because it set them on the road to assimilation'.[28] In part, the Labour Movement became an alternative as much as an additional point of Catholic loyalty and identification, and after 1945 their growing reliance on public-sector employment and housing tended to relate Catholic perceptions of declining sectarian discrimination by a Protestant 'boss class' to a wider erosion of social injustice.

Such trends widened in the 1970s and 1980s with the emergence of 'social justice' as an orthodoxy — and increasingly an ecumenical orthodoxy — amongst many Scottish clergy. In the context of rising unemployment, industrial decline, and the contraction of social security and social services under the Conservative Government elected in 1979, significant co-operation developed between the Church of Scotland and the Roman Catholic Church in social-policy initiatives at both national and local levels. The consequences of these trends are still developing. On the one hand, it is possible to detect a growth of hostility to the economic and social ideology of the Thatcher government — notably in the reaction to the Prime Minister's so-called 'Sermon on the Mound' in 1988, when she expounded to the General Assembly of the Church of Scotland on her belief in the Scriptural foundations for her government's policies of disengagement from state intervention. On the other hand, there has been a growth of practical work by clergy at parish level. There was notable clerical assistance in organising during the 1970s and early 1980s defence campaigns against industrial closures (such as at the steel plants of Ravenscraig and Gartcosh, and in the shipbuilding and sewing-machine industries of Clydebank). Similarly, Catholic and Protestant clergy have played significant roles since the early 1980s in community economic-development campaigns and youth-training programmes.[29]

The apparent 'radicalisation' of social theology in the last two decades has not been without controversy both within and outwith the churches. For the Church of Scotland in particular, the growing radicalism of many clergy in inner-city and peripheral-housing-scheme parishes has conflicted with the much more conservative (and Conservative) inclinations of the eldership and the membership. The role that the churches lost early in the century through the abolition of local democratic institutions has not been replaced with a clearly defined alternative, and the absence of a consensus *popular* view on what social theology should be leaves the churches' position uncertain and vulnerable.

                                    V

In addition, the very content and structure of organised religion itself was being cast in doubt during the century.[30] In the Protestant churches, liberal biblical interpretation — the 'higher criticism' — had since the late 1890s been a subject which had spread from the theological colleges to the public domain, with a younger generation of clergy promoting more seasoned doubt as to the literal interpretation of the Bible. Diminishing puritanism in Lowland presbyterianism went hand-in-hand with a liberalising of public taste in leisure and recreation. The advent of the shortened working week — a five or five-and-a-half day week for most workers by the inter-war period — promoted Saturday sport (especially football), dancing, cinema and gambling as weekly 'secular' competition to the religious 'recreation' of the Sabbath. The churches tried to compete with ever more 'secular' congregational activities: the militarism and adventure of the Boys Brigade, Scouting, the Girls Guildry, church sports clubs (especially for football, golf, curling, rambling and swimming), and dramatic societies. Churches became entertainment centres, and suites of church halls appeared in the 1920s and 1930s: many churches has as many as five halls for their various organisations. The churches were starting to suffer serious 'goal displacement' where the religious objective of their activities was being overtaken by 'secular' enticements.

Accompanying this process was the sharp demise of denominational schismaticism within presbyterianism. Evangelical puritanism in the United Free Church was in disarray in the first two decades of this century. Even when it formed in 1900 out of the union of the Free and United Presbyterian Churches, it no longer represented 'suffering presbyterian remnants' but a highly suburban and bourgeois denomination with several 'millionaire congregations'. It had declining confidence in evangelical social policy with the rise of the Labour Movement, and its self-confidence and identity was of diminishing importance. From 1904 the United Frees were negotiating for the disestablishment of, and union with, the Church of Scotland. Ecclesiastical and parliamentary lobbying in the 1900s and 1910s gave way to a spate of legislation in the 1920s which made union possible in 1929. Practically all presbyterians were united thereafter in a Church of Scotland shorn of nearly all its state support, leaving only small numbers of dissenters in the Highland Free and Free Presbyterian churches and in the liberal United Free Church (Continuing) of the Lowlands.

The ecumenical momentum built up within presbyterianism to 1929 was translated in the 1930s into negotiations for union with the Scottish Episcopal Church. Presbyterianism was under assault from within, led predominantly by liberal 'high-church' clergy. Attempts in the 1930s, 1950s and 1980s to institute bishops in the Church of Scotland as a prelude to union with episcopacy were rejected, but wider ecumenical initiatives with nearly all Scottish Protestant churches (and involving the Catholic Church at the margins) have been part of a wider and sometimes imperceptible struggle between high-church liberal ecumenicalists and traditional 'low church' presbyterians. Occasionally conflicts have arisen to split congregations, but as the Church of Scotland's central administration faces declining current-account income, falling rolls, and empty and collapsing churches, ecumenism becomes a strategy for ecclesiastical rationalisation.

The experience of the Catholic Church has been somewhat different. As the statistics examined earlier indicate, decline in active Catholic adherence started considerably later — in the 1960s and 1970s — and has been of a much smaller scale than in the Church of Scotland. Still, the signs are growing of increasing disaffection. The Catholic Church by the mid 1980s was suffering an even greater shortage of clergy than the Church of Scotland, and the disaffection of the young was becoming strikingly evident in falling mass attendance. Various 'internal' factors may be identified as contributing to this trend. For some Catholics, the Second Vatican Council of the 1960s represented an undermining of old certainties, whilst for others it thwarted a liberalisation of lifestyles — especially in the areas of divorce and contraception; nevertheless, Scots Catholics are still the most 'conservative' on moral issues of all Catholics in Britain.[31] The rising scale of mixed Catholic-Protestant marriages (which, for Catholic-solemnised occasions [ie. excluding non-Catholic and civil ceremonies], rose from 36 per cent of the total in 1966 to 48 per cent in 1977) has possibly also reduced the religious unanimity of the Catholic family. And the rise of divorce of Catholic-solemnised marriage partners (which almost doubled between 1971 and 1977 alone) has followed trends in other church and civil marriages.[32]

Whilst the Catholic Church has clearly been affected like most others by the liberalising trends in popular lifestyle and attitudes since the mid 1960s, what is perhaps significant is that this disaffection from the Church has been occurring at the end of the period of most rapid Catholic assimilation into Scottish society. The Catholic community that has emerged since the 1960s presents a sharp contrast to that which commenced the century. The Victorian Catholic development of a 'fortress mentality' in the face of discrimination in employment and Protestant hostility in politics and popular culture, was sustained through difficult times of transition during the first four decades of this century. Elements of assimilation were becoming evident through the absorption of Catholic schools into the state system of education after 1918, the slow growth of a small Catholic middle-class (in which teachers probably predominated), by the rapid switch of Catholic political allegiance from Liberalism to the Labour Movement between c.1906 and 1922, and by the appearance of some openings for Catholics in the traditionally Protestant skilled jobs in heavy industry during the First World War.

But such developments merely helped to instigate a Protestant backlash during the inter-war years. In the early 1910s, events in Ireland heightened militant Orangism in Scotland, and intensified the religious divide between Scottish football clubs (symbolised by Protestant Rangers and the predominantly Catholic Celtic). The advent after 1918 of state schools segregated between Catholic and 'non-denominational', (in practice Protestant) schools instigated near riotous education authority elections between 1919 and 1929 in which opposition to 'Rome on the Rates' became a rallying call for Protestant agitators. The general assemblies of the Church of Scotland and the United Free Church became embroiled in eugenic commentary on how the Catholic Irish of Scotland threatened 'the loss of the Scottish race to civilisation', and Catholics were blamed for the failure of plebiscites to curb the 'evil' of the public house and the drinks trade. The economic slump of 1929–33, and the demise of *ad hoc* authority elections in 1929, transferred electoral sectarianism to town-council elections in Glasgow and Edinburgh in which anti-Catholic parties gained significant numbers of votes, culminating in Edinburgh with a riot in Morningside in the summer of 1935 when a Catholic Eucharist Congress was surrounded by a Protestant mob reputedly thirty-thousand strong.

The period between 1919 and 1935 was arguably Scotland's most intense episode of sectarian animosity since the seventeenth century.[33] It ended with economic recovery in the late 1930s and the outbreak of war in 1939. War-time labour shortage, and the post-war advent of full-employment and integrated social welfare reduced tensions and increased the prospects of Catholic assimilation. Entry to state housing and skilled manual jobs in the 1950s and early 1960s was followed by widening openings in higher education and white-collar jobs in the later 1960s and 1970s. At the same time, political assimilation has come through the dominance since the 1960s of the Labour Party (to which to Catholic vote has been thirled since the 1920s).[34]

Despite such trends, the Catholic community retains a stronger proletarian character than any major Lowland denomination. Its adherents are more likely to live in council housing schemes, to have lower educational attainment, to have manual jobs, and to suffer low incomes and unemployment than non-Catholics. This spectrum of distinction provides the context in which Protestant-Catholic sectarian hostility has survived the relative affluence of the post-war decades.[35] However, the nature of sectarianism has changed. No longer do Church of Scotland General Assembly reports proclaim, as they did in the 1920s, that Catholics are undermining 'the purity of the Scots race'. The violence of the Glasgow sectarian gangs of the 1930s — the 'Norman Conks (Catholic) and the 'Billy Boys' (Protestant) — has become much rarer in the post-war period. Though the annual 'marching seasons' of Orange parades has not diminished the fear of public disturbance in the 1980s, the sectarian face of industrial Scotland tends now to be more associated with Rangers-Celtic football rivalry.

Presbyterian decline has proceeded so far by the 1980s that the Catholic Church is now Scotland's largest denomination in terms of churchgoers. Though the decline of church connection has not eliminated sectarian divisions in society at large, the size and increased social integration of the Catholic community in modern Scotland ensures that secularisation is now felt across the religious spectrum. At the same time, ecumenism is widespread within the Scottish Christian churches. Whilst only one church union of any significance has been achieved since 1930 (the cross-border formation in 1970 of the United Reformed Church, which united the Churches of Christ in Scotland with the Congregationalist and Presbyterian churches in England and Wales), the latest of three sets of inter-church 'conversations' towards union of the Church of Scotland and the Episcopal Church in Scotland has involved other reformed churches with the Roman Catholic and Baptist churches as observers. The desire for interdenominational *rapprochement* has achieved significant compromises — especially on the presbyterian side — on the the nature of baptism and the Eucharist, but presbyterian reluctance to surrender distinctive church government has repeatedly stifled significant progress.

More generally, though, the growth of inter-church communication at many levels — the parish, theological, social action, and social policy — has all but eradicated the denominational rivalries of previous centuries. Though union of any kind between the Church of Scotland and the Catholic Church is unlikely, these two churches — which in 1984 accounted for 84 per cent of all churchgoers — have produced leadership groups who have come to acknowledge a joint responsibility for the moral (and, as some would have it, the political) destiny of Scotland. For others both within those churches and in other reformed churches, ecumenism amounts to surrender to the economic pressures of church decline (which, for example, necessitate the sharing of church buildings) and to surrender of principle.

VI

Scotland takes its place in a very complex pattern of recent religious development.[36] It has shared a common experience with England and Wales of a peak of popular church adherence occurring around the turn of the century. In contrast, some countries have experienced a later peaking of religious adherence — such as the United States in the early and mid 1950s. But unlike those Protestant-dominated nations, religious decline commenced later in most Catholic countries in Europe — in the

4. The packed Kelvin Hall, Glasgow, at one of the meetings during Billy Graham's crusade, 1955. T. Allan (ed.) *Crusade in Scotland* (1955).

1960s, 1970s and 1980s. Indeed, looking at it another way, the decline of adherence has been evident in Protestant churches from early in the century, with acceleration after 1950, whilst for the Catholic Church nearly everywhere (including Scotland) it has only commenced within the last two decades. However, there are a minority of countries where religious decline is not only imperceptible, but where adherence and religious observance are extremely high: notably Poland, the Republic of Ireland, Northern Ireland, Hungary, and the Baltic republics of the former U.S.S.R. (Latvia, Lithuania and Estonia).

A number of reasons have been attributed for the differences between Protestant and Catholic experience: the Catholic Church's refusal to follow Protestant compromise with liberalisation of behaviour and doctrine; the Catholic avoidance of membership 'leakage' caused by ecumenical union of previously hostile Protestant churches; the role of the Catholic Church as a point of ethnic identification for groups of minority immigrants; and the stronger proletarian character (and inner-city location) of the Catholic Church compared to more middle-class (and suburban) Protestant churches. Such factors have had important bearings on Scotland. Scots Catholics are more conservative over doctrinal and moral welfare issues (such as abortion, homosexuality and divorce) than either most Protestants in Scotland or Catholics in England and Wales.[37] Their greater working-class character, combined with Protestant hostility in the workplace and in higher education, has sustained the Catholic Church at the core of distinctive Catholic leisure organisations. And the reunification of presbyterianism has created one of the most denominationally-united Protestant communities in the world, but one in which the erasure of puritan tradition has cost the loyalty of many adherents.

As well as those general reasons, the strength of religious adherence in some countries and regions is attributed to sectarian tension — notably in Northern Ireland, Yugoslavia and the southern republics of the former U.S.S.R.. Where communities of different religions have lived in close proximity and have a heritage of antagonism, popular identification with churches has kept religious adherence buoyant. The Protestant-Catholic hostilities of Northern Ireland have been evident also in Scotland, and though they do not compare in severity with the Ulster situation, none the less they have been during some decades more prominent than at any period since the seventeenth century.

Another factor has been suggested to explain the strength of religious identity in certain countries: the association of religion with national pride and identity. In Ireland, the struggle for national independence was enveloped in a religious schism which identified Catholicism with liberation — an association which has remained during statehood. In the United States, by contrast, religious adherence within three main traditions (of Protestant, Catholic and Jew) is split between literally hundreds of different churches, sects and ethnic communities which collectively constitute a 'civil religion' in which a patriot is seen to be a churchgoer. In the case of Poland and some other East European countries, Soviet domination in the political sphere redirected thwarted nationalism into identification of nation with church (either Roman or Orthodox Catholic Churches).

A similar analysis has been suggested for Scotland. Whilst the general level of religious adherence has been falling here since 1906, the level has remained higher in Scotland (and also in Wales) than in England. Some commentators have suggested that this marks the identification of religion (presbyterianism) with a thwarted nationalism in the same way — but not nearly to the same degree — as in East European countries. More widely, there has been a growing trend since the 1950s for clergy in the Church of Scotland to see themselves as upholders of Scottish identity. Since 1980 this has been reinforced by the growing theological resistance in both the Church of Scotland and the Catholic Church in

Scotland to the Thatcher government. Whilst the 'new right' of British Conservatism claims a heritage deriving from an eighteenth-century Scot, Adam Smith, the economic and social doctrines of 'Thatcherism' are regarded by some clergy as 'alien' and 'immoral' impositions upon Scotland. In this way, erstwhile Christian socialism is being transformed in Scotland into a mixture of nationalism and welfare socialism. The process is, however, limited. Though some clergy are prominent in extra-parliamentary processes like the Scottish Constitutional Convention — which seeks to create a consensus in favour of Scottish devolution across political parties and voluntary bodies like the churches — there is little evidence that the Scottish public identifies the churches as in any sense embodying a revivified 'nationhood'. No matter how far links can be made between presbyterianism and national identity in the eighteenth and nineteenth centuries, little positive connection can be made between crisis-hit religion and the advent of political nationalism in post-war Scotland. Indeed, if anything, an *inverse* relationship between the two is a more likely hypothesis.[38]

The survival of neo-peasant society in parts of the Highlands and Hebrides of Scotland has strong parallels with other areas where religion has fared better in relatively backward economies: maritime and North Wales, and the peasant countryside of Catholic Europe (ranging from Portugal to Poland). Equally, though, it has been observed that amongst otherwise declining Protestant churches, it is the so-called 'fundamentalist' or puritanical reformed churches — which have avoided compromise with liberal values in doctrine and secular life — that have suffered least from declining adherence. This is perhaps best exemplified by the conservativism of the American 'Bible Belt', whilst in Scotland the Free and Free Presbyterian churches of the Highland region and the Brethren of the north-east have retained strong holds in crofting and fishing communities. At the same time, the dynamic yet strict 'new religions' (like the Jehovah's Witnesses and especially the Latter Day Saints) have grown dramatically in Scotland as in Britain as a whole since the early 1960s, and have a modest though solid following amongst the lower middle classes.

Scotland thus fits into a variegated experience of religion in the modern western world. In trying to place Scotland, it is fair to conclude that its experience is much closer to that of England and Wales than to that of Northern Ireland, the United States or continental Europe. Religion has not been sufficiently sustained by nationalism or by civil religion in Scotland to resist the advance of a sweeping secularisation that has enveloped mainland Britain. In its response, the Scottish churches have grown closer to the English churches through joint organisations like the British Council of Churches, through combined campaigns on issues as diverse as unemployment, Sunday trading and abortion, and through ecumenical links towards Christian co-operation. It is difficult to avoid the conclusion that the underlying impulse to ecumenism and church liberalisation since the 1960s is the unprecedented diminution in practising Christian faith amongst Scots. The legacy of the 'swinging, hippy sixties' is certainly underestimated if it is not acknowledged that it initiated the greatest and swiftest decline of religious adherence in Scottish history.

NOTES

1. B. Wilson, *Religion in Secular Society* (Harmondsworth, 1969); A. D. Gilbert, *The Making of Post-Christian Britain* (London and New York, 1980). But compare the different early 1950s' perspective contained in G. S. Spinks *et al.*, *Religion in Britain since 1900* (London, 1952), and the idiosyncratic Christian revisionism in J. Kent, *The Unacceptable Face: The Modern Church in the Eyes of the Historian* (London, 1987).

2. Analysis of Scottish twentieth-century religious statistics is contained in C. G. Brown, *The Social History of Religion in Scotland since 1730* (London and New York, 1987); C. G. Brown, 'Religion' in R. Pope (ed.), *Atlas of British Social and Economic History* (London, 1989), pp. 211–223; and J. Highet, *The Scottish Churches 500 Years After The Reformation* (London, 1960). The most vital raw statistics are to be found in R. Currie *et al.*, *Churches and Churchgoers: Patterns of Church Growth in the British Isles since 1700* (Oxford, 1977); R. Currie and A. Gilbert, 'Religion' in A. H. Halsey (ed.), *Trends in British Society since 1900* (London, 1972); J. Darragh, 'The Catholic population of Scotland, 1877–1977' in D. McRoberts (ed.), *Modern Scottish Catholicism 1878–1978* (Glasgow, 1979); J. Highet 'The Churches' in J. Cunnison and J. B. S. Gilfillan (eds.), *The Third Statistical Account of Scotland, vol V Glasgow* (Glasgow, 1958), pp. 713–50 and 956–7; and P. Brierley and F. Macdonald (eds.), *Prospects for Scotland: Report of the 1984 Census of the Churches* (Edinburgh, 1985).

3. Calculated from data in R. Currie *et al.*, *op. cit.* 132–138.

4. P. Thompson *et al.*, *Living the Fishing* (London, 1983), pp. 227–368; C. G. Brown, *Social History*, p. 215.

5. T. Allan (ed.), *Crusade in Scotland: Billy Graham* (London, 1955).

6. C. G. Brown, *op. cit..*, p. 87.

7. An important recent attempt by the Church of Scotland to investigate the social context of religious decline was marred by poor conceptualising and social-survey techniques; Church of Scotland Board of Social Responsibility (A. Robertson), *Lifestyle Survey* (Edinburgh, 1987).

8. Calculated from data for estimated Catholic population in *The Catholic Directory for Scotland*, 1980–1986.

9. The peak of baptisms in the Church of Scotland after 1929 came in 1962 (51,

767), followed by an unprecendented fall of 13 per cent (to 44,974) by 1965. Church of Scotland baptisms as a proportion of Scottish live births minus Catholic baptisms were as follows:

1951–55	65.1 per cent	1961–65	63.0 per cent
1956–60	67.7 per cent	1966–70	56.1 per cent

10. So little research has been undertaken on the social history of religion in twentieth-century Scotland that general ecclesiastical texts must be referred to. Two stand out: the excellent integrated essays in D. W. Bebbington (ed.), *The Baptists in Scotland: A History* (Glasgow, 1988), which have been written as much from a social history perspective as from a denominational one; and the thematic essays in D. McRoberts (ed.), *Modern Scottish Catholicism 1878–1978* (Glasgow, 1979). Presbyterianism is extremely poorly served, with nothing recently comparing to the work of J. R. Fleming, *A History of the Church in Scotland 1875–1929* (Edinburgh, 1933), and A. H. Dunnet *The Church in Changing Scotland* (London, c. 1933).

11. Research on religion in the Highlands and Hebrides since 1900 has been sparse and sporadic in its coverage. Important perspectives on Gaelic and religion are to be found in C. W. J. Withers, *Gaelic in Scotland 1698–1981* (Edinburgh, 1984), and V. E. Durkacz, *The Decline of the Celtic Languages* (Edinburg, 1983), Social anthropology provides F. G. Vallee's study of the Catholic island of Barra in 'Social structure and organisation in a Hebridean community', unpublished Ph.D. thesis, University of London (L.S.E.), 1954; and T. M. Owen's 'The "Communion Season" and presbyterianism in a Highland community', *Gwerin* 1 (1956), pp. 53–66. Denominational histories detail aspects of church life but with varying quality; compare the puritanical zeal of A. McPherson (ed.), *History of the Free Presbyterian Church of Scotland 1893–1970* (Inverness?, 1973) with the balanced and professional treatment in D. E. Meek, *Island Harvest: A History of Tiree Baptist Church 1838–1988* (Edinburgh, 1988).

12. G. N. M. Collins, *The Heritage of Our Fathers: The Free Church of Scotland: Her Origin and Testimony* (Edinburgh, 1976), pp. 110–111.

13. The following extracts were transcribed by the present author from the cassette tape, *Lewis, Land of Revival: The story of the 1949–52 Lewis revival as told by the islanders* (Belfast, 1983), and are published with the kind permission of Ambassador Productions Ltd.

14. A. Maclean, *Night Falls on Ardnamurchan: The twilight of a crofting family* (London, 1984), pp. 165–67.

15. Scotland awaits comparable studies to D. Clark, *Between Pulpit and Pew: Folk religion in a North Yorkshire fishing village* (Cambridge, 1982); and R. Moore, *Pitmen, Preachers and Politics: The effects of Methodism in a Durham mining community* (Cambridge, 1974). But see Thompson, footnote. 16.

16. Quoted in P. Thompson *et al.*, *Living the Fishing* (London, 1983), pp. 205, 256–63.

17. M. Weir, *Best Foot Forward* (London, 1972), pp. 69–71.

18. Testimony of Mrs W. I. Stirling Women's Oral History Archive, Smith Museum, Stirling.

19. On Lowland rural religion, the most valuable analytical starting point is J. Littlejohn, *Westrigg: the sociology of a Cheviot parish* (London, 1963). An interesting though overly-detailed account of a minister's life in his parish (at Lumphanan in Aberdeenshire), as recounted by his daughter, is to be found in H. Gilbert, *As a Tale That is Told: A Church of Scotland Parish 1913–1954* (Aberdeen, 1983).

20. N. Morgan, 'Property ownership in Victorian and Edwardian Glasgow', unpublished E.S.R.C. Research Grant Final Report (D00232126), p. 16.

21. On the churches' responses to slum clearance, rehousing and wartime evacuation, see A. Muir, *John White* (London, 1958), pp. 286–348; C. G. Brown, 'Religion' in J. Hood (ed.), *The History of Clydebank* (Carnforth, 1988), pp. 47–50, 100–102, and 195–199; T. A. Fitzpatrick, *Catholic Secondary Education in South-west Scotland before 1972* (Aberdeen, 1986); and D. Bebbington (ed.), *op. cit.*

22. Figures calculated from data in Fitzpatrick, *op. cit.*, pp. 156–167.

23. K. J. Panton, 'The Church in the community: A study of patterns of religious adherence in a Scottish burgh', in M. Hill (ed.), *A Sociological Yearbook of Religion in Britain* vol 6 (London, 1973), p. 190.

24. Figures from I.L.S. Balfour, 'The twentieth century since 1914' in D. Bebbington (ed.), *op. cit*, pp. 68–70. On success of conservative churches, see S. Bruce, *Firm in the Faith* (Aldershot, 1984), pp. 37–40.

25. On church and social class in urban Scotland, see D. R. Robertson, 'The relationship between church and social class in Scotland', unpublished Ph.D. thesis, University of Edinburgh 1966; D. R. Robertson, 'The relationship of church and social class in Scotland', in D. Martin (ed.), *A Sociological Yearbook of Religion* vol 1 (London, 1968); P. L. Sissons, *The Social Significance of Religion in the Burgh of Falkirk* (Edinburgh, 1973); K. J. Panton, *op. cit*; and M. Maxwell-Arnot, 'Social change and the Church of Scotland' in M. Hill (ed.), *A Sociological Yearbook of Religion in Britain*, vol 7 (London, 1974).

26. The moral and religious foundations of Scottish local government between the 1870s and the 1930s have not been studied in detail, but important contributions include B. Aspinwall, 'The Scottish religious identity in the Atlantic world 1880–1914', in S. Mews (ed.), *Religion and National Identity* (Oxford, 1982); B. Aspinwall, *Portable Utopia: Glasgow and the United States 1820–1920* (Aberdeen, 1984); W. M. Walker, *Juteopolis: Dundee and its textile workers 1885–1923* (Edinburgh, 1979); C. G. Brown, *The Social History of Religion*, chapter 6; and, on the local-veto plebiscites, E. King, *Scotland Sober and Free* (Glasgow, 1979).

27. Littlejohn, *op. cit*, p. 42; Vallee, *op. cit*, pp. 214–5.

28. T. Gallagher, *Glasgow: The Uneasy Peace: Religious Tension in Modern Scotland* (Manchester, 1987), p. 350.

29. C. G. Brown, 'Religion 1945–1980' in J. Hood (ed.), *The History of Clydebank* (Carnforth, Lancs., 1988), pp. 196–198.

30. On growth of secular entertainment and the Labour Movement, see C. G. Brown, *op. cit.* On ecumenism and presbyterian reunion, see R. Sjolinder, *Presbyterian Reunion in Scotland 1907–1921* (Edinburgh, c.1962).

31. See below, note 37.

32. J. Darragh, 'The Catholic population of Scotland, 1878–1978' in D. McRoberts (ed.), *Modern Scottish Catholicism 1878–1978* (Glasgow, 1979), pp. 237–8.

33. On Protestant-Catholic sectarianism since 1914, see T. Gallagher, 'Protestant extremism in urban Scotland 1930–1939: its growth and contraction', *Scottish Historical Review* lxix (1985); T. Gallagher, *Edinburgh Divided: John Cormack and No Popery in the 1930s* (Edinburgh, 1987); S. Bruce, *No Pope of Rome: Anti-Catholicism in Modern Scotland* (Edinburgh, 1985); and B. Murray, *The Old Firm: Sectarianism. Sport and Society in Scotland* (Edinburgh, 1984). The place of sectarianism in Victorian and Edwardian Scotland is poorly researched, and its strength has been generally

underestimated; compare for example J. Smith, 'Labour tradition in Glasgow and Liverpool', *History Workshop* 17 (1984) and T. Gallagher, 'Protestant militancy and the Scottish working class before 1914', *Radical Scotland* 10 (1984), with the critique in M. Montgomery, 'Sectarianism and the Labour Movement in Clydeside, with special reference to Govan, 1912–1950', unpublished B.A. dissertation, Dept. of History, University of Strathclyde, 1989.

34. The major treatment of the 'emergence' and 'assimilation' of the Catholic community in twentieth-century Scotland is T. Gallagher's *Glasgow: the Uneasy Peace* (Manchester, 1987).

35. J. Panton, *op. cit*; G. Payne and G. Ford, 'Religion, class and educational policy', *Scottish Educational Studies* vol 9 (1977).

36. Important international perspectives on twentieth-century religion include H. McLeod, *Religion and the People of Western Europe 1789–1970* (Oxford, 1981); D. Martin, *A General Theory of Secularisation*, (Oxford, 1978); R. Wuthnow, *The Restructuring of American Religion: Society and Faith since World War II* (Princeton, 1988); and M. Pomian-Srzednicki, *Religious Change in Contemporary Poland: Secularization and Politics* (London, 1982).

37. M. P. Hornsby-Smith, 'The statistics of the Church', in J. Cumming and P. Burns (eds.), *The Church Now: An inquiry in to the present state of the Catholic Church in Britain and Ireland* (Dublin, 1980), p. 62.

38. On religion and nationalism in Scotland, see the essays by Sefton, Aspinwall, Bebbington and Robbins in S. Mews (ed.), *Religion and National Identity* (Oxford, 1982).

APPENDIX

Graph 1

Abbreviated Technical Explanation

This graph displays the annual estimated membership/active adherence/Sunday-school enrolment of major churches as proportions of total Scottish population in a stacked-graph format. For most of the period data are based on actual church-collected figures, though figures for the Scottish Episcopal Church after 1972 and for the Methodist Church after 1970 are estimates. Manifest discontinuities in membership series were weighted to the longest time-run. Population figures for Scotland are from the decennial censuses and, after 1981, from the Registrar General, Scotland. All gaps in data, including between population censuses, were then filled by linear extrapolation. Communicant data for the Free Church and the Free Presbyterian Church were then multiplied by a factor of 3.9 (to compensate for the low level of communion in those denominations), and data on estimated Catholic population were divided by a factor of 1.75 to produce a series of national mass attenders. Sunday-school data in all cases are enrolments. Original church and Sunday-school data are from R. Currie *et al.*,, *Churches and Churchgoers: Patterns of Church Growth in the British Isles since 1700* (Oxford, 1977), pp. 128–129, 133–135, 137 (fns, 7–8), 143–144, 145 (fn. 4), 150–151, 153, 169–170, 173–174; D. W. Bebbington (ed.), *The Baptists in Scotland: A History:* (Glasgow, 1988), pp. 338–339; *The Church of Scotland Yearbook* 1971–1988; *The Catholic Directory for Scotland*, 1971–1988; *Scottish Episcopal Church Yearbook and Directory*, 1969/70–1985/86; *Yearbook of the Congregational Union of Scotland*, 1971–1988; *Handbook of the United Free Church of Scotland*, 1971–1986. Original stacked graph generated by *Supercalc 3*.

CHAPTER 3

Schooling

Andrew McPherson

The wheel has come round almost full circle from individualism to collectivism, from competition to co-operation. and from the doctrine of laissez-faire to that of state control.

— Duncan MacGillivray, 1919[1]

Introduction: the Progress of Progress

MacGillivray was President of Scotland's largest teachers association, the Educational Institute of Scotland (EIS), and this was his view of the trend of economic and political change in the fifty years before the First World War. He thought that schooling too had been transformed and had

> merged in the great communal current in which are united all the forces and agencies making for social amelioration and national progress

Ameliorist aspirations for schooling influenced the Education (Scotland) Act of 1918 (hereafter called 'the 1918 Act', with other Education (Scotland) Acts similarly named) and, strengthened by the education and welfare legislation of the first majority Labour government (1945–1951), were shared by successive governments until well into the 1970s. The Conservative governments of the 1980s, however, aimed to reduce the role of the state by introducing competition into the provision of public utilities, housing, health, and education, and they attributed Britain's national decline to the very features that MacGillivray and his contemporaries, or at least the Liberals amongst them, had thought were the forces of progress.

Scotland had a special place in the Conservative critique of the 1980s. Scotland, Ministers claimed, was deviant, was the most entrenched case of the 'dependency culture' produced by the British welfare state. But it was also a culture at odds with Scotland's past:

> . . . traditional Scottish values are essentially conservative, and individualistic, though in recent years these characteristics have been set aside by a collectivist, socialist ethos that denies personal responsibility and self-improvement.[2]

80

To reassert these values in education required, Ministers said, more popular (as opposed to public) control, less control by educational professionals, and a return to analogues of the pre-twentieth century grammar school and local school board. Ironically, whilst the rhetoric of the Conservative critique was undeniably Scottish, its aim was to justify policies that were not the personal responsibility of the majority of Scottish voters, only a quarter of whom had supported Conservative candidates in the 1987 general election. Like most major legislation for Scottish education since 1872, the statutory introduction for Scottish state schools of school boards (1988) and of the option of self-government (1989) were both occasioned by companion legislation for England and Wales, as had been the introduction of parental choice earlier in the decade (1981).

If it was novel to hear Conservative Ministers complain of the alienation of the schools from the people, there was nothing novel as such in the critique of state control. It has been a recurrent theme this century of radical teachers, of teachers who wanted greater professional autonomy, and of a more diffuse spectrum of opinion that thought that education should somehow be kept out of politics. Nor was it unusual that the Conservative search for political legitimacy in the late 1980s should reopen questions of Scottish history and identity. It was a Conservative Secretary of State for Scotland in the 1930s who wrote evocatively of Scotland's 'democratic intellectualism'[3], and appeals to national tradition have figured regularly in policy debate and commentary in the course of the past two centuries.[4] Here, to take a recent instance, is Allan Rodger, until the 1960s a senior official of the Scottish Education Department (SED):

> I would say that the democratic tradition is the most powerful historical influence in modern Scottish education. You see, if you go right back to John Knox's Book of Discipline of 1560, he envisaged a school in every parish. He envisaged that the best pupils of these schools should go to a more centralised secondary school; the best of these should go to the universities. In short, he was really talking about promotion by merit, a meritocracy, from as early as 1560. Everybody went to school. They got the same chance; equality of opportunity; if you had the ability, you rose. I think that this was a remarkably democratic tradition to be spelt out as early as 1560. It was a long, long time till it was implemented, and indeed, in some respects, it wasn't fully implemented till the 1918 and the 1945 Acts, but it had its influence all along in Scotland.[5]

Essentially, this is MacGillivray's view of national progress, but extended to Rodger's own times. And it was a view that was widely shared amongst Rodger's contemporaries in government and education. Until the late

1960s, the dominant interpretation of Scottish schooling was framed in terms of 'the rise and progress of Scottish education' (the title of a book by a contemporary of MacGillivray's who was Principal of Moray House Teacher Training College where Rodger himself had once lectured).[6]

In many ways the pre-occupation with progress was understandable. For MacGillivray's generation, and even for Rodger's, the memory of the social and educational transformation following the 1872 Act was still vivid. In the 1960s, new perspectives began to emerge, in Osborne's comparative studies (1966 and 1968) and in James Scotland's history (1969).[7] But fresh approaches were required, and it was not until the 1980s that the most important works of reappraisal appeared, particularly Anderson's studies which placed Scotland's universities and post-primary schools in a European context for the period 1820–1939.[8] There were also new insights in the collection of essays edited by Humes and Paterson (1983).[9] These and other studies emphasised the part played by social class in the growth of state education and they questioned the egalitarian claims of the older ameliorist perspective. In doing this they also raised questions about the perspective itself. If it were partly or entirely invalid as an historical account, was it merely ideological? Alternatively, might not the very power of an ameliorist ideology over the decades itself have shaped the reality of schooling in its own image? Thus the reappraisal was also concerned with the character of contemporary Scottish schooling, and with the potentially ideological role of interpretations of the past, themes pursued concurrently in a body of work by sociologists and others.

One example of the reworking of the ameliorist theme is Paterson's account of Scottish post-primary schooling 1900–1939. MacGillivray used the ideas of competition and co-operation to mark out the path of progress. For Paterson, however, the self-same terms describe the polarities of an enduring conflict in Scottish society born, ultimately, of poverty:

> The more remote the prospect of any kind of fair share in the few material goods available, the stronger the forces driving people towards both solidarity and division, and the more definite the polarisation of the society between ideals of both co-operation and competition. This would then explain more fully the twin Scottish drives towards both egalitarianism and elitism — it makes more sense of that common Scottish phenomenon known as 'meritocracy'.[10]

For Paterson, meritocracy was not 'democratic', as it was for Rodger, but:

a particularly Scottish solution of the problems involved in sieving a nation, by the device of mass schooling so as to recruit talent to the leader class whilst, at the same time, placating and controlling the many who would never reach such heights.[11]

The themes of selection ('sieving') and social control have been given wider exposure in two later studies. Humes writes of a 'leadership class' of officials that has governed Scottish education in recent decades essentially in its own interests.[12] By contrast, Smout (1986) takes a more benign view of officials, and gives them the major credit for improvements in social conditions since 1945. But he arranges much of his account of twentieth century schooling around Paterson's core thesis talking, not of the progress, but of the 'failure' of education before 1950 and of its damaging consequences for Scottish economy and society up to the present day.[13] This judgement, I think, is too severe. But it is likely to be the single judgement on Scottish schooling best known to students of Scottish social history, and I return to it in the final section of the chapter.

The new historiographical mood and the new conservatism may sometimes point in different directions politically, but they are both responses to the declining faith in ameliorism, and this brings us back to the changes that came with the turn of MacGillivray's wheel.

Citizenship and Compulsion

One aspect of the revolution that MacGillivray had in mind was a fundamental change in government's attitude to welfare. The nineteenth century had left the pauper beyond the pale of citizenship and dependent on the parish or on individual charity. But, by 1914, the British state had accepted a limited responsibility for the welfare of its citizens, and had recognised that education was both a component of welfare and also essential to 'national' or 'social' 'efficiency'. The change originated in the provision of universal elementary schooling for the basic education and moral regulation of sections of the population that were losing religion but winning the vote. It was strengthened during the First World War by social unrest at home, by Bolshevik revolution abroad, and by the massive extension of the franchise for the General Election of 1918. In 1923, Scottish Day Schools (non-secondary schools) were required

to bring up the children in habits of punctuality and thrift, of good manners and language, of cleanliness and neatness, and also to impress upon them the importance of cheerful obedience to duty, of consideration and respect for others, and of honour and truthfulness in word and act.

Thus the state's concern for education already extended beyond the 'three R's' of reading, writing and arithmetic, to which we can clearly add righteousness and respect. It also encompassed, in varying degrees, secondary, technical and commercial education, teacher training and higher education and research. It was accepted, too, that children could not learn if they were individually 'inefficient', that is, ill, poorly nourished, verminous, hungry or tired. The 1908 Act had given schools powers of feeding, clothing and medical inspection, and there were age and hours restrictions on juvenile employment that were to be tightened by subsequent Acts. Half the Scots population in 1911 lived in one- or two-roomed houses and working-class fertility was high, but improvements in public health had started to reduce the high rate of infant mortality. If an inefficient and discontented working-class threatened national efficiency, the remedy of social amelioration was not without its dangers either. There were fears, formalised by eugenicist arguments, that a growing working class would swamp its social superiors and reduce the quality of the national stock. Birth control was seen as one solution, and emigration a second, especially emigration to British dominions overseas. But it was education that offered a surer solution, if only because it was not voluntary.

The 1918 Act consolidated the growing state commitment to public education and established a framework for subsequent developments, though some of these were decades in coming to fruition. Like the 1945 Act, the 1918 Act was occasioned by wartime moves for social reform. But the impetus soon faltered. The Liberal decline broke up the reforming alliance of earlier decades, whilst the party that came eventually to represent most of the intended beneficiaries of reform did not form a majority administration until 1945. Furthermore, the 1918 Act was followed by the financial crisis of 1921, by cuts in public spending, and by years of recession leading to a further crisis and cuts in 1931.

In this sense too, the 1918 Act set the pattern for the future. For six of the eight decades of our period, education has been conducted in a climate of restraint on public spending. It is true that there have been restraints on levels of aspiration and provision that were themselves rising. But financial restraint characteristically led to Treasury demands for greater selectivity in educational expenditure and in effect, for a damping down of educational expansion and change. The few years in which restraints on spending were relaxed, roughly between the early 1960s and the mid 1970s, were also years of significant expansion and of major changes both in institutions and in ideas.

Nevertheless, the broad framework of our contemporary institutions, ideas and practices was largely in place by 1914. In particular, the state was winning the struggle over compulsion. Though school attendance rates were to fall during the two World Wars, the first four decades of universal elementary education following the 1872 Act had established the habit of schooling among the young, and it was easier, thereafter, to get their own young to school. Officially recorded attendance rates for primary schools increased steadily from a post-war low in 1918 to reach what was considered their realistic maximum of around 90 per cent in the early 1930s. Attendance could still be erratic among children of migrant populations, such as agricultural labourers and miners moving to new seams. However, SED officials in the inter-War period no longer regarded non-attendance as a problem of mass regulation, but as a problem of delinquent individuals, of households in crisis, and of individually ineffective or unattractive schools.[14]

The 1918 Act was intended to extend compulsion in two main ways. First, it provided nationally for the extension of the period of compulsory schooling from 14 to 15 years, and limited the grounds for exemption that had earlier allowed the schooling of many children to end at 12 or 13 years. This power was stronger than the provision made in the 1918 Education Act in England and Wales which left the raising of the age to local bye-law. National implementation in Scotland was delayed, however, by the crisis of 1921, and then by the crisis of 1931 which frustrated the plans of the minority Labour government to raise the age. The Act of 1936 provided for universal and compulsory secondary education to 15 years with effect from August 1939. But the operation of these provisions was suspended a few weeks after the outbreak of the Second World War. The minimum leaving age was finally raised to 15 years in 1947, and then to 16 years in 1973, again after a delay owing to restraints on public-spending.

Second, the 1918 Act provided for 320 hours annually of compulsory education and training for 15–18 year olds no longer at school. This provision too was a casualty of financial crisis and recession. Although voluntary enrolments in day-continuation, as it was then called, rose between the Wars, attempts to create systematic national links between education and training for this age group were renewed only towards the end of the 1950s. By then, however, high youth wages were inhibiting demands for training, and the universal entitlement of young school leavers to training developed only after the virtual collapse of the youth labour market in the early 1980s. By the end of that decade, something approaching the intentions of the 1918 Act had finally been realised:

5. Primary 1, Skene Square Primary School, Aberdeen. 1938. Courtesy of Mrs Jean Fraser.

two-thirds of Scottish 17 year olds received full- or part-time education, or training off the job. But continuation was still not compulsory, and vocational education was still a poor relation to the academic route to which policy had given priority until the 1970s.

Post-primary Schooling 1914–1962

A major issue which the 1918 Act did not resolve was the organisation of post-primary schooling. Universal elementary education, and higher education were already well established and did not change in any fundamental way until the 1960s. But what should lie between elementary and higher education? In particular, should secondary schooling be regarded as a stage of education common to all, or as a level of education only for some?

At the heart of the post-primary issue lay the polarities of social organisation identified in Paterson's analysis (above). Was the school system to be organised on the principles of co-operation or competition, of egalitarianism or elitism? The question had implications for the character of schooling at all levels, and it took decades to resolve. The obligation of the state to provide free secondary schooling for all was acknowledged in the Act of 1936, though a small minority of education-authority schools was allowed to charge fees until the 1970s. An obligation to provide secondary education in the same type of school was enjoined with comprehensive reorganisation in 1965, and the principle of the same type of course for all pupils in compulsory schooling was first recommended in 1977. But the delivery of common courses through the Standard grade examination started only in the mid 1980s and was not due for completion until the early 1990s.

Although the 1918 Act did not resolve the post-primary question four provisions of the Act were essential to its eventual resolution. First, the Act created a larger and more effective local education authority. It replaced the 987 School Boards with 38 (later 35) County (and 'County of City') education authorities (EAs). Initially these were *ad hoc* authorities with powers only over education. But in 1929 the model of the 1902 English Act was adopted and the EAs became part of the *ad omnia* local authorities that had powers over the full range of local services. The scale of the EAs was enlarged again when they became part of the 12 mainland and island authorities created by the reform of local government in 1975.

Second, Section 6A of the 1918 Act for the first time gave the F ʒ powers and responsibilities for all public post-primary schooling, rc quiring them to produce schemes for 'the adequate provision of all forms of primary, intermediate and secondary education in day schools . . . without payment of fees' ('intermediate' education is explained below).

Third, the scope of these duties was substantially enlarged by the requirement that EAs accept responsibility for all voluntary schools whose trustees wished to transfer control to them. The majority of these schools were Catholic, and it was here that contemporaries found a particularly persuasive case for state intervention. Despite a massive voluntary effort over the previous half century, Catholic provision in 1918 lagged far behind the non-denominational sector, serving mainly an immigrant Irish population whose squalid conditions of life and work in the urban industrial settlements of west-central Scotland exemplified the worst consequences of *laissez faire*. The Secretary of the SED feared that, if their schools were not funded to the same standard as others, Catholics would become a 'pariah class', 'inefficient' as individuals, and incapable of using the opportunities to be offered by an increasingly efficient system. Under the Act, the control of virtually all Catholic schools was to pass to the EAs, with provisos concerning religious observance and teacher appointments. Accommodation and staffing problems were so acute that it was to be 50 years before the quality of Catholic secondary provision approached that of the non-denominational sector. By the end of the 1970s, however, and through the 1980s, Catholic schools were performing highly effectively.[15]

Fourth, Section 4 (1) of the 1918 Act gave EAs the right to spend money to ensure 'that no child . . . who is qualified for attendance at an intermediate or secondary school, and . . . shows promise of profiting thereby shall be debarred therefrom by reason of the expense involved'. Similar support was also allowable for the attendance of 'duly qualified' persons at college or university. What underpinned these provisions was the notion of equality of opportunity. It was not yet a strong version of equality requiring that all pupils have the same secondary education. This was to come only with comprehensive reorganisation after 1965. But it did recognise the principle that, above a certain level of 'promise', neither material nor intellectual factors should restrict access to any level of the national system, including higher education.

All sides to the debate over post-primary education agreed this principle. But two issues divided them. One was whether the overriding purpose of secondary schooling should be the preparation of pupils for higher education, as the SED insisted. The other was whether 'promise of profit' should be generously interpreted to encompass a relatively large proportion of the age-group or even, as the EIS argued, 'secondary education for all'. The SED favoured limited access to secondary schooling, and in the early 1920s it imposed its own blueprint for the development of post-primary schooling along bi-partite lines. Circular 44 of 1923 set the pattern of post-primary schooling until comprehensive reorganisation in the 1960s. But the introduction of the policy was widely criticised by contemporaries for breaking with a long-standing and socially more open strand of the Scottish educational tradition, and it was resisted in many localities.[16]

One part of the SED's bi-partite plan was an enlarged secondary sector of some 250 schools. Hitherto, the Department (*ie* the SED) had recognised only some 55 such schools, mainly in the pre-industrial population centres of the east and north. But, in 1923, it extended full secondary-school status to around 200 of the schools in the Higher Grade sector. This sector had been reorganised and greatly enlarged between 1902 and 1908 and had offered a broadly liberal education, with some vocational emphasis, to pupils between the ages of roughly 12 and 15 or 16 years. Most Higher Grade schools had presented pupils at 15 or 16 years for the Intermediate Certificate awarded by the SED, and some had also presented pupils for Highers.[17]

The other part of the bi-partite model was a new Advanced Division sector into which the rump of the former Higher Grade schools passed. This sector was administered under a Day Schools Code that allowed lower staffing and other standards than the Code for secondary schools. The new Advanced Division sector was intended for all pupils who had failed to qualify at around 12 years for secondary schooling, but who had attained the standard that marked the end of primary schooling. In practice, many of these Advanced Divisions were located as separate units either in primary schools or in full secondary schools. In many urban areas, however, new 'central' schools were created solely for Advanced Division work. These schools were the forerunners of the 'junior-secondary' school sector that began to emerge in the late 1930s and that provided the main alternative to 'senior-secondary' schooling after 1945. Similarly, the senior-secondary sector 1945–1965 comprised the vast majority of the schools whose secondary status was granted or confirmed by the SED in the early 1920s.

The SED intended the reorganisation of 1923 to 'raise the standard' of secondary schooling by wholly separating the secondary and non-secondary sectors of post-primary schooling after the age of 12. In doing this, the Department acted on the basis of a socially and academically elitist conception of secondary education that had its Scottish origins principally in the endowed secondary schools that were created or reorganised for the urban professional classes in the 1870s and 1880s. The Department wished to restrict secondary schooling to pupils whose 'promise of profiting' from the full five-year course for Highers (until 1951 awarded as a Group Leaving Certificate) could be demonstrated at the age of 12 years. This notion of secondary education was contested both at the time and in following decades. In practice, most secondary-school pupils left school before Highers, and there was little other than the potent cachet of secondary status to distinguish their schooling from that of the much larger numbers of pupils leaving Higher Grade schools.

The alternative, and more open, conception of secondary schooling derived from the Higher Grade schools and from memories of the parish school. Here the essential idea was that elements of secondary education should be widely available to 13, 14 and 15 year olds who should not be deterred from embarking on a course by the premature expectation that they take it to 17 years. At the same time, such courses should also keep open the route to higher education for those who chose. The Intermediate Certificate was thought to provide this articulation because it was taken both by Higher Grade and by secondary-school pupils. It provided a focus for the work of the Higher Grade schools and it was an intermediate rung in the ladder leading to Highers. Higher Grade enrolments had increased substantially during the First World War. An open model would have built on this growth by retaining the Intermediate Certificate and by yielding to the evident parental and pupil demand for greater access to the early stages of secondary schooling. Such a model was proposed in 1921 by the Scottish Advisory Council on Education, which numbered MacGillivray among its members, and it was supported by the EAs. But the SED, mindful one presumes of Treasury restrictions, rejected the Advisory Council's recommendations and, in 1924, abolished the Intermediate Certificate.

The school reorganisation of the 1920s set the pattern of post-primary schooling for the next half century. It created two levels of provision based on a concept of secondary schooling that was bound to condemn the majority of the school population to the 'failure' of 'early' leaving. This, in turn, made it likely that, in populous areas served by more than one school, the privileged form of schooling (secondary and, later, senior-secondary) would be located in a socially-favoured neighbourhood, a correlation still clearly evident in the 1970s, and one which contributed to social-class differences in attainment.[18] But the 1920s reorganisation also brought gains. Because the newly recognised secondary schools were much better distributed over the new centres of population, the reorganisation greatly increased access to secondary schooling, and it helped to achieve levels of participation in the inter-War period that were substantially higher than those in England and Wales and that compared favourably with major European countries.[19] Nevertheless, the full potential of the reorganisation was never realised. The abolition of the Intermediate Certificate denied pupils a major incentive for embarking on secondary schooling. The inhibiting effect of this change on participation was graphically illustrated in the 1960s when the restoration of an examination at 16 years led immediately to a sustained increase in post-compulsory enrolments and presentations for Highers (below).

The Acts of 1945 and 1946 introduced no major new educational principle to Scotland, but they did set the problems of the inter-War years in a new context that was to lead directly to the changes of the 1960s. Universal secondary education meant that access to secondary schooling could no longer be determined by attainment (stage) but by age. This made the treatment of junior-secondary pupils more visible and distinctive than the treatment of their predecessors in the Advanced Divisions. Hitherto, many pupils had been held back by a year or more in primary school in the hope that they might qualify for secondary schooling. The majority of Advanced Division pupils thus entered late and did less than the full two-year or three-year course. Moreover, many of these courses were themselves located in primary schools. However, with the raising of the minimum leaving age to 15 years, it was clear that there must be a 'clean cut' for all pupils at 12 years and that they should go to a non-primary school. Henceforward junior-secondary pupils would be more than an administrative category; they would be a distinct and visible group (even in many *omnibus* schools, which, in smaller population centres, took all the children from the local community, the junior- and senior-secondary courses were located in separate buildings). Junior-secondary schools were poorly accommodated and staffed, and there was little prospect of a solution to these problems even by the end of the 1950s when children born in the post-1945 'bulge' were approaching secondary education. The thrust behind comprehensive reorganisation in 1965 was partly a moral protest at this long-standing inequality, established by the reorganisation of 1923 and made socially transparent in the conditions of the junior-secondary school after 1945.

Meanwhile the rationale for junior-secondary schooling was also being undermined by changes in the senior-secondary sector. Rebuffed by the SED in the early 1920s, and sceptical of an Advisory Council mechanism that was now tightly controlled by the SED, the EIS and the EAs in 1928 established the Scottish Council for Research in Education (SCRE). As part of its attempt to develop thinking on post-primary schooling, the SCRE made a major research effort to operationalise the concept of 'promise of profit'. Interpreting this as an evens chance at age 12 of eventual success in the Higher School Leaving Certificate, research published in 1944 showed that at least a third of an age-group had the ability to be admitted to senior-secondary courses.[20] Many EAs had disregarded the Department's restrictive approach to secondary provision in the 1920s and 1930s, and most after 1945 followed the SCRE guideline or improved on it. By the early 1960s, it is estimated, 38 per cent of the Scottish age-group was admitted to a selective secondary course (including private schools) as compared with 30 per cent gaining admission to places in grammar schools, direct grant schools or private schools in England and Wales. Fewer Scottish than English pupils were in private schools, but the higher level of EA provision in Scotland meant that the chances of access to selective schooling for a working-class child in Scotland were as high as a middle-class child's chances of access to selective schooling in England and Wales.[21] The SED, however, thought the provision of senior-secondary courses too generous because of the continuing incidence of 'early' leaving at 15 years. It was to reduce this 'wastage' that a decision was made in 1955 to introduce the SCE O-grade examination in fourth year in 1962.

The new examination showed what had been lost with the abolition of the Intermediate Certificate in 1924. True, by now, to form, schools and EAs ignored the SED's wish to restrict the SCE O grade to the senior-secondary course pupil. Instead they treated the O grade, like the Intermediate Certificate before it, both as a rung in the ladder leading to Highers and as a course in its own right for pupils who might never take Highers. Secondary schooling was immediately opened up. Rates of staying-on rose. Between 1964 and 1974 the percentages of school leavers gaining certification increased from 27 to 66, and the percentages passing Highers rose from 16 to 28.[22] At the same time, three-year junior-secondary schools 'grew' a fourth year and began to present pupils successfully for the examination. To the moral argument against junior-secondary schooling could now be added a pragmatic demonstration that selection at 12 years into non-certificating courses was neither valid nor efficient.

Schooling after 1962[23]

The fifteen years following the introduction of the O grade in 1962 saw major changes in the ideas and practices of Scottish schooling and in its politics and government. So much changed in this period, and global and local movements were so intertwined, that it is not easy to identify all of the factors making for change or to grasp all of the consequences. One important outcome, however, was an emphatic and lasting shift in the moral basis of schooling. With the rejection of the bi-partite policy, the quality of secondary schooling provided for a child became less dependent on attainment at primary school or on family background, religion, neighbourhood or region. Levels of participation and attainment rose, though relative inequalities of outcome between the social classes remained.[24] There were also related changes in the politics and administration of schooling. These did not guarantee that the move towards more equal school provision was irreversible, still less that more equal provision would produce more equal educational outcomes. But they did mean that arguments about purposes and resources were less easily resolved to the palpable disadvantage of one group or another.

A second and related change was that more was expected both of individual schools and of the school system as a whole. The end of bi-partism has meant that all schools are expected to be effective in the same way, and for all of their pupils. Initially this was true only of primary schools. It did not become true of secondary schools until the Munn and Dunning reports of 1977 clarified the curricular implications of comprehensive reorganisation and of the 1973 raising of the school leaving age.[25] No political party or government agency has since challenged this expectation. Indeed, more schooling, though sometimes of a different sort, has since been consistently advocated as a solution to Britain's economic problems. Furthermore, the significance of the changes sought in the 1980s through the consumer-based policies of parental choice, school self-government, assisted places, and the abortive attempt to introduce technology academies is precisely that the formal differentiation of state secondary schools was no longer considered legitimate or politically viable. Similarly, it is significant that a recent curricular innovation like the Technical and Vocational Education Initiative (TVEI) (introduced in 1984) should be a cross-curricular strategy for all pupils, and not, as it would have been at any time before 1977, a principle for differentiating sectors of schooling.

The enhanced expectation of secondary schooling is linked to two further changes: in the purposes of secondary schooling, and in understandings of equality. Until the 1960s, the purpose of secondary schooling was set in terms of a pupil's attainment of an external standard, in this case the standard required for entry to higher education. Thereafter, it was also understood in terms of the pupil's development, primarily intellectual development, but also aesthetic, moral and social development. In primary education the beginnings of this change can be discerned much earlier, in the late 1920s. The Schools Inspectorate began to realise that a system organised around an arbitrary external standard — in this case, the qualifying standard for a form of secondary education intended to lead only to higher education — would continue to present intractable problems of failure, whereas all children could be expected to grow intellectually, whether or not they reached a particular level of attainment. The change was one of emphasis and not of kind, but its implications for curriculum and assessment were profound. They can be seen in the child-centred philosophy of the Primary Memorandum of 1965,[26] in the Standard grade reforms of the 1980s, and in the growing concern for the articulation of secondary education with further and higher education. Paradoxically, the change of policy emphasis was to produce the very outcome that the earlier policy had sought as more and more pupils succeeded in qualifying for entry to higher education.

The move in the 1960s and 1970s towards a model of schooling based on pupil growth was accompanied by a change in the understanding of equality. The notion of equality implied by the 1918 Act had been based on an external standard (intermediate or secondary education) and was aimed selectively at individuals (those who showed 'promise of profit' therefrom). The new emphasis on growth was universal to all pupils. It therefore entailed equality, not of opportunity, but of treatment; that is, giving all individuals the conditions in which they could continue to develop. And, because it was universal, it implied policies that could and should be directed at whole communities, and not just at individuals. Thus the instrument of the earlier notion of equality was the bursary, whilst the instrument of the later notion was the area comprehensive school.

Comprehensive reorganisation was quickly implemented in Scotland, mainly because the large EAs were Labour controlled and because small, Conservative controlled, EAs were compelled by arguments of economy. The free all-through, six-year neighbourhood school was universally adopted except in some rural areas where short-course 'feeder' schools were still needed. Fees were finally abolished in the few EA schools that still charged them, but most of the grant-aided schools became private, sometimes amalgamating with others.

The significance of the area comprehensive school was not that it eliminated group differences in educational outcomes. It did give a particular boost to the attainment of female pupils and working-class pupils, and this showed that the large social-class differences in attainment that remained were not wholly intractable. But comprehensive schooling was working against the legacy of a bi-partite system that had educationally disfranchised whole groups and neighbourhoods for more than half a century. This was especially true of the cities where the residential segregation of the social classes was greatest and where there was no tradition of secondary (later senior-secondary) education in many areas including the peripheral housing estates. It was not true of the New Towns; there the local secondary-school systems were most truly comprehensive in terms of social mix, and social-class differences in attainment were smaller than in the cities. Nor was it true of the rural and smaller urban, communities served by the one, *omnibus* post-primary school. These were the archetypal Scottish communities sometimes supposed in a nostalgic reading of the democratic tradition. But they were only a small part of twentieth century Scotland.

Comprehensive reorganisation enfranchised previously disadvantaged groups and communities by extending to them the same standards of provision serving the same purposes that applied in other schools. This standardisation is itself an aspect of the qualitative change that began in the 1960s. It is also evident in the adoption in the 1970s of a national structure of promoted posts for teachers and of national staffing standards to replace those set by the local EA. It was reinforced, too, by the reduction in the number of EAs themselves, and by the continuing reduction in the number of secondary schools, from around 900 in 1945, to around 600 in 1965 and 450 in the late 1970s. Again, standardisation did not mean that the quality of provision no longer varied between schools. But it did provide a framework for the reduction of this variation, and it did make the quality of local school provision less dependent on the social character and educational history of the neighbourhood. Nevertheless, the pull of tradition remained a potent factor among parents once they had the statutory right to choose a school. By the mid 1980s one pupil in ten had been relocated in this way. The net movement resulting from parental choice was towards the schools of older foundation, and towards those with socially favoured pupil intakes[27]. Thus the effect of the policy was to sharpen again the contours of the older system.

Another aspect of standardisation was the spread of national certification in the 1960s and 1970s to 'less able' pupils. The O-grade curriculum had not been designed for such pupils, but it rapidly displaced the vocationally oriented courses that the SED had wished to see expanded. Employers, nevertheless, used the O grade to select among school leavers, thereby extending the 'bond' between school certification and the youth labour market[28]. Standard grade courses were the first to be designed with an entire age-group in mind, and they incorporate a greater variety of aims and methods. In this sense they are less standard than the O-grade. Nevertheless, they are universal, nationally assessed, and based on curriculum guidelines that comprehend all pupils. Thus comparable pupils in different areas are now more likely than in earlier decades to be doing similar courses. This, and the fact the new courses are universal, makes national certification a yet more effective means of control and change.

Even so, the massive increase in the aims and delivery of the school system from the 1960s onwards could not be accomplished without changes in its governance. Until the 1950s, the SED had been reluctant to share its responsibilities with outside bodies or individuals. It had fallen out with the Advisory Council in the 1920s over policy for secondary schooling. It fell out with it again in the 1940s when the Council, backed by a Labour Secretary of State for Scotland, proposed reforms that would have replaced the bi-partite organisation of schooling with a comprehensive system, and would have given educationists greater control over public examinations and teacher-training[29]. But the expansion that the SED finally and inadvertently released with the introduction of the O-grade in 1962 forced the Department to create a new structure of extra-governmental agencies to administer the growing undertaking that schooling was becoming. Participants in this enlarged policy community were carefully selected by the SED. To begin with, they tended to share the same professional background as the HMI itself, a background dominated by early professional experience in the older-established secondary schools. Their educational ideas tended to be similarly traditional. But, in the 1970s, there were changes both in thinking and in personnel. Many more teachers were recruited to the policy community from Catholic schools, from new comprehensive schools, from schools serving mainly working-class areas, and from schools in the west of Scotland where the provision of secondary education before 1923 had been relatively weak.

This, too, was a form of enfranchisement, essential to help the SED to run an enhanced undertaking, but also empowering the claims of previously neglected areas of the system. Changes in local government also worked in this direction. The larger unit of the region was more appropriate to the growing scale of education, and the business of most regions came to be organised along party-political lines. Through Strathclyde region alone, Labour controlled almost half of Scottish school provision, and its control extended over most of the other authorities. This broader policy community was distrustful of policies than might reverse the trend towards more equal provision. In 1987, for example, it forced the Conservative government to scale down its plans to give Scottish schools powers of self-management comparable to those for schools in England and Wales. Even in its modified form, however, the Scottish legislation of 1988 and 1989 presented its authors with a difficult problem of legitimacy which, as we have seen, they attempted to solve by an appeal to a version of traditional Scotland.

The changes of the 1970s made for a very different politics of education. It was no longer possible, as it had been between the Wars, to limit public spending by giving a raw deal to women teachers, or to the Advanced Divisions or junior-secondary schools, which, in effect, meant to working-class pupils, Catholic schools and schools in the west of Scotland. The moral basis of educational discourse had changed, and this change was reinforced by the standardisation of secondary provision both in its own right, and because of the fillip that standardisation gave to union activity. Teachers now were less divided among themselves and were able to exert pressure through effective industrial action.

The result was that schools and government were both overstretched as they attempted to provide for an expanding and rapidly changing system. The pressure on resources might have been relieved by the substantial fall in the number of pupil entrants that worked its way through the secondary sector from the late 1970s onwards. But, here too, the political response merely illustrated how few options there now were, other than to cut the cake in equal parts. Local authorities were reluctant to achieve the economies that demography made possible and to close schools. Moreover, even though absolute pupil numbers were falling, the proportions who entered post-compulsory schooling increased in the 1980s, partly as a result of recession and partly because of rising levels of attainment at 16 years.

Much of this rise in attainment is to be explained by a process of continuing feedback, from schools to pupils, and then from those pupils as parents to their own children at school. In 1935 the SED remarked:

> [T]he last half century has seen a steady improvement in the attitude of parents towards the schools. Fifty years ago, the pupils were children of parents some of whom had never attended school and a few of whom had done so long or regularly. . . . Now, however, the pupils are, with few exceptions, children of parents who themselves attended school up to the age of fourteen and who feel that school is the proper place for their children[30].

Similarly, the rising level of education in the parental population continued to boost attainment at school in the 1980s[31]. One consequence was that, slowly but inexorably, the focus of policy attention broadened to include the organisation and funding of higher education, and its relations with the rest of the system. By the beginning of the 1990s, a majority of Scottish pupils volunteered for post-compulsory schooling and one quarter entered higher education by the age of 21 years. In 1990 the official projection was that this quarter would rise to 40 per cent by the year 2000.

Higher Education

Robert Anderson has argued that, apart from the admission of women, there was no fundamental change in the social role of the Scottish universities between the 1880s and the Second World War. The numbers of male students changed little and the universities 'were actually reaching a smaller proportion of the population in the 1930s than in the 1880s'[32]. In the 1950s, the proportion of the Scottish age group that entered university started to rise. However, it had reached only 5.1 per cent by 1962, the year before the Robbins report recommended a major expansion of higher education in the United Kingdom. A further 4.8 per cent entered non-university higher education, making a total of 9.9 per cent who entered some form of higher education. This compares with 8.4 per cent in England and Wales, but only 3.9 per cent of the age group in England and Wales entered university. In the early 1960s the numbers of Scottish school leavers increased and so, dramatically, did the rates of qualification for higher education. These had risen slowly from 4.2 per cent in 1953 to 6.8 per cent in 1961[33]. With the new SCE O grade now in place as an intermediate bridge to Higher, they then shot up, faster than in England and Wales, to reach 11 per cent in 1965 and 17 per cent in 1970[34]. The supply of places was now clearly insufficient to meet demand.

Pressure on places in higher education had hitherto not been high, partly because of the SED's reluctance to see secondary education expanded, and partly because of the relative 'generosity' of the settlement of the Scottish universities in the late nineteenth century. Although the introduction of matriculation and universal graduation in the 1890s had confirmed the trend towards a higher age and standard of entry, the universities had remained much more accessible than in England and Wales. There were more places per head of population; the student culture was less collegial; and the costs of attendance were lower, partly because larger proportions of students lived at home. The majority of students came from middle-class backgrounds, especially in the professional faculties where the tendency of sons to follow fathers was not measurably less than south of the Border. Working-class students comprised around a fifth of the student body throughout much of our period, but their representation suffered during the Depression years. So too did the representation of women which peaked at just over a third in the mid 1920s, fell away to a quarter in the mid 1930s, and had barely improved on that by the start of the 1960s[35].

Until the 1970s when the problem of teacher supply was finally contained, women's experience of higher education was closely related to arrangements for the recruitment and training of teachers, and so too was the experience of working-class students of both sexes. The pattern had been set in the nineteenth century when teacher-training was the main form of higher education available to women, and when the pupil-teacher route was an important avenue of access for poorer students (both to college and to concurrent university education). This route disappeared after the First World War, but the cultural configuration continued and was reinforced by the ban on married women teachers and by the requirement, introduced in 1924, that all male teachers be graduates. It made little economic sense for a woman who contemplated teaching as a career and marriage as a possibility to aim for an Honours degree. The most economical route into teaching was through the college course. Failing that, the Ordinary degree, completed in three years, offered a less costly route than the four-year Honours degree. Male Honours graduates could benefit over a full career from the higher earnings that their qualification gave them. Even so, male students from working-class backgrounds commonly took the shorter, Ordinary degree route into school teaching[36].

The marriage ban was lifted after the Second World War and equal pay for women was achieved in the 1950s. But, there was still social stratification of the college- and Ordinary degree routes into teaching. The gendering of teaching was exploited yet again in the 1960s when the need for more teachers was met largely by the provision of non-graduating courses for women in colleges of education (as they came to be called in 1958). Thus, until primary and secondary schools were staffed to standard, as they were for the first time in the 1970s, the system's need for teachers was met by a lower-level, mainly liberal-arts, track from secondary school through higher education, catering mainly for women, working-class men and Arts students. In 1962, 40 per cent of all graduates from Scottish universities (other than medical graduates) entered school teaching. For women graduates in arts and related areas, the proportion was almost two thirds[37]. By the 1970s, however, there was no longer any need to encourage or to tolerate the underattainment of women. Nor were women themselves as likely as in the past to accept traditional expectations. By the end of the 1970s, girls were leaving school better qualified on average than boys, and they were close to achieving parity of entry to higher education despite the contraction of teacher training in that decade.

The proportions of young people qualifying for entry to higher education increased more slowly in the 1970s than in the 1960s, possibly because of the strains that were placed on the schools by the raising of the school-leaving age in 1973. But the decade saw the central institutions begin to take an increased market share of higher-education provision, degree and non-degree until, by the mid 1980s, they more than matched the universities' share of provision for new entrants. This trend had seemed at first to be no more than a short-term reaction to the conviviality of the 1960s and to the oil crisis of 1973, but it proved to be of lasting significance. Costs were lower in the central institutions and there was greater flexibility, especially in the provision of part-time and short courses. If higher education were to continue to expand, could the university share of provision be maintained at anything like its historic level? For a time the question was obscured by the financial crisis that the monetarist policy of the government visited on the universities in the first half of the 1980s. But qualification rates for higher education continued to rise in Scotland in the 1980s and were by now well in excess of rates for Britain overall[38]. The lasting issues were clearly ones of student access, and of cost, flexibility and rationalisation, but not of the restoration of an earlier *status quo*.

The universities had opposed political devolution in the 1970s, and they were wary too of proposals by an SED advisory committee in 1985 for some form of unified funding structure for all Scottish higher education. But attitudes were changing. In 1991 the government announced its intention to transfer the control of the Scottish universities from the Department of Education and Science to the SED in 1993 or 1994[39]. Viewed from Whitehall, this was not so much a concession to Scottish Office aggrandisement, or to national sentiment, as a piece of administrative tidying-up necessitated by the ending of the binary divide of higher education in England and Wales. Viewed from Scotland, however, it offered the opportunity of an integrated and distinctive approach to the provision of mass higher education. Only a minority feared that it would deliver the universities to the fate that MacGillivray thought must come with the turn of the wheel: 'the fate reserved by Polyphemus for Odysseus, to be eaten last'[40].

Reflections

Was Scottish education in 1990 still distinctive? Clearly yes. The great expansion of provision and uptake had been accomplished within an institutional structure that remained in many ways unaltered. In higher education, the creation of new universities and colleges did not change either the basic structure of honours and ordinary degrees or the essentially vocational nature of the public-sector colleges. More accommodation was provided for students but the collegial model was confined to the University of St Andrews. Universities and colleges remained essentially non-residential institutions with strong local ties. The model was flexible, capable both of supplying a surplus of higher education to the rest of the United Kingdom and of educating higher proportions of Scotland's own.

In this respect, the higher-education system has built on the continuing advantage which Scottish schooling gives the young. For 40 per cent of young Scots in the year 2000 to enter higher education would imply a level of development of higher education comparable with that of secondary education in the inter-War period and of senior-secondary schooling in the period up to 1965. It is not surprising, therefore, that a tertiary-education question has emerged that in many ways recapitulates the earlier debate on post-primary schooling. How far should the provision of higher education be differentiated in level and content? Who should pay? Can it be made equally accessible to all social groups? And, above all, should tertiary education be regarded as a stage of education open to all or, like secondary education before 1945, as a level of education suited only to some? In thinking these issues through, there is clearly much to be learned from the parallel with the post-primary question this century, and from the form of organisation that characterised the Scottish universities before the settlement of 1889. However the issues are resolved, the prospect of a separate funding council for all higher education in Scotland makes it more likely that the solutions will be distinctively Scottish. Moreover, such a council can only strengthen the case for greater accountability to the Scottish electorate and hence for a Scottish Parliament. But it is striking that Scottish educational institutions have retained their distinctive character in the absence of such powers.

At secondary level, too, the system has remained distinctive. Relative to England and Wales, the private sector remains surprisingly small despite a great increase in disposable income. All state schools are comprehensive and virtually all are run by the education authorities. There are no equivalents in Scotland to the city technology colleges or grant-maintained schools found in England. The Higher continues to offer a broader and more accessible qualification than the GCE A level. The delivery of curriculum remains distinctively Sottish, as in the case of the National Certificate and the Scottish Certificate of Education, or else is well able to adapt external innovations to prevailing Scottish circumstances, as in the case of the TVEI.

More intangibly, but no less important, the system's sense of its own distinctiveness also remains despite the loss of moral certainty that came with the ending of bi-partite secondary schooling in the 1960s and 1970s. Elsewhere in Britain there was a wider loss of confidence in the ameliorist perspective. But it is doubtful whether this decline has been anything like as severe in Scotland which has seen no Black Papers on education, no Great Debate on schooling, and no crisis of confidence in educational standards. It is true that a substantial minority of Scottish parents now exercises its right to choose a school. In spite of this, perhaps even because of this, support for the system of public schooling is high. The solidarity of parents with teachers survived the teachers' industrial action of the mid 1980s and was consolidated by opposition to the government's programme for testing in primary schools in 1990. No group of parents has taken a school out of education-authority control. Indeed, there are signs that school boards, far from promoting opting-out, are becoming a focus of resistance to market-led policies for education both locally and nationally. Whilst the Scottish Office has become a more powerful instrument of change since 1950, it is a power that relies on, and that is circumscribed by, the consensual support of a wider educational policy community with roots in a distinctive civil society. At the beginning of the 1990s, there was a widespread consensus across this community in respect of key areas, among them the organisation of secondary schooling, the role of the Higher, the organisation of higher education, the importance of the local education authority, and the importance of the integration of the system at national level.[41]

Is the story of twentieth century Scottish education, then, indeed the story of the rise and progress of a system that has promoted talent regardless of social origin? Smout, as I have indicated, would argue not:

> In the twentieth century, Scottish education has been marked by the same attitude that branded it in the nineteenth, which regarded it as a matter of low social priority once the perceived needs of the middle classes had been attended to, and once a channel had been opened for a limited number of working-class children to use secondary school and university as a means of upward social mobility. Neither the Scotch Education Department . . . nor the teaching profession, nor the public at large, expressed much interest in achieving high standards for the bulk of the population, or even in discovering what the world outside Scotland considered high and appropriate standards for an efficient, modern nation.[42]

And later:

> Perhaps, then, it is in the history of the school more than in any other aspect of recent social history that the key lies to some of the more depressing aspects of modern Scotland. If there are in this country too many people who fear what is new, believe the difficult to be impossible, draw back from responsibility, and afford established authority and tradition an exaggerated respect, we can reasonably look for an explanation in the institutions that moulded them.[43]

In its way, this too is a diagnosis of a dependency culture, but it is a diagnosis that is made possible only by giving too small a place to government, to politics, and to social change. It disregards the conflicts of purpose between the SED and the rest of the Scottish educational world, and it misrepresents the achievements of both.[44] Scotland provided more places in secondary and higher education than England and Wales, and thereby provided more opportunities for working-class children than were available to their counterparts south of the Border. Other Scottish children also profited from the higher levels of provision in Scotland, with the result that social-class relativities in access and attainment within Scotland resembled relativities elsewhere. But there was, nevertheless, more opportunity in Scotland.[45] Furthermore, there was also a strand in the Scottish educational tradition which wanted to see these relativities eroded. I have argued that what happened after 1923 was that the SED, itself constrained by a wider governmental context, imposed a bi-partite model for secondary schooling over the claims and practice of a more open model. It also tried to represent that model as the authentic Scottish tradition. This was an ideological gloss prompted by the Department's need to maintain its legitimacy and effectiveness in the face of opposition. By the time of the Conservative governments of the 1950s and 1960s, the gloss had been widely accepted and had put down roots in the educational policy community. But the vision of a more open and generous system survived and was expressed in the practice of the schools and in the work and thinking of the local authorities. In turn this fuelled, and was fuelled by, a social demand for more and better education, a demand which diffused and grew across the generations and which fed the pressures for change. Smout argues that improvements in twentieth century Scottish welfare are to be explained by

> the rise of the modern collectivist state that relied on the mixed economy and the guidance of a bureaucracy of professional government-financed experts.[46]

In education, however, the major changes came in the 1960s and 1970s when the experts were challenged, by comprehensive reorganisation and by the expansionary practice of the schools. And they came as a result of demands that were no less embedded in Scottish educational culture than the form of organisation that was imposed on an unwilling system after the First World War.

Acknowledgement

The author is grateful to Lindsay Paterson for his comments on an earlier draft of this chapter.

NOTES

1. Duncan MacGillivray, 'Fifty Years of Scottish Education', in John Clarke (ed.) *Problems National Education* (London, 1919), pp. 1–41.

2. Malcolm Rifkind, *A Vision for Scotland* (Edinburgh, 1988) p. 3.

3. Walter Elliot, 'The Scottish Heritage in Politics' in the Duke of Atholl and others *A Scotman's Heritage* (London, 1932), pp. 53–65.

4. Stimulated in recent decades by George Elder Davie, *The Democratic Intellect: Scotland and her Universities in the Nineteenth Century* (Edinburgh, 1961); and George Elder Davie, *The Crisis of the Democratic Intellect: The Problem of Generalism and Specialisation in Twentieth-Century Scotland* (Edinburgh, 1986).

5. Quoted in Andrew McPherson and Charles D. Raab, *Governing Education: A Sociology of Policy Since 1945* (Edinburgh, 1988), p. 413.

6. Alexander Morgan, *Rise and Progress of Scottish Education*, (London, 1927).

7. G. S. Osborne, *Scottish and English Schools: A Comparative Survey of the Past Fifty Years* (Pittsburgh, 1966); G. S. Osborne, *Change in Scottish Education* (London, 1968); James Scotland, *The History of Scottish Education, Volume 2, From 1872 to the Present Day* (London, 1969).

8. Robert Anderson, *Education and Opportunity in Victorian Scotland: Schools and Universities* (Oxford, 1983). Also, for example, Robert Anderson, 'In Search of the "Lad of Parts": The Mythical History of Scottish Education', *History Workshop*, 19 (1985), pp. 82–104; Robert Anderson, 'Education and Society in Modern Scotland: A Comparative Perspective, *History of Education Quarterly*, 25 (1985), pp. 459–481.

9. W. M. Humes and H. M. Paterson (eds.), *Scottish Culture and Scottish Education 1800–1980* (Edinburgh, 1983).

10. H. M. Paterson, in Humes and Paterson, *op. cit.*, p. 198.

11. *Ibid.*, p. 200.

12. W. M. Humes, *The Leadership Class in Scottish Education* (Edinburgh, 1986).

13. T. C. Smout, *A Century of the Scottish People 1830–1950* (London, 1987, paperback edition), pp. 229, 259, 273, 275 and chapter IX.

14. Reasons for non-attendance and non-enrolment were discussed regularly in the annual reports to Parliament of the Committee of Council on Education in Scotland.

15. T. A. Fitzpatrick, *Catholic Secondary Education in South-West Scotland before 1972: Its Contribution to the Change in Status of the Catholic Community of the Area*, (Aberdeen, 1986); J. H. Treble, 'The Development of Roman Catholic Education in Scotland 1878–1978' in David McRoberts (ed.) *Modern Scottish Catholicism 1878–1978* (Glasgow, 1979), pp. 111–139; Andrew McPherson and J. Douglas Willms, 'Certification, Class Conflict, Religion and Community: A Socio-Historical Explanation of the Effectiveness of Contemporary Schools' in Alan C. Kerckhoff (ed.), *Research in Sociology of Education and Socialization (Volume 6)* (Greenwich, Connecticut, 1986).

16. N. Wade, *Post-Primary Education in the Primary Schools of Scotland 1872–1936* (London, 1939), pp. 126–127; and John Young, 'The Advisory Council on Education in Scotland 1920–61', PhD thesis, University of Edinburgh, 1986. Evidence of local failure to follow the policies and practices recommended by the Department appears regularly in the Committee of Council on Education reports to Parliament for the years after 1924.

17. This paragraph and the following four draw in part on Anderson, 'Education and Opportunity in Victorian Scotland', and on Wade *op. cit.*.

18. McPherson and Willms, 'Certification, Class Conflict, Religion and Community'.

19. 'England had 8.1 [secondary] pupils per thousand population in 1921 and 9.9 in 1931, and Scotland 13.5 and 16.8. . . .', Anderson, 'Education and Society in Modern Scotland', p. 475, (my parenthesis) (see also his note 55, p. 481). The Scottish figures include pupils in Advanced Divisions in secondary schools. Excluding these pupils would reduce the Scottish ratios by about 12 per cent of the ratio leaving them still considerably higher than the ratios to England and Wales — estimated from SED, Report of the Committee of Council on Education in Scotland for the Year 1928–29 (London, 1929), Cmd. 3312, pp. 16 and 17. Note also that the ratios are not adjusted for the later age of transfer in Scotland to post-primary schooling. Anderson mentions population ratios of 7.6 for France in 1936, and 11.9 for Germany in 1931. In 1938, a third (32 per cent) of Scottish pupils aged between 13 and 14 years were in the secondary departments of secondary schools — calculated from Education (Scotland) Reports, etc Issued in 1939 (Edinburgh, 1940), p. 89, Table IVB. This compares with the figure of 13 per cent given in Brian Simon, *The Politics of Educational Reform 1920–1940* (London, 1974), p. 366, Table 4. All British figures in this note exclude pupils in private schools.

20. W. McClelland, *Selection for Secondary Education* (London, 1942).

21. J. W. B. Douglas, J. M. Ross, S. M. M. Maxwell and D. A. Walker, 'Differences in Test Score and in the Gaining of Selective Places for Scottish Children and Those in England and Wales', *British Journal of Educational Psychology* 36 (1966), pp. 150–157. The study also found that the proportion of working-class pupils was higher in Scotland than in England. About 20 per cent of the age group entered grammar school in England and Wales in the early 1960s, see Committee on Higher Education (CHE), *Higher Education* (London, 1963), Cmnd. 2154 (The Robbins Report), Appendix One, Annex K, Table K3, p. 233.

22. SED, *Assessment for All: Report of the Committee to Review Assessment in the Third and Fourth Years of Secondary Education in Scotland* (Edinburgh, 1977) (The Dunning Report), Table C1, p. 131. 'Gaining certification' means one or more SCE O grade awards at A-C grade.

23. This section draws on McPherson and Raab, *op. cit.*.

24. J. Gray, A. F. McPherson and D. Raffe, *Reconstructions of Secondary Education: Theory, Myth and Practice since the War*, (London, 1983), Chapters 12 and 14; Andrew McPherson and J. Douglas Willms, 'Equalisation and Improvement: Some Effects of Comprehensive Reorganisation in Scotland', *Sociology* 21 (1987), pp. 509–539; and Lindsay Paterson, 'Social-Class Inequalities in Scottish School-Leaver Entry to Higher Education', in H. Maguiness (ed.) *Educational Opportunity: The Challenge of Under-Achievement and Social Deprivation* (Paisley, in press), ISBN 0.903655-20–9.

25. SED, *Assessment for All*; SED, *The Structure of the Curriculum in the Third and Fourth Years of the Scottish Secondary School* (Edinburgh, 1977) (The Munn Report).

26. SED, *Primary Education in Scotland* (Edinburgh, 1965).

27. SED, 'Placing Requests in Education Authority Schools', *Statistical Bulletin*, No. 9/B6/1987, Tables 1 and 6B; F. Echols, A. F. McPherson and J. D. Willms, 'Parental Choice in Scotland', *Journal of Education Policy* 5 (1990), pp. 207–222. See also Adler, Petch and Tweedie, *op. cit.*

28. Geoff Payne, *Employment and Opportunity* (London, 1987), Chapters 5 and 6; and D. Raffe, 'The Extension of Certification and the Tightening Bond', in Gray, McPherson and Raffe, *op. cit.*, Chapter 7.

29. SED, *Secondary Education: A Report of the Advisory Council on Education in Scotland* (Edinburgh, 1947), Cmd.7005; and Young, *op. cit.*

30. SED, *Report of the Committee of Council on Education in Scotland for the Year 1935* (London, 1936), Cmd.5140, p. 18–19.

31. P. M. Burnhill, C. L. Garner and A. F. McPherson, 'Parental Education, Social Class and Entry to Higher Education, 1976–1986', *Journal of the Royal Statistical Society* Series A, 153 (1990), pp. 233–248.

32. Anderson, 'Education and Society in Modern Scotland', p. 467.

33. CHE, *op. cit.*, Appendix One, Section 7, Tables 31 and 32, pp. 148 and 149, and Section 4, Table 12, p. 115.

34. SED, 'School Leavers Qualifications', *Statistical Bulletin* No. 10/E2/1986. The percentages are those of school leavers who passed at least three Highers. The British rate (including Scotland, but mainly reflecting the proportions of young people in England and Wales gaining two or more GCE A levels) did not reach Scotland's 1970 level of 17 per cent until 1988 (Department of Education and Science, unpublished series), by which time the Scottish rate was 23 per cent (SED, 'School Leavers Qualifications 1987–88', *Statistical Bulletin* No. 15/E2/1989, Table 1).

35. Anderson, 'Education and Opportunity in Victorian Scotland'; Anderson, 'Education and Society in Modern Scotland'; Robert Anderson, *The Student Community at Aberdeen 1860–1939* (Aberdeen, 1988); Andrew McPherson, 'Selections and Survivals: A Sociology of the Ancient Scottish Universities', in R. Brown (ed.) *Knowledge, Education and Cultural Change: Papers in the Sociology of Education* (London, 1973), pp. 163–201; Alison Kelly, 'Family Background, Subject Specialisation and Occupational Recruitment of Scottish University Students: Some Patterns and Trends', *Higher Education* 5, (1976), pp. 177–188; Lindsay Paterson, 'Social-Class Inequalities in Scottish School-Leaver Entry to Higher Education'; CHE, *op. cit.*, Appendix Two (A), Table 10, p. 25.

36. Anderson, 'Education and Opportunity in Victorian Scotland'; Helen Corr, 'An Exploration into Scottish Education', in W. Hamish Fraser and R. J. Morris (eds.) *People and Society in Scotland*, vol 11, 1830–1914 (Edinburgh, 1990), pp. 290–309; M. Cruickshank, *A History of the Training of Teachers in Scotland* (Edinburgh 1970); Judith Fewell and Fiona M. S. Paterson, *Girls in Their Prime: Scottish Education Revisited*, (Edinburgh 1990); and G. Mercer and David C. Forsyth, 'Some Aspects of Recruitment to School Teaching Among University Graduates in Scotland, 1860–1955', *British Journal of Educational Studies* XXIII (1975), pp. 58–77.

37. CHE, Appendix Two (B), Annex P, Tables p. 5 and P.6, pp. 466 and 467.

38. SED, 'Revised Higher Education Projections for Scotland', *Statistical Bulletin* No. 6/J1/1985; *Higher Education: Meeting the Challenge* (London, 1987), Cm 114, Figure D.

39. *Higher Education: A New Framework* (London, 1991), Cmd.1541; *Access and Opportunity* (Edinburgh, 1991), Cmd.1530.

40. MacGillivray, *op. cit.*, p. 23.

41. Andrew McPherson, 'The Howie Committee on Post-Compulsory Schooling' in D. McCrone and L. Paterson (eds.), *The Scottish Government Yearbook 1992* (Edinburgh, 1992); Pamela Munn, 'Devolved Management of Schools and FE Colleges: A Victory for the Producer Over the Consumer?', in McCrone and Paterson, *op. cit.*

42. Smout, *op. cit.*, p. 223.

43. *Ibid.*, p. 229.

44. Also, the leading figures in educational research and teacher training in the period

1920 to 1960 were actively involved in the international scientific and progressive movement in education. Their interest in the standards and values of other systems is reflected in, for example, William Boyd's *A History of Western Education* (London, 1921) which was revised and regularly republished in subsequent decades; see also Robert E. Bell, 'Educational Studies in the Scottish Universities, 1870–1970', PhD Thesis, University of Edinburgh, 1986. For a further assessment of Scottish meritocracy, see Keith Hope, *As Others See Us: Schooling and Social Mobility on Scotland and the United States* (Cambridge, 1984).

45. This conclusion is also supported by Mueller and Karle's recent analysis of data on men in various European countries, including Scotland, England, Northern Ireland and the Republic of Ireland, who were born in the first half of this century. See Walter Mueller and Wolfgang Karle, 'Social Selection in Educational Systems in Europe', Paper Prepared for the Meetings of the International Sociological Association Research Committee on Social Stratification, XIIth World Congress of Sociology, Madrid, July, 1990, p. 22.

46. Smout, *op. cit.*, p. 259. It is difficult to reconcile Smout's de-politicised concept of the 'expert' with the fact that the expertise of educational professionals was always contested.

Note: A version of this chapter with more extensive footnotes is available from the author.

CHAPTER 4

Class, Work and Trade Unionism in Scotland

W. Knox

It is universally recognised that the twentieth century has so far brought about important changes in the nature of class relations, technology, the organisation of the workplace and in industrial relations, with the prospect of still more to come in the light of the Thatcher revolution. Yet, in spite of this, social and labour history has rarely applied its tools of analysis to detail the reasons for and the outcomes of these significant changes in modern Scotland. The historical research which has been carried out has focused on the collapse of heavy industry, the rise of Labour and, more recently, the emergence of nationalism as a potent political factor. This means that whole areas of study concerning gender and workplace relations, the development of trade unionism and the impact of the state and unemployment upon it, the demise of the craft culture and the terrain of white-collar work and organisation remain neglected. The neglect of these important issues has a number of causes, but, perhaps, the major one might be the decreasing distinctiveness of Scottish labour institutions. The lack of research makes it impossible to survey and evaluate the writing of Scottish historians in these crucial areas of historical inquiry. Thus this essay draws together the work of economists, historians and sociologists, all of whom, for their own reasons, have interested themselves in these matters. This multi-disciplinary approach is also made inevitable given the period under review as it would be unfair to criticise historians for not taking an interest in current problems, except, of course, where they throw up historical questions.

The major themes under investigation include changes in the labour market, the impact of economic and technological change on work and workplace relations, the growth and development of trade unionism, particularly the rise of white-collar unionism, and the influence of the state and unemployment on organisation and bargaining strategies. Central to these concerns is the decline of the craft culture, and this phenomenon will form the leitmotif of the essay. The disappearance of the male, skilled and Protestant dominated labour movement is perhaps the most important consequence of economic and technological change and something which, although not fully understood, will have a profound impact on the organisation and conduct of trade unions for years to come. However, while the essay will inevitably focus on craft unionism and the staple industries, where possible and appropriate it will attempt to compare them with the experience of at least a few segments of the labour market dominated by semi-skilled and unskilled workers.

1. The Changing Labour Market

As changes in the labour market are inextricably bound up with changes in the economy and the structure of industry it is important to outline the main features of Scottish economic development in the twentieth century. By 1914 Scotland was an industrial economy heavily dependent on the staple industries of coal, engineering and shipbuilding, and, to a lesser extent, textiles. It was an export orientated economy particularly vulnerable to shifts in world trade and whose ownership was based on the family firm. Even before the First World War the economy was experiencing relative decline, but its weaknesses were obscured by the prosperity of the war years and the restocking boom which followed the end of hostilities. After 1921 the shortcomings inherent in the industrial structure were cruelly exposed as world demand for capital goods fell sharply and depression set in, leading to decline in all the major sectors of the economy and mass unemployment. Depression was a feature of the inter-war Scottish economy and was only alleviated by the rearmament boom of the late 1930s and the outbreak of war itself in 1939. The economy as a result of war enjoyed a brief period of prosperity but the trends observable in the inter-war period reasserted themselves with equal intensity after 1945. Since the end of the Second World War the Scottish economy has experienced a profound process of industrial restructuring, inducing a shift away from heavy industry to the service sector and high tech light engineering. This shift, particularly marked in the 1970s, brought about the collapse of traditional manufacturing industry and has led to a rise in the number of foreign-owned firms and the decline of the family-style of ownership typical of Scottish industry pre-1945.

The structural changes taking place in the economy have inevitably had considerable effects on the occupational profile of Scotland. The main change has been the decline of manufacturing employment and the increase in white-collar jobs. Employment in the service sector took off after 1945 with the expansion of state and local authority public services and the growing importance of retailing and financial institutions in the economy. The restructuring of the labour market has led to a growth in the number of working women, especially married women. (The reasons for this development are dealt with in McIvor's separate essay.) Such a transformation in employment patterns has been accompanied by a loss of manufacturing jobs at a faster rate than the service sector can absorb. Between 1960 and 1975, 10,000 men a year were losing jobs in the manufacturing sector and this rate nearly doubled in the period 1979–87. Employment in skilled work has been particularly badly hit with the loss of 80,000 jobs in the decade 1961–71 alone; a loss larger than the previous fifty years. By the mid-1980s the new electrical and electronic industries were employing more than double the numbers employed in coal, shipbuilding and steel.[1] The Association of University Teachers in Scotland currently has a larger membership than the National Union of Mineworkers.

In short, since 1914 the Scottish economy has moved from being a manufacturer of capital goods to a producer of services. As industry

6. Metal workers at the furnace in Beardmore's works, Glasgow, 1934. Glasgow University Business Archives.

7. Pneumatic riveters at work, John Brown's shipyard, 1937. Glasgow University Business Archives.

has declined and the service sector substantially increase its demand for labour there has been a corresponding reduction in skilled work and manufacturing employment in general. This transformation has given rise to the development of the branch plant system of production, in which the locus of control of the firm lies outside Scotland, and, at the same time, it has created thousands of part-time jobs, mainly for women. These developments pose new challenges to the labour movement in Scotland.

2. Work and Workplace Relations

The changing structure of the economy and the labour market was related to the pace of technological change. Normally, innovations in techniques and machinery will occur more extensively and rapidly in conditions of rising demand in an economy, and will decline or stagnate in conditions of falling demand. Scotland in the twentieth century was to prove no exception to the general rule of technological advance. Declining demand in the inter-war years for capital goods and other products was a disincentive to producers to improve the methods and machinery of production and, therefore, in the absence of innovation employers displayed a greater willingness to extend and refine existing technology throughout industry. In the construction industry the mechanisation of the joiner's shop which began in the decades before 1914 spread rapidly in the post-war period. The use of metal and plastic rather than wooden components accelerated the development of prefabricated building methods. The availability of plastics revolutionised the iron and steel industry as did the demands of mass production. The switch from steam to electric power in the jute industry and the introduction of high speed spinning machinery saw spinners attend to four 96 spindle frames. In engineering the use of semi-automatic machinery of the post-1880 period was further extended and refined. For example, whereas only one or two milling machines were available before 1914, in the inter-war period there around twenty models 'each designed to perform a different range of work with different degrees of accuracy'.[2] In the related field of shipbuilding the most innovatory feature of the inter-war period was welding; an innovation which ultimately led to prefabricated shipbuilding after 1945. Coalmining experienced further mechanisation and by 1935 72 per cent of Scottish output was cut by machine compared to only 50 per cent for Britain as a whole. Additionally, the old 'pillar and stoop' method had been abandoned in many pits and replaced by the longwall method which simplified the process of coal-getting and facilitated even greater mechanisation.

As a result of the economic depression technical change in the interwar years, although not static, was more concerned with the extension and reinforcement of existing processes rather than altering them in a fundamental way. The post-Second World War economic boom provided the commercial incentive that was lacking in the 1920s and 1930s and consequently the pace of technical change considerably quickened. In building, the process of prefabrication had developed so extensively that as early as 1947 the president of the Amalgamated Society of Woodworkers considered that many of the jobs in the industry could be done by 'mere process workers'. As tanker building begun to dominate the output of the Clyde in the 1950s it called for flowline methods using the maximum amount of prefabrication. This increased the demand for welding skills and proportionately reduced the need for rivetting skills. The steel industry saw key processes fully automated in the 1960s, and the same could be said of the jute industry which in the 1950s invested £11m in automatic machinery. In the late 1950s coalmining also experienced profound technological change with the introduction of power-loading machinery, which would take coal off the face layer by layer and simultaneously load it to an armoured conveyor which followed along the face. Coal could now be cut on all shifts whereas before only one shift cut and the others prepared and cleared.

Technological change also affected other workers normally assumed to be outside the dynamic sectors of the economy. Farmwork, for example, was becoming more mechanised as tractors replaced horse drawn implements. In 1939 there were 6,250 tractors in use in Scottish farming. This figure rapidly increased to 20,158 in 1944 as wartime demand and falling supplies of labour forced producers to become more capital intensive. Shopwork also underwent a revolution with the growth of large retail outlets. The new enterprises reduced much of shopwork to filling shelfs and running tills, and the prepackaging of goods led to the abandonment of the six year grocery apprenticeship. As point of sale equipment became more sophisticated, leading to the electronic till of the present, even simple addition skills became redundant. Surveys have shown that a high percentage of staff in checkout work in supermarkets suffer from musculoskeletal problems including headaches, eye strain and pains in various parts of the body. Dockwork is another unskilled occupation to have undergone profound change. Formerly it was based on the muscle power of a largely casual workforce, but since the 1960s automatic methods of cargo handling and containerisation has eliminated the physical aspects of dockwork and reduced the numbers employed in the industry.[3] In the 1970s and particularly the 1980s the use of micro-processors has enhanced the possibility of fully automating the production process and threatens to revolutionise white-collar office work, but whether this has eliminated the need for human labour is something which will be discussed later.

The motives behind the introduction of new machinery were primarily economic as employers hoped it would lower production costs and/or increase output. However, it also created opportunities to challenge skilled labour's independence in the workplace and open skilled work to intrusion from semi-skilled and unskilled workers. Thus accompanying changes in technology were changes in supervision and industrial discipline. The latter could be implemented either directly through attacks on traditional customs and habits and greater effective supervision, or indirectly through subtle paternalistic or quasipaternalistic strategies and incentive payments. During the inter-war years employers favoured more direct methods of confronting worker independence. In spite of higher levels of unemployment and falling demand workers were forced to work harder. Shift work became more common as did longer hours. Among motormen in the 1920s shifts of nineteen and twenty hours were not unusual. After the 1922 lock-out engineering workers experienced a loss of control over their working times as the convention of 'minutes of grace' at starting times and meal breaks were abolished. Other petty restrictions were introduced including a ban on smoking, eating and unnecessary movement during working time.

The agency by which the gospel of hard work and the other imperatives of management were mediated was the foreman. Known in shipbuilding as the 'bastards in bowlers', foremen were, as the visible reminder of the power of capital, objects of fear and loathing. Control over the hiring and firing process gave them, in times of high unemployment, 'the power of life and death over you . . . [they] could stop you putting bread on the table'.[4] The power could often border on arrogance, especially in trades like dockwork where the work was casual. As one dockworker put it: 'they did'ne treat you like human beings. You were only there for their convenience'.[5] Foremen were at the core of day-to-day activity in the workplace making decisions, in the absence of strong managerial structures, over the various aspects of the production process and the organisation of labour. However, the degree of autonomy exercised by the foreman varied from place to place. As a rule, the more the work process was dispersed and the greater the heterogeneity of the workforce, as in shipbuilding, the more the foreman was assured of a place in the hierarchy of authority. In other trades more suited to Taylor-like ideas on scientific management, such as engineering, the greater was the reduction in the all-round authority of the foreman.

Using the physical presence of the foreman to control the workers was not the only option open to employers. Various schemes were used to enhance the power of the employers, ranging from paternalism and sub-contracting to the wage bargain itself. In the 1920s and 1930s industry was in the strong grip of family firms and paternalism was by extension a natural strategy to extend employer power and to command the loyalty of the worker. In the coal industry employers traditionally provided housing and other amenities for their workers; in the linen industry of Fife the firm of Fergus and Company built the industrial village of Prinlaws; while in shipbuilding yards employers were more concerned with building houses for supervisory workers. Internal sub-contracting was also a favoured strategy for imposing industrial discipline in occupations where work was dispersed over a wide area.

The system was based on the contracting of key workers to produce an agreed amount of output at a given price, they being responsible for the recruitment, discipline and payment of their assistants. Sub-contracting was well-established in the coalfields of Fife and the Lothians, as well as among platers in shipbuilding. Innovations in payments systems maximising individual effort were also a feature of the inter-war economy. The growth of piece rate payment was well-entrenched in engineering before 1945 and it was calculated that by 1944 more than 70 per cent of fitters and turners were working on the piece.[6]

The post-1945 era saw a revolution in workplace ideas on authority and discipline. New systems of control were introduced as the old systems proved incompatible with greater bureaucracy and increased workers' power. The power of the foreman was markedly reduced as the introduction of time measurement for jobs presumed that wages clerks and personnel departments in large firms took responsibility for recruitment. Foremen were downgraded to supervisors responsible for discipline and with some control over the pace and intensity of work, but no longer an indispensable part of the structure of management. The decline of family ownership also reduced the scope for paternalistic control of labour. This was assisted by the extension of local authority housing and by the opening up of alternative forms of employment in areas of Scotland previously dominated by a single industry. The exercise of power by employers had to be achieved in other ways. However, vestigial aspects of the system can be found in the labour practices of manufacturing firms like IBM and various financial institutions, which offer higher wages and certain fringe benefits in return for worker loyalty and, in the former case, non-unionism. Similarly, the system of internal sub-contracting has broken down as employers have moved towards greater bureaucratic control of the production process.

Because of the problems associated with the previous methods of workplace control employers have since 1945 increasingly resorted to the wage packet as the best way of securing power over the workforce. The system of piece-rate payment which linked the level of wages to output and encouraged individual rather than collective bargaining was widespread in the 1940s and 1950s. Half the workforce in coalmining, including almost all face workers, were on piece-rate, and it was nearly universal in engineering.[7] However, the emergence of full employment and a stronger trade union movement saw employers move away from piece-rate to a measured day work system [based on hourly rates and performance standards established by work measurement techniques] first in coalmining in the 1960s, and later in engineering, shipbuilding, dockwork and the motor car industry. The old system was only found to be effective in enlarging management's power in times when a reserve pool of labour exerted a downward pressure on wages, conditions which did not exist in the economic boom of the post-1945 period. The decline of the piece-rate system has had two contradictory effects on workers. On the one hand, it enhances collective bargaining by establishing uniform national rates for all workers in an occupation, and, on the other, it increases the degree of supervision. The motor car industry saw the number of supervisors increase from three to run the plant, to a supervisor for every 25 men, and this was also true for the coal industry.[8] Changes in workplace relations would tend to point to a loss of control by labour of the pace and intensity of the work rythmn. Was that experience mirrored in the changing nature of the skill itself?

3. Deskilling and Scottish Workers

Economic and technological changes combined with the shifting patterns of industrial discipline and supervision have been seen by some as part of management's strategy to control the labour process.[9] A key part of the strategy is the destruction of craft control of production by sub-dividing work task into simple operations and in the process taking technical knowledge out of the hands of the worker and placing it with the functionaries of capital. Deskilling — the separation of planning from execution — allows management to substitute skilled labour by unskilled and this not only cheapens the cost of labour, but also the ability of workers to resist intensified exploitation as their labour is easily substitutable.

On the surface, the evidence seems to strongly favour the deskilling thesis. The introduction of the longwall method of coal-getting and increased mechanisation in coalmining destroyed the formerly independent collier's power to control the labour process. The new methods and machines sub-divided mining skills and created larger numbers of unskilled workers. In the process it reduced the collier to 'the status of a living tool'.[10] There was a similar decline in the numbers of skilled workers and a rise in the amount of semi-skilled and unskilled workers in the engineering industry. In 1914, 60 per cent of engineering workers in Britain were classed as skilled with the remainder equally split between semi-skilled and unskilled. By 1933 the respective figures were 32 per cent skilled, 57 per cent semi-skilled and 11 per cent unskilled. Additionally, female labour was being used in greater proportions rising from a mere 3 per cent of the total number of operatives in 1907, to 10 per cent in 1930, and 13.2 per cent in 1935. With the changing balance of skilled requirements apprenticeship began to undergo serious decline. An AEU enquiry in 1938 found that only 16 per cent of engineering firms in Britain took apprentices.[11] Dissatisfaction with specialisation and routine work led to apprentices' strikes in 1937 in Scotland. The increasing importance of unskilled labour in shipbuilding was reflected in the narrowing of wage differentials between those workers and time-served men. In 1914 an unskilled worker earned 57 per cent of the skilled wage, by 1932 it had increased to 68 per cent.[12] Boilermakers also faced the prospect of further dilution as the introduction of the multiple punch and welding threatened the livelihoods of platers and rivetters. In foundry work the changes in materials and technology meant that by the late 1940s 'the highly skilled are no longer a majority in the industry'.[13]

Since the Second World War technological change and the growth of the branch plant economy in Scotland has accelerated the trend towards the destruction of craft-based skills. This has resulted in augmenting the demand for semi-skilled labour, particularly in assembly work. From the 1960s onwards more of manufacturing industry has been subject to automation and computerisation, as has various forms of white-collar work. Automation, because it is less dependent on human activity and intervention, increases and strengthens managerial control over the production process and its speed of operation, while in office and clerical work it enhances centralised control and functional specialisation. Thus, even in areas outside manufacturing, the direction of change seems to have been towards the deskilling of the worker and the proletarianisation of those employed in white-collar jobs. Thus the empirical evidence would appears to strongly favour the deskilling thesis. However, before pronouncing an affirmative verdict a number of important areas have to be explored.

The first point to make regarding deskilling is that the extent to which it can be carried out is determined by the interplay of three important factors: the nature of the product, the structure of the market, and the degree of worker resistance. These factors operate most obviously in the area of skilled work, but they are also influential in occupations that are considered unskilled or labelled as white-collar. In the shipbuilding industry the lack of a standardised product and the vulnerability of the trade to shifts in world demand made Scottish employers reluctant to add substantially to fixed overhead capital. Thus they continued to rely on skill intensive methods of production. As late as 1978 a shop steward described the Robb Caledon yard as 'an industrial museum', adding 'we have a shaping machine dated 1910, a borer that no one knows the age of and a pipe-bending machine that was taken as reparations in 1918 from the Germans'.[14] According to a Department of Trade and Industry Report in 1973, 'Except in yards building warships, control of quality and dimensional accuracy is provided by the workplace'. Where management was successful in introducing new machinery and working methods, such as the multiple punch and welding, they were appropriated by the Boilermakers. McKinlay found that the latter were able in the inter-war period to extend 'craft controls to every single innovation irrespective of the impact of it on materials, techniques, or skilled requirements'.[15] Markets, products and reliance on skilled labour had effectively checked employer control of the labour process in shipbuilding. Similarly, the unstandardised nature of much of engineering work meant that new techniques were inapplicable to many establishments. Thus a situation arose in which technical and managerial stagnation coexisted with technical advance and managerial enterprise. Steelmaking was in a comparable position to engineering. Until recently steelmaking, in spite of new techniques and materials, relied on the knowledge of the craftsman in the casting process. Understanding of the process was built up over an apprenticeship of thirty to forty years and written down in the leading hand's 'Bible', which was passed at the age of retirement on to the next in line for promotion. It was these highly experienced workers who controlled the output of the steelworks and, in fact, as one steelworker put it, 'made the steel'.[16] In printing the introduction of new type-setting technology in the newspaper industry in the 1960s reduced the skill of the compositor to a level below that of the traditionally inferior machine-minder. However, the force of custom and the strategic position held by compositors in the production process continued to afford them high wages and the power to counter managerial authority in important ways.

Those outside the realm of skilled work were not without the means to challenge and constrain managerial authority even in industries, such as dockwork, which were based on casual labour. Casual labour gave dockside employers the power to control and maintain labour discipline and to regulate its supply in accordance with trading conditions. But it had one very strong disadvantage for employers in as much as at high points in the trade cycle it was impossible to guarantee the efficient performance of work as the best workers would go where the money was greatest, often without giving notice. The supply of labour was therefore an uncertain factor. Improvements in cargo handling and the introduction of mechanised road transport in the 1920s and 30s reduced the demand for labour but did nothing to solve the problem of efficiency. To overcome the problem it was decided by employers and unions alike to introduce a labour registration scheme. Such a strategy did not appeal to the majority of dockers, especially in Scotland, where union organisation was strong enough to afford preferential employment to members. Glasgow especially had a good record of limiting recruitment to match the available employment. Even the attempts by the dockers' union to get their agreement was opposed in Scotland and led in 1932 to the breakaway Scottish Transport and General Workers' Union. It was only the intervention of the state in the form of the National Dock Labour Scheme of 1947 which ended casual labour in the docks, although not without widespread industrial conflict. Workers in the modern and increasingly computerised sector of the economy also have similar opportunities to control the labour process. In automated plants workers are generally seen to have greater freedom to organise their work and the speed at which it is performed. Computerisation has increased the demand for high level skills in the areas of programming, systems analysis, as well as in management information systems.

The second point is that while technological change can result in the disappearance of traditional skills, at the same time it can also change the nature of existing skills or, indeed, create new ones. The extension of semi-automatic machinery in engineering in the inter-war period did away with much of the manual dexterity of the time-served man, but it also had the effect of increasing the need for greater technical awareness on his part. More modern developments in the industry have seen the demise of traditional engineering skills and an increase in the number of technicians. In 1963 the Technical and Salaried Staffs Association [TSSA] listed seven categories of technical worker, including draughtsman, designers, tracers, estimators, planning engineers and other technicians. Ten years later the list had grown to 468, of which 400 were of a technical nature and the rest clerical or supervisory.[17] In coalmining too new methods of production made the old collier's skills redundant, but they also created a greater demand for skilled maintenance staff and electricians. In 1957 maintenance craftsmen accounted for six per cent of the total mining workforce of Britain; by 1981 the figure had increased to twenty per cent.[18] In the highly automated electronics industry there has been an appreciable rise in the level of skill, a phenomenon which poses a threat to the jobs of semi-skilled workers as hand preparation of printed circuit boards declines. Therefore, the impact of technological change can be contradictory and does not necessarily presume an irresistible move

8. Lone pneumatic riveter at work, John Brown's shipyard. Note the absence of any ear muffs or any form of protection against noise. Glasgow University Business Archives.

in the direction of a deskilled proletariat of the kind envisaged by Braverman and others.

However, what is clear from the discussion is that traditional craft skills have gradually disappeared over the course of the twentieth century and with them the existence of a culture and system of values to which they gave rise. The independent craftsman symbolised in the ownership of tools, the extensive system of rituals and ceremonies which served to emphasise his status in the workplace and underpin the values of craft pride and solidarity, disappeared with the arrival of the stopwatch, quality control, planning offices and modern technology. In his place emerged the semi-skilled assembly worker and the technician, more specialised and subject to greater managerial discipline.

Although the decline of the craft culture is perhaps the most striking and obvious feature of the changing labour market in Scotland, it should not act as a base for nostalgic longings for the 'old days'. Other workers outside the field of skilled work have also witnessed the disappearance of established habits and customs, indeed, a whole way of life. The introduction of the National Dock Labour Scheme and the decline of employment in port transport destroyed a distinctive culture and community. Family networks in dockwork established by patrimonial custom all disappeared. The same point could be made with respect to mining communities in the 1980s in Scotland. Furthermore, it has to be appreciated that deskilling often results in increased opportunities for upward mobility, if measured in terms of the wage bargain, for those classed as unskilled. Although specific figures for Scotland do not exist, it would appear, at least within a British context, that the twentieth century witnessed a narrowing of differentials between skilled and unskilled workers. The main causes of this trend have been the improved efficiency of the labour market and the long economic boom which followed the end of war in 1945. Between 1935 and 1955 average wages for our unskilled workers increased by 337 per cent over their 1935 level, while the corresponding increase for skilled workers was 319 per cent. From the 1960s onwards differentials further narrowed, and this was particularly marked in the 1970s due to the egalitarian effects of incomes policies. However, a return to mass unemployment has seen a large number of unskilled workers out of work compared to the skilled and this has caused differentials to widen.[19] In spite of recent trends, the magnitude of the changes described above have had important consequences for the character and development of trade unionism in Scotland, as has the impact of mass unemployment in the 1920s and 1930s, and the growth of state intervention in the labour market and the workplace, particularly after 1945.

4. The Character and Development of Trade Unionism

During the nineteenth century trade unionism in Scotland was characterised by weakness and fragmentation. As late as 1892 there were only 147,000 trade unionists, which amounted to a mere 3.7 per cent of the total adult population. (In England the corresponding figure was 4.9 per cent.) Scottish workers were divided on occupational and sectarian lines which made solidarity difficult to achieve. The unions that did emerge were noted for their insularity and nationalism. There were a hundred unions active on Clydeside alone in the final decade of the twentieth century, and out of these only twenty could claim 500 or more members, and 37 less than 100. The powerful desire for local autonomy meant Scottish unions refused to amalgamate or merge with larger British organisations. Anti-Englishness played an important part in their intransigence. Indeed it was this sentiment that led to the formation of the Scottish Trades Union Congress (STUC) in 1897. The strength of national sentiment can be guaged from the fact that of the total number of trade unionists in Scotland in 1892, two-thirds were members of exclusively Scottish unions. However, since then the trade union movement in Scotland has undergone a transformation both in terms of membership and national identity.

For the first half of the twentieth century the most reliable guide to the level of trade union membership in Scotland is that provided by Bell. According to his estimates, the number of trade unionists increased from 536,000 in 1924 to 900,000 in 1947, or from 11 per cent of the total adult population to 17.7 per cent, with the respective figures for Britain at 5,554,000, or 12.6 per cent, in 1924, and 9,145,000, or 18.2 per cent, in 1947. In terms of size the average Scottish union was small in the 1920s. Of the 227 unions organising in 1924 129 organised fewer than 5,000 workers, while 36 organising 5,000 plus members. In terms of density the 36 largest unions accounted for four-fifths of the total membership in Scotland. The 1940s witnessed a decline in the number of unions with only 125 unions operating north of the border. Of these the eight largest accounted for over 50 per cent of total membership, while the largest seventeen accounted for over 70 per cent, making the degree of concentration higher than that for the United Kingdom as a whole.[20] The rise in union membership in Scotland was accompanied, however, by a decline in the number of exclusively Scottish unions. In 1924 39.8 per cent of union members in Scotland belonged to independent Scottish unions; by 1947 this figure had declined to 15.1 per cent. Occupationally the bulk of union members were located in 1947 in coalmining, construction, metals and machines, transport, including the railways, and general labouring. The high representation of traditionally male-dominated trades in the labour movement emphasised the sexual division of labour in Scottish society. Between 1924 and 1947 there was an increase in the number of women trade unionists in Scotland from 14.6 per cent to 18.1 per cent of the total number.[21] However women, in spite of the growing numbers entering the labour market, were still poorly organised in Scotland.

Since 1950 Scottish trade unionism has undergone a transition in keeping with that taking place in the wider economy. The main characteristics of this have been firstly, an increase in white-collar and a decline in industrial trade unionism; secondly, an expansion of general unions at the expense of those based on occupations; and, lastly, an increase in the number of women joining trade unions. Unfortunately, given the level of amalgamations taking place between English and Scottish unions since 1945, accurate density figures are not available separately for Scotland. Therefore, in dealing with the empirical dimensions of the transformation it has been necessary to rely on affiliations to the STUC as the best way of estimating the numbers of trade unionists in Scotland.

Hunter estimates that in 1951 there were 85 unions affiliated to the STUC with a combined membership of 730,000. But by 1980 the number of unions had declined to 73, while the total membership had increased to 1,070,000. The degree of concentration had become more marked with eleven unions accounting for 71 per cent of the total.[22] Within this overall figure there was a massive shift in the occupational composition of the membership. In 1960 the industrial section of the STUC (mining and quarrying, railways, transport, metals and machines, construction) accounted for 57 per cent of the total affiliated membership, while the service section (distributive trades, public employees and general workers) contained 26 per cent. Ten years later the industrial section had decreased to 48 per cent, while the latter had grown to 42 per cent, in spite of an alteration in classification. By 1980 sections 8 and 9 (civil and public servants and non-manual workers) alone were accounting for 45 per cent of affiliated membership.[23] The rise in the representation of non-manual workers is partly attributable to an increase in the organisation of women workers in Scotland, a phenomenon discussed by McIvor elsewhere in the volume.

These broad changes in the pattern of trade unionism in Scotland throw up two important questions; firstly, what were the motive forces behind the transformation of the occupational profile of the movement; and, secondly, how did the decline of the craft and/or manual unions alter the character of Scottish trade unionism? In answering the first it is obvious that the economic and technological changes discussed above are crucial as they altered employment patterns and created the conditions for an increase in white-collar unionism. However, although the potential for growth in the latter area undoubtedly existed, its realisation was problematical. As we have seen, organisation among white-collar workers was negligible in the inter-war period and it was only after 1945 that it became important. Thus short-term factors must be explored before the question of growth can be resolved.

The years following the end of the Second World War saw the

expansion of welfare and greater state involvement in the economy in the form of public ownership of utilities and important industries. There was also an expansion in local government services and a general increase in bureaucratic business methods in the private sector. These trends considerably increased the demand for white-collar labour, but organisation lagged behind recruitment. As one might expect, it was in the public sector that trade unionism was first to gain a major foothold, but in the decade 1969–78 union growth exploded in all sectors. By 1978 the number of white-collar trade unionists in Britain had grown by two million; a two-thirds increase on the 1968 figure. In Scotland the National Association of Local Government Officers (NALGO) saw its affiliated membership to the STUC increase from 24,409 in 1969 to 62,043 in 1979. The respective figures for the Association of Scientific, Technical and Managerial Staff (ASTMS) were 9,036 and 32,629.[24] The state helped to create the climate of expansion through setting up the Donovan Commission and the subsequent extension of collective bargaining rights which followed its recommendations. The Industrial Relations Act of 1971 and the Employment Protection Act of 1975 were instrumental in securing recognition and bargaining rights for white-collar workers. Economic stimulus was also important. Historically high levels of inflation as well as prices and incomes policies led to an erosion of white-collar workers' real wages and this led them to join unions in increasing numbers to protect their standard of living. The success of the unions in achieving this goal simply reinforced the process. The question which arises from this account of the changing structure of union participation is whether it transformed the character of the movement in Scotland.

Although in the closing decades of the last century the unskilled were beginning to organise, the movement was essentially based on skilled, male Protestant workers. The twentieth century showed no immediate tendency to undermine the position of the craft workers in the hierarchy of trade unionism and their values and interests continued to dominate the movement in Scotland. Their hegemony was only slowly eroded in spite of economic and technological change and the mass unemployment of the inter-war years. The strength of the craft culture can best be shown in relation to unskilled and women workers, both of whom, although especially the former, posed a direct threat to the power and skilled status of the craftsman.

The First World War and the years that followed provided direct challenges to the integrity of the craft unions. Dilution, unemployment and the failure of industrial action, culminating in the General Strike of

1926, placed craft workers under increasing pressure from semi-skilled and unskilled workers. This was reflected in the narrowing of wage differentials. In 1920 a bricklayer's rate was 235 per cent that of 1914, his labourer's 300 per cent; the engineering craftsman's rate was 231 per cent of that of 1914, that of this labourer 309 per cent.[25] In engineering, too, the semi-skilled machinist was gaining ground at the expense of fitters and turners in terms of new recruits. Falling membership and industrial defeats forced the craft unions to incorporate the lower skilled into their culture, albeit on a subordinate basis. In printing the Scottish Typographical Association (STA) opened an auxiliary section in 1919 for machine minders and other workers; the Amalgamated Engineering Union (AEU) established sections V and Va for all male workers regardless of their jobs, skills or experience; plumbers followed the trend and in 1923 opened their ranks to all those earning a livelihood at any branch of the trade. Other trades, such as shipbuilding, were less open to dilution and, therefore, under less pressure to recruit members outside the ranks of the time-served men. But those unions who did, maintained the craft basis of the union by keeping the less skilled in sections which had lower contributions, fewer benefits and, most important, inferior voting rights. It took, for instance, until the 1950s for the auxiliary section of the STA to gain a place on the executive.[27]

The subordinate position of unapprenticed labour within the structure of craft unionism was sometimes not enough to nullify the prejudice of the ordinary journeymen. Repeated attempts to incorporate the STA's auxiliary section into full membership were defeated on the basis that it would transform the Association from a craft to a general union. In engineering the AEU executive in 1927 had to send a directive to branch secretaries 'informing them that they were not in order in refusing to accept members for sections V and Va'.[28] In his study of engineering shop stewards in inter-war Glasgow, McKinlay found that they made no efforts to recruit semi-skilled millers, grinders or drillers into the AEU.[29] Moreover, by demanding the skilled rate for the job, regardless of whether or not it was performed by skilled or semi-skilled labour, the AEU placed pressure on employers to hire the former, which explains why over 70 per cent of the automatic and semi-automatic lathes were operated by skilled workers on Clydeside. Indeed, the 'overwhelming majority of semi-skilled workers on the Clyde [during the inter-war period] were in fact time-served men'.[30] Given this situation it is hardly surprising that by the end of 1929 sections V and Va in Scotland comprised less than a sixth of the total employed in this work. It was only after 1935 when the industry was once more enjoying a resurgence of activity did the total reach 50 per cent.[31] Thus in a period of mass unemployment the AEU was still able to preserve craft control over the distribution of work and insist on the skilled rate for the job, even if the rate fell sharply over the period. How the activities of the skilled unions were perceived by the unskilled is a mystery. Few union histories dwell on this difficult area, although it would appear that women in engineering made their protest by joining general unions like the TGWU.

However, in spite of these long-term problems, craft unionism displayed a dogged resistance to the forces of change, as did occupations such as dockwork. In shipbuilding the unions employed a strategy based around control of the labour process. The traditional belief among the labour force that once work was lost it would be forever led to demarcation disputes in the 1950s and 1960s. Platers and burners fought with each other to control flame cutting and planing machinery and, later, this extended to computerised cutting heads. Welders restricted entry to the trade and refused to allow unemployed members of other shipbuilding trades to operate welding equipment. Boilermakers used apprenticeship and separate agreements governing their terms of employment to maintain differentials with related trades. These differentials were maintained even during the 1972 Upper Clyde Shipbuilders work-in. Payments to those taking part in the work-in were made on the basis of take home pay prior to the industrial action.

Religion also played a part in maintaining craft exclusiveness. In the early decades of the century it was rare for Catholics to become apprenticed to the engineering trade in Glasgow and in certain shipyards on the Clyde the presence of a strong Orange group excluded the former from specific yards and occupations, particularly boilermaking. Sectarianism continued into the inter-war years as Alex Ferry, later president of the AEU, makes clear. He recalled that as a Catholic in the 1940s it was difficult to find an apprenticeship in the engineering trade. When out of his time he found work in the Singer Sewing Machine Company; the only Catholic out of 300 workers.[34] The power of the foreman to hire and fire, as well as the close-knit occupational networks, made it possible to use religion to police the boundaries of skill and status. However, this kind of exclusionism broke down in the 1950s and 1960s when skill shortages developed and the number of foreign-owned firms began to increase. Those in charge of hiring became less concerned with what school a boy attended and more with his qualifications and aptitude for the work. In these conditions the policy of occupational sectarianism proved inoperable.

The 1960s and 1970s witnessed the demise of the male, skilled Protestant culture as industrial restructuring brought about the collapse of the industries in which it was most entrenched. However, it would appear that the new breed of highly skilled technical workers were susceptible to craft attitudes since they had come through an apprenticeship system themselves. This meant that educational status could not be used as a source of division between manual and white-collar labour. Working on the shop floor as part of their training led to the formation of strong links between non-manual and manual workers and this was reflected in membership of other engineering unions such as the Draughtsmen and Allied Technicians Association. Changing employment conditions have seen manual and non-manual sections of the engineering industry come together in the Amalgamated Union of Engineering Workers (AEUW). Another example of craft transfer

9. Clerks at Falkirk Foundry, c. 1925. Note the exclusively male character of the workforce and the absence of mechanical equipment. Glasgow University Business Archives.

was the motor car industry. Large numbers of redundant engineering and shipbuilding workers found their way into car plants, such as Linwoods, which led to mounting industrial conflict. Many of the labour disputes which beset the industry in the 1960s were the consequence of traditionally autonomous workers adapting to the routinised demands of assembly-line production. Between 1963 and 1969 there were 300 stoppages in the Scottish car industry.[35] Although the number of strikes declined in the 1970s, the industrial unrest remains a potent example of the difficulties created by cultural readjustment on the part of skilled workers and the way patterns of industrial relations were transferred from one industry to another. Craft attitudes were, at least for a time, kept alive in a totally different working environment.

Another way of sustaining the craft culture and its material base was through influencing government policy, particularly with consensus-minded governments. To succeed, trade union policies regarding minimum wage fixing, legal immunities, health and safety standards, and so on, have often needed government support. The continued support by the state for the staple industries has also been important in this respect. However, at the local level politicians have also played a significant part in helping to preserve the craft culture. Even during the inter-war depression town councillors ensured that nationally negotiated wages and conditions were implemented by councils and that non-union shops received no council contracts. The main vehicle for ensuring that the craft unions had an influential voice in policy-making circles has been the STUC and its General Council. It is the latter body which nominates union representatives for important government committees. For most of the twentieth century the General Council has been dominated by the numerically superior craft/industrial unions, and even in the changing conditions of employment which emerged after 1945, the skilled unions were able to maintain their power base within the STUC. In 1960 skilled unions made up 32 per cent of the affiliated membership represented on the General Council — the largest single grouping — and, in spite of deindustrialisation, twenty years later it was still a respectable 28 per cent. Although skilled unions have been overtaken in terms of membership by general unions, such as the TGWU, it must be remembered that in recent years mergers have meant that the latter contain skilled sections. The boilermakers, for example, are now part of the General and Municipal Workers' Union and through it are still able to exercise an influence, albeit a reduced one, on the wider movement. But what is the nature of this influence?

The predominantly male culture in which trade unionism emerged, and the stress it has placed on the family wage, have led to active opposition to the unionisation of women in certain industries and the maginalisation of women's issues within the movement. It has also discouraged women members from taking an active part in the running of the unions in which they form a substantial majority of the membership. This issue is explored elsewhere in the volume. What is important from the perspective of this essay is that the unions' attitudes to women workers, although influenced to a large extent by the desire to earn the family wage, have been part of a search for acceptance and respectability in the wider society. Operating within this gender-bounded culture the 'masculinity of the skilled worker especially could be a force for all sorts of understanding with employers (a "boss" in his sphere as the worker in his home)'.[36] The bargaining strategy of the family wage and the desire to keep women in the home underwrote union policy in the First World War and in the depression that followed. Both employers and the state supported this position and helped to lay the basis of attempts to build a corporatist approach to industrial relations.

Although the inter-war period is generally remembered as a time of industrial warfare, with workers pitched against the employers and the state, it was also an era in which the modern trend towards corporatism was established. During the First World War trade unionists served on various government advisory councils and some were in the war cabinet. But as wartime controls were abandoned, direct influence in policy-making declined proportionately. In spite of this, stronger links with employers were established through the setting up of joint councils in industry, of which there were 73 in 1921. A number of these failed to survive the post-war economic slump and five years later the number had fallen to 47, where it stayed for the rest of the inter-war period. Links with the state were, however, tarnished by the 1926 General Strike and the Trades Disputes Act which followed. The legislation of 1927 forced civil servants into isolation from the rest of the labour movement and forbade public authorities from demanding union membership of employees. It also stipulated criminal liabilities for strikers involved in attempts to 'coerce' the government and restricted the right to picket. Notwithstanding these measures, the state tended to adopt a non-interventionist policy towards industrial relations. But it had no need to as employers and unions reacted to the General Strike by adopting a more conciliatory attitude to each other.

It was the onset of economic depression in the early 1930s which led to a revision of the state's attitude to industrial relations. From this period more direct attempts were made to incorporate the representatives of labour onto state-sponsored policy bodies. The STUC along with leading industrialists and the Scottish Office set up the Scottish Economic Council in 1936 and by 1938/9 trade unionists were serving on twelve government committees affecting the interests of labour. The Second World War enormously expanded the role of trade unions in government and the economy. As the price of wartime sacrifices the state awarded labour an extension of collective bargaining and statutory regulation of conditions in weakly organised sectors of the economy. By 1950 80 per cent of British workers were covered by joint voluntary negotiating machinery or by statutory machinery. In addition the Attlee government repealed the 1927 Act and restored the position of organised labour to where it stood after the Liberal government's Act of 1913. It meant that civil servants were free to affiliate to the TUC and the STUC and several of them did so, including the Civil Service Clerical Association and the Union of Post Office Workers. There were other pieces of legislation affecting the legal position of unions, including the Fair Wages Resolution of 1946 which encouraged collective bargaining by stipulating labour relations standards for public contractors, and wages councils laid down a minimum legal wage in selected industries. Lewis summed up the labour legislation of the Attlee government as 'abstentionist', in as much as it was designed to 'legislate judges out of trade disputes by providing special immunities from judge-made liabilities'.[37]

The trade union legislation of the Attlee government was part of the process of meaningful incorporation of the unions into the state and quasi-state bodies. One example of this was the membership of the STUC of the Scottish Council for Development and Industry (1946), which also included representatives from local authorities, chambers of commerce, banks, trade associations, corporate bodies, lord provosts and county convenors. Since then the STUC's role has expanded to include most of Scottish social and economic life. Craigen estimated that in 1973 well over 1500 trade unionists in Scotland were serving on boards and committees as diverse as the Scottish Postal Board, the Parole Board for Scotland, the Consultative Committee for Edinburgh Airport, as well as the main government economic committees.[38] The corporate structure of industrial relations established in 1945 survived beyond the lifetime of the Attlee government and was an integral part of Conservative policy towards the economy and industry. However, incorporation, like any other political/industrial strategy, is open to periodic renegotiation in order that some balance in class forces might be obtained. What is an appropriate strategy for one set of economic conditions may not be suitable for another. The oil price rise of 1973 and the world recession which followed fundamentally altered the relationship between the unions and the state.

Governments tried to cope with worsening economic conditions by resorting to incomes policies in the hope that they would lower production costs and restore profitability to British industry. Their attempts were generally failures and led to mass strikes and rising inflation. Eventually low paid workers in the public sector, Ford car workers and lorry drivers protested in a mass wave of strikes against pay restraint in the 1979 'winter of discontent'. Their action led to the fall of the Labour government and the election of a Tory government pledged to curb what they saw as excessive union power. Defeat of the trade unions became an essential part of the Thatcher government's anti-inflation policy and legislation followed which considerably weakened trade union power and influence. The hostility towards the unions was demonstrated in the virtual ending of the closed shop; the outlawing of secondary picketing and sympathy strikes; the introduction of compulsory ballots for the election of officials and the holding of strikes; and, finally, the institution of a system of 'contracting in' in terms of the political levy. Thus a century's work of building a viable corporate structure of industrial relations has been swept away in the last decade or so by a Conservative government.

Although corporatism has been abandoned by the state in recent years, the building of it during the twentieth century involved the official leadership in redefining its relationship with the rank-and-file of the labour movement. As defeat of the extreme left was a precondition of incorporation, the Communists were the first challenge to be overcome. Communists had won the support of significant sections of the working class by setting up the Minority Movement in the early 1920s to encourage rank-and-file militancy in face of downward pressures on wages and increased managerial power. Reform committees were established in the mining areas of Fife and Lanarkshire to challenge the old labourist leadership and democratise the county unions. In 1925 the Glasgow Trades Council (GTC) affiliated to the Minority Movement as did the Clydeside AEU in spite of an executive ruling against affiliation. After the failure of the General Strike a mood of conciliation emerged in the labour movement and was symbolised by the Mond/Turner talks of 1927/8. As a result of the talks union leaders declared support for arbitration and conciliation rather than conflict as means of settling disputes.

The new mood saw an intensification of the campaign of the labour leadership against the Communist Party and the Minority Movement. The TUC ruled in 1928 that no person associated with the Minority Movement would be eligible to attend the annual conference of trades councils and this was the signal for removing Communists from official positions in the unions themselves. The Scottish Carters, the Jute and Flax Workers, the Boilermakers, the Engineers and the GTC all initiated procedures to exclude from office members of the Communist Party and its affiliated organisations. In response the Communists set up rival unions, but the only one to enjoy a measure of success was the United Mineworkers of Scotland (UMS). With the support of the larger and highly mechanised pits in Fife, the UMS exploited the mineworkers' dissatisfaction with the reformist leadership of the county unions and deteriorating conditions. None the less the UMS never recruited more than 3,000 members and eventually disbanded in 1935 when it became an embarrassment to a party attempting to build a united front with other labour organisations against fascism and unemployment. With the decisive defeat of communism in the inter-war years, those on the extreme left of the labour movement were reduced to influencing union development through winning leadership positions, once the ban was lifted after 1945, and by gaining support for various policy stances. Successes were evident, as for example Communist control of the Scottish mineworkers' union and in opposition to nuclear rearmament and pay policies of the 1960s and 1970s, but they were less the result of ideology and more because of proven ability in negotiations and organisation. Unions with Communist leadership have shown no less inclination to play by the rules than unions with moderate officials.

A more persistent and successful counterpoint to the power of the official leadership and a buttress against total incorporation has been workshop organisation, in which the locus of power is the shop steward. For most of the nineteenth century the weakness of the trade union structure in Scotland raised the importance of informal workshop organisation. One of the consequences of this development was the emergence of the shop steward as a key figure in industrial bargaining. The First World War confirmed and strengthened the power of the steward as the industrial truce between the unions and the Asquith government left it to the former to articulate the grievances and aspirations of the working class. Among Clydeside engineers and shipbuilders a Shop Steward and Workers' Control Movement emerged during the war in opposition to dilution and war profiteering and demanding workers' control of industry. The organisation was suppressed by the state, with the leaders either deported or imprisoned. Its swan song came in the 1919 Forty Hours strike and failure saw the movement collapse and official trade unionism restored once more as the legitimate voice of Scottish workers. However, in the engineering industry the wartime struggles had confirmed the shop steward as an integral part of the bargaining process and this was recognised by the employers and unions alike.

Two factors explain the continued importance of the shop steward in engineering; firstly, the move towards piece-rate payment meant that fixing time and rates for specific tasks were the concern of shop floor organisation; and, secondly, following the success of the 1922 lock-out the employer-determined 'Provision for Avoiding Disputes Agreement' institutionalised the position of the shop steward as negotiator on behalf of individual workers with specific grievances. However, it should be noted that shop steward power was conditional on a particular set of economic set of circumstances and a conducive structure of industrial relations. The employers victory in 1922 pushed the AEU to the verge of bankruptcy, with its financial reserves falling from £3.25m in 1920 to £35,572, and led to a dramatic fall in membership in Scotland of around 38 per cent, mainly in Clydeside.[39] Unemployment furthered the process of decline and as morale plummeted there was a concomitant fall in the numbers of shop stewards. Lancaster noted that while in normal times there were around 30 to 40 stewards in Beardmore's Parkhead Forge, plus a full-time convenor, by 1923 there was not a single steward to be found at Beardmore's or John Brown's. There was also a corresponding fall in the Edinburgh district of the AEU from a peak of 85 in 1923 to 46 in 1928.[40] Coalmining was similarly affected with the blacklisting of those active in the miners' strike of 1926. A prominent example of victimisation was Abe Moffat and his family.

The continuing presence of mass unemployment kept workplace organisation on the defensive until the rearmament boom of the mid-1930s onwards. In engineering improving employment prospects and the desire of the AEU, the employers and the state to avoid politicising industrial relations saw a resurgence of workplace trade unionism and an increase in the number of shop stewards. There was a gain of 150 stewards in the Glasgow district of the AEU in 1937. The war and the economic boom which followed it strengthened shop steward power. Between 1947 and 1961 the density of stewards in British engineering increased by 50 per cent, and in dockwork workplace organisation was said to have replaced official unionism as the medium of worker/employer relations.[41] The foundation of shop stewards' power lay in the wage bargain and the complicated systems of wage calculation.

Even in dockwork where national bargaining structures existed the 'complicated and ever-changing wage system of port transport required constant adjustment at . . . the quayside. Shift arrangements, manning questions, the revision of registers, the enforcement of discipline, were all matters which demanded immediate solutions when and where they arose'.[42]

One of the consequences of plant bargaining was an increase in the frequency of strikes. During the period 1952–80 Scotland averaged twice the number of stoppages of the UK, with the number of workers involved on average 40 per cent above the national rate, and the number of working days lost about 55 per cent higher.[43] The shift to the measured day wage system and the strengthening of national bargaining procedures as recommended by the Donovan Commission have seen the number of unofficial stikes decline, although this may also be the result of worsening economic conditions and the declining level of manufacturing employment. Whatever the determining factor both the frequency and duration of strikes in Scotland have declined in recent years. In the period 1978–80 an average of 664,000 working days were lost through strikes; in 1981, the figure had fallen to 240,000.[44] As centralisation has increased in the trade union movement militancy has waned. However, it would appear that recent legislation governing picketing and sympathy strikes is pushing industrial relations in the direction once more of plant by plant bargaining. This can only lead to a resurgence of shop steward power and workplace organisation and, possibly, an increase in unofficial activity.

5. Conclusion

The twentieth century has witnessed a marked change in the structure of the Scottish economy. As the old staple industries have declined there has been a corresponding rise in employment and output in the service sector. The transformation of the labour market has been partly the result of technological change. Older craft-based work has been progressively deskilled and this has destroyed the workplace culture of the time-served man. The old boiler-suited, respectable and Protestant craftsman has given way to the white-coated technocrat. As a result the trade union movement in Scotland has altered its character. The unions of the miners and the skilled workers are no longer the dominant force in the movement and have been replaced by general and white-collar unions. As we move into the 1990s the unions face new challenges, not the least being the existence of a government hostile to their interests.

In the workplace the presence of large numbers of part-time female workers, unorganised and lacking the protection of labour legislation, pose fundamental questions for unions. Another problem is that of the ownership and scale of Scottish industry. Investigations into the electronics industry in Scotland have shown that around two-thirds of firms do not recognise unions. These are mainly small establishments employing less than 100 workers and have been in business a relatively short space of time. And while seven out of ten of the larger plants did afford recognition, it must be remembered that since the 1960s smaller firms are more likely to constitute new manufacturing units than are large ones.[45] Moreover, it was found that multi-unionism was far less common in plants set up in the 1980s than in the 1970s, and that in 1987 white-collar unionism was only running at 26 per cent of those employed in electronics, electrical and instrument engineering.[46] Finally, there is the declining public sector and the growth of privatisation. As the private sector assumes a greater control of all aspects of economic and social life then one might expect a fall in the number of white-collar trade unionists, recently the most dynamic sector of growth. It would appear that the years ahead will be of historic importance as unions adapt to a changing economic and political landscape. What we have traced in this essay is the closing of one chapter in the history of trade unionism in Scotland. We sit uneasily as we open the next.

NOTES

I would like to thank Helen Corr, Robert Knox, Alan McKinlay, Bob Morris, Chris Schmitz, Christopher Smout and, not least, the editors of this volume, Jim Treble and Tony Dickson, for their advice and criticism. Needless to say they bear no responsibility for any errors and misinterpretations on my part.

1. J. MacInnes, 'Economic Restructuring Relevant to Industrial Relations in Scotland', Centre for Urban and Regional Research, University of Glasgow, *Discussion Paper*, No 26, (1987), p. 11.

2. J. Jeffreys, *The Story of the Engineers, 1800–1945*, (1948), pp. 201–2.

3. G. Phillips and N. Whiteside, *Casual Labour: the unemployment question in the port transport industry, 1880–1970*, (Oxford, 1985), pp. 261–3.

4. A. McKinlay, *Making Ships, Making Men: working for John Brown's between the wars*, (forthcoming, 1989).

5. A. Davidson, *Leith Lives: memories of work*, (Edinburgh, 1985), n.p.

6. W. McLaine, 'Payment By Results in British Engineering', *International Labour Review*, vol 49, (1944), p. 630.

7. A. Moffat, *My Life with the Miners*, (1965), p. 122.

8. *14th Report on the Motor Vehicles Industry*, PPXXV, (1974–5), pp. 371–2; R. Price, *Labour in British Society*, (1986), p. 235.

9. H. Braverman, *Labour and Monopoly Capital* (1974).

10. A. B. Campbell, 'From Independent Collier to Militant Miner: tradition and change in the trade union consciousness of the Scottish miners, 1874–1929', (paper delivered at the British Sociological Association Conference, Edinburgh, 1988), p. 8.

11. R. Penn, 'Trade union organisation and skill in the cotton and engineering industries in Britain, 1850–1960', *Social History*, vol 8, (1983), pp. 50–1; Jeffreys, op. cit., p. 207.

12. D. MacKenzie, 'Labour Conditions and Industrial Relations', *Third Statistical Account of Scotland: Glasgow*, ed J. Cunnison and J. B. S. Gilfillan, (Glasgow, 1958), p. 592.

13. H. J. Fryth and H. Collins, *The Foundry Workers: a trade union history*, (Manchester, 1959), p. 252.

14. *7 Days*, 17 March 1978.

15. A. McKinlay, 'Employers and Skilled Workers in the Inter-War Depression: Engineering and Shipbuilding on Clydeside, 1919–1939', (D. Phil, University of Oxford, 1986), pp. 247–8.

16. P. Pagmanenta and R. Overy, *All Our Working Lives*, (1984), p. 77.

17. C. Smith, *Technical Workers: class, labour and trade unionism*, (1987), p. 91.

18. R. Penn and R. Simpson, 'The development of skilled work in the British Coal Mining Industry, 1870–1985', *Industrial Relations Journal*, vol 17, (1986), pp. 339–49.

19. C. Routh, *Occupations and Pay in Great Britain, 1906–1979*, (1980), pp. 182–8.

20. J. D. M. Bell, 'Trade Unions', in *The Scottish Economy*, ed. A. K. Cairncross, (Cambridge,1954), pp. 282, 292–3; J. M. Craigen, 'The Scottish Trades Union Congress, 1897–1973: a study of a pressure group', (M. Litt, Heriot-Watt University, 1974), p. 139.

21. Bell, op. cit., pp. 284–6.

22. L. Hunter, 'The Scottish Labour Market', in *The Economic Development of Modern Scotland 1950–1980*, ed. R. Saville, (Edinburgh, 1985), p. 177.

23. STUC, *Reports* (1960, 1970, 1980).

24. Ibid. (1969, 1978).

25. Routh, op. cit., p. 138.

26. Jeffreys, op. cit., pp. 207–8.

27. S. C. Gillespie, *A Hundred Years of Progress: the record of the Scottish Typographical Association, 1853–1953*, (Glasgow, 1953), p. 148.

28. Jeffreys, op. cit., p. 236.

29. A. McKinlay, 'Depression and Rank and File Activity: the Amalgamated Engineering Union, 1919–1939', *Journal of the Scottish Labour History Society*, No 22, (1987), p. 25.

30. A. McKinlay, *Thesis*, pp. 136–8.

31. E. Kibblewhite, 'The impact of unemployment on the development of trade unionism in Scotland, 1918–1939: some aspects', (Ph.D., University of Aberdeen, 1979), p. 3.

32. McKinlay (1989), op. cit., p. 4.

33. A. McKinlay, 'The Inter-War Depression and the Effort Bargain: shipyard riveters and the 'workman's foreman', 1919–1932', *Scottish Economic and Social History*, vol 9, (1989), p. 59.

34. T. Gallagher, *Glasgow. The Uneasy Peace: religious tension in modern Scotland*, (Manchester, 1986), pp. 252–3.

35. S. Checkland, *The Upas Tree: Glasgow, 1875–1975*, (Glasgow, 1976), p. 53.

36. P. Joyce, 'Labour, capital and compromise: a response to Richard Price', *Social History*, vol 9, (1984), p. 75.

37. R. Lewis, 'The Historical Development of Labour Law', *British Journal of Industrial Relations*,' vol XIV, (1976), pp. 5–6.

38. Craigen, op. cit., pp. 358–9.

39. McKinlay, *Thesis*, p. 143.

40. E. Lancaster, 'Shop Stewards in Scotland: the Amalgamated Engineering Union between the wars', *Journal of the Scottish Labour History Society*, No 21, (1986), pp. 31–2.

41. Price, op. cit., pp. 215–6.

42. Phillips and Whiteside, op. cit., p. 233.

43. Hunter, op. cit., pp. 179–80.

44. D. Bell, 'The Changing Labour Market in Scotland', in *The Scottish Government Yearbook 1983*, ed. D. McCrone, (Edinburgh, 1983), p. 202.

45. J. R. Firn and J. K. Swales, 'The formation of new manufacturing establishments in the central Clydeside and west Midlands conurbations', *Regional Studies*, vol 12, (1978), pp. 199–213.

46. A. Sproull and J. MacInnes, 'Trade Union Recognition, Single Union Agreements and Employment Change in the Electronics Industry in Scotland', Department of Economics, Glasgow College of Technology, *Discussion Paper*, No 6, (1988), pp. 26–7, 35–6.

CHAPTER 5
Women and Work in Twentieth Century Scotland

Arthur J. McIvor

The aim of this chapter is to explore continuity and change in the experience of Scottish women at work within the context of an intensely patriarchal society through the course of the twentieth century. The definition of work utilised here is a broad rather than a narrow one, encompassing unpaid domestic labour within the home and family as well as employment for wages within the formal and informal 'black' economy. The underlying assumption is that the distinctly female experience of work in Scotland merits separate attention and more detailed analysis. The task involves a synthesis of published work but also traversing some uncharted terrain because historical research on work remains scanty and has tended to concentrate on male-dominated industries. The emphasis in the discussion will be laid on developments in the formal economy, not least because homework and domestic labour in Scotland remains seriously under-researched. Section I investigates female participation rates within the Scottish economy, outlining the contours and discussing the causes of changing female occupational patterns and gender segregation in the job market in Scotland since 1900. Sections II and III, focussing on the interwar years and the post-1945 period respectively, move beyond the Census data to exploit oral testimony and other sources in order to probe in a little more depth the work milieux, relationships and environment, attitudes to work and trade unionism in an attempt to determine what work really meant for Scottish women and to what degree the nature of work altered through time. Here a central theme will be the dogged persistence throughout this century of structural inequalities, discrimination and subalternation of women at the point of production.

I

Our starting point is with the census data which illustrate the broad parameters of change in the type of work performed by women in Scotland since the turn of the century.

Table 1. Female Employment in Scotland, by Principal Economic Sector, 1901–1981 (in thousands)

Sector	1901	1921	1931	1951	1971	1981
Services (misc)	186.6	161.0	175.9	114.8	122.8	157.0
domestic, indoor	*143.7*	*122.3*	*138.7*	*73.3*	*46.3*	*7.4*
Textiles	123.0	101.6	100.7	73.6	41.6	21.9
Clothing	77.9	42.0	27.8	30.8	27.7	23.1
Agriculture	40.7	24.9	16.4	15.1	11.6	7.4
Paper, Printing	16.8	18.8	20.1	20.8	19.7	14.0
Food, Drink	15.3	33.6	39.4	36.8	40.6	34.6
Engineering, Metals	3.0	17.5	16.1	40.6	60.3	42.8
Transport & Communic.	8.1	7.4	15.3	28.4	26.6	14.9
Distribution	53.8	114.4	127.7	130.3	156.6	153.4
Insurance, Banking	.2	7.6	7.1	11.0	31.1	59.5
Public Administration	2.2	6.1	20.0	23.5	37.5	67.0
Professions, Science	30.2	45.0	48.9	65.0	193.3	206.3
Teachers	*17.4*	*23.8*	*25.6*	*25.5*	*37.8*	*44.2*
Nurses	*8.4*	*13.5*	*16.0*	*27.5*	*45.2*	*68.1*
TOTAL EMPLOYED	591.6	638.6	667.3	667.9	814.0	861.6
TOTAL FEMALE POPULATION AT EMPLOYABLE AGE *	1790.2	1967.1	1909.5	2046.1	2050.2	2040.3
PARTICIPATION RATE	33.0%	32.5%	34.9%	32.6%	39.7%	42.2%

Sources: Census of Scotland; CH Lee, *British Regional Employment Statistics, 1841–1971* (1979)
Note: * 1901: 10 years and over; 1921: 12 years and over; 1931: 14 years and over; 1951: 15 years and over; 1971/81: 16 years and over.

Several features of these statistics can be highlighted. At the very broadest level, there has been a marked shift from manual, industrial, primary, productive labour towards tertiary, clerical, service and distributive work. Numbers of Scottish women employed in agriculture declined between 1901 and 1981 to insignificant proportions as new labour shedding technology diffused throughout the sector and total agricultural employment contracted sharply. Again, female employment in the personal services sector experienced a remarkable transformation. Perhaps the most significant single change in the occupational profile of women workers in Scotland in the twentieth century has been the virtual extinction of the indoor domestic servant, the largest single occupation for women before World War Two. However, job opportunities for women in the non-servant component of the personal services sector rose markedly, especially after 1950, with the expansion of private and state sector employment, including institutional

People and Society in Scotland

Table 2. *Proportion of the Female Force in Scotland Employed in Principal Economic Sectors, 1901–1981 (expressed as a percentage of total occupied females)*

Sector	1901	1921	1931	1951	1971	1981
Services (misc)	32	25	26	17	15	18
domestic, indoor	*24*	*19*	*21*	*11*	*6*	*1*
Textiles	21	16	15	11	5	3
Clothing	13	7	4	5	3	3
Agriculture	7	4	3	2	1	1
Paper, Printing	3	3	3	3	2	2
Food, Drink	3	5	6	6	5	4
Engineering & Metals	1	3	3	6	8	5
Transport, Communications	1	1	2	4	3.	2
Distribution	9	18	19	20	19	18
Insurance, Banking	0	1	1	2	4	7
Public Administration	0	1	3	4	5	8
Professional & Scientific	5	5	10	15	24	24
Teachers	*3*	*4*	*4*	*4*	*5*	*5*
Nurses	*1*	*2*	*2*	*4*	*6*	*8*

Source: Census of Scotland; CH Lee, *British Regional Employment Statistics, 1841–1971* (1979)

cleaners and caterers. Female employment in the manufacturing sector in Scotland has also undergone notable change through the course of the twentieth century. The traditional sectors of textiles and clothing, where over a third of all women in the Scottish labour market found employment before World War One, suffered catastrophic contraction as foreign competition eroded markets, forcing closures, rationalisation and the belated adoption of labour saving technologies and scientific management techniques. On the other hand, the process of technological change, new mass-production assembly-line techniques, deskilling and more sophisticated division of labour led to a substantial increase in the proportion of females employed in light industry, food and drink processing and transport and communications, though most of this expansion was over by the late 1960s. Perhaps the most notable growth area within the manual sector for female labour has been the growing electrical, electronic and instrument engineering sectors in Scotland, where 42 per cent and 50 per cent respectively of the labour force were female by 1971 (the comparable figures for 1901 were 0 per cent and 4 per cent).[1]

Numerically, the major employment growth area for Scottish women — as in England — in the twentieth century has been the non-manual, services sector, what Jane Lewis has termed the 'white blouse' occupations — insurance, banking, business services, public administration, local government, teaching, nursing and shopwork. Indeed, 75 per cent of all Scottish women employed in the formal economy were clustered in the services sector in the mid-1970s, compared to less than 20 per cent in 1901. The twentieth century has witnessed a revolutionary transformation in the gender composition of clerical labour in Scotland, though this has been confined to the junior and 'middling' levels with relatively few females achieving managerial and higher administrator status. Secretarial, typing, sales and routine clerical work have become dominated by female labour, with female employment in banking, insurance and public administration increasing almost fourfold since World War Two. Between 1961 and 1981 male clerical labour declined by 20 per cent to 60,000 whilst the number of female clerical workers rose by almost 50 per cent to 181,000. Shopwork also became a major employer of female labour in the twentieth century, though job opportunities in this sector stagnated in the 1970s, partly as a consequence of the growth of giant stores and the penetration of labour-saving micro-chip technology. A further component of the expansion of opportunities for women in the white-collar sector has been increased employment in the professional and scientific sector. Whilst the 'higher professions' remained almost exclusively male-dominated, employment of women in the 'lower' professions — including teaching and nursing — expanded dramatically, a consequence largely of post-war expansionary initiatives in state health and education. Hence between 1951 and 1981 the numbers of Scottish female nurses and teachers doubled.[2]

Thus, the first point to be made about the female labour market in Scotland during the twentieth century is that there has been a major reorientation in the type of work women performed, from manual to non-manual. Since the Second World War another important change has taken place. While participation rates of Scottish females in the formal economy appear to have remained remarkably constant between 1901 and 1951 thereafter the proportion of adult women in such employment rose sharply, from 32.6 in 1951 to 42.2 per cent by 1981. Taking a rather different index — the proportion of women either in employment or classified as seeking employment — Kendrick argues that the increase was even more dramatic, from 33.6 per cent in 1951 to 46.6 per cent in 1981.[3] The major element in this marked increase in female participation rates in Scotland since 1950 is the rising proportion of married women re-entering the formal economy, a trend already evident before 1951, as Table 3 indicates.

Table 3. Female Employment in Scotland, by Marital Status, 1911–1981 (by percentage of total females employed)

	Married	Single		Widowed/Divorced
1911	5.3	87.3		7.4
1921	6.3	86.7		7.0
1931	8.5	85.9		5.6
1951	23.4	69.0		7.3
1961	38.7		61.3	
1971	57.8		42.2	
1981	62.0	30.0		8.0

Source: Census of Scotland

A pincer movement has been operating here. Since World War Two, the pool of single women in the labour market has shrunk because of earlier marriage, rising school leaving age and longer periods spent in full-time education. On the other hand, and most significantly, the enhanced labour market participation by married women has been facilitated by smaller family size. Crucially, the child bearing and rearing period has been cut, on average, by more than ten years between 1900 and 1980. Expanding, more attractive job opportunities, rising real wages, smaller families, rising education standards and expectations — fuelled not least by the feminist movement of the 1960s/70s — and the effects of labour saving technology in the home have all played a part in encouraging this increased involvement of women in the formal labour market. The impact of the technological determinant in this process, however, is more marginal than many commentators have suggested.[4]

There has been a marked rise in part-time employment within the Scottish economy, particularly since World War Two and this accounts for a considerable proportion of the rise in female participation rates. Between 1951 and 1981 the proportion of total female jobs in Scotland that were part-time (i.e. a working week of under 30 hours) rose from less than 5 per cent to 41 per cent, whilst at the latter point, only around 7 per cent of all male Scottish employees worked part-time. Most female part-timers were married and clustered in the low-paid clerical, catering, entertainment, cleaning and distribution sectors. For example, over 40 per cent of female shop assistants and over 80 per cent of cleaners in 1981 worked part-time. This is not to imply, however, that part-time employment was insignificant before World War Two. A number of commentators have shown how deficient the official Census statistics are in this respect, in that they obscure a considerable, undefinable amount of part-time, informal work, such as child-minding, washing and mending, knitting, typing, toy making, performed by married women often desperate to supplement the meagre and insecure earnings of their partners. Such evidence exposes the fallacy that working class families existed solely on the 'family wage' of the male 'breadwinner'. Nevertheless, the 'bi-modal' or M-shaped profile of female employment undoubtedly became more prevalent in Scotland as the twentieth century wore on; typically with an initial eight to ten year period of work outside the home until reaching early-mid twenties, followed by a period of several years of unpaid work within the home, rearing and nursing children, and capped off by a return to work in the formal economy (i.e outside the home), on a full or part-time basis until retirement.[5]

Before we leave our introductory survey of female employment patterns in Scotland it is perhaps worth noting three further points. Firstly, despite the changes noted above, a distinct sexual division of labour continued to characterise the employment market in twentieth century Scotland. Gender segregation in employment undoubtedly became more blurred by the 1980s, compared to the 1900s, but it remained pervasive none the less. Many areas of manual employment continued to be monopolised by male workers, women patently failing, for example, to penetrate in any significant numbers the traditional bastions of shipbuilding, coal mining, metal production, heavy engineering and construction which dominated the Clydeside economy. Within 'newer' occupations, moreover, women tended to be clustered, or more appropriately ghettoised, into the lowest status, poorest paid, menial jobs, whilst male workers were located in the most skilled, responsible and best paid jobs. Hence, as I. Watt has argued, two distinct, gender specific primary and secondary labour markets persisted through the post-World War Two decades.[6] Deep-rooted patriarchal concepts of the 'lesser value' of female labour clearly proved difficult to eradicate. We shall return to this point later in the discussion.

Secondly, despite some narrowing, over the course of the twentieth century, marked variations in female participation rates and job opportunities continued to exist between social classes and different regions within Scotland. Generally speaking, a lower proportion of rural women participated in the formal economy, whilst such areas exhibited a higher proportion of women workers in the service industries than in urban areas. Differences also existed within urban labour markets. Contrast Glasgow with its diversified female labour market with many of the metal working and mining towns and villages of Fife and Lanarkshire with extremely constrained opportunities for employment outside the home.

Many small towns in the Borders were dominated by wool production, Paisley by cotton thread and Dundee by the manufacture of jute, all industries which employed a high proportion of female labour. In the early part of our period, Dundee had unusually high proportions of married females working outwith the home and a distinctive factory culture not dissimilar to many of the cotton weaving towns of North Lancashire.[7] The recent penetration of multi-national companies into the Scottish economy, predominantly anti-unionist, employing large female labour forces in new towns like East Kilbride, Cumbernauld and Glenrothes has created a further permutation.

Thirdly, the ten-yearly Census fails to register the enormous, albeit temporary, escalation in economic activity rates of women during the two world wars, 1914–18 and 1939–45, when the industrial 'reserve army' of women was utilised on the home front to replace male workers called up to the armed forces. At peak, four in every five married women without children in Britain were employed during World War Two and with the wartime expansion of nurseries and works creches a much larger proportion of mothers were drawn inexorably into the wartime economy. Both wars marked important periods in the work experience of Scottish women, not least because of their exposure to a much broader range of employment. The next section moves beyond the rather bland statistical data to investigate the nature of women's work in Scotland in a little more depth, starting with developments during the Great War, 1914–1918.

II

The First World War was an emancipating experience and a consciousness raising episode for the vast swathes of Scottish working class women who flooded into the munitions factories, the railways, the trams, and other jobs replacing male labour drawn into the armed forces. In their own memories of this period women articulated mixed feelings of strain and fatigue, of release, freedom, pride and satisfaction — what Gail Braybon has termed 'a new sense of self-worth'[8] Changes in women's experience of work played an important part in this process. Through wartime 'dilution', large numbers of women suddenly became exposed to a wide range of skills and tasks previously denied to them, to the cameraderie of large factories, to higher wages, to more mechanised production, and to trade unionism. The demystification of cherished male dominated crafts, as women came into closer contact with such work, had an important, liberating effect, as did the physical transistion from stultifying domestic service — characterised by uniformed servitude and relative isolation — to large scale factory production. Scottish women also found themselves at the sharp end of escalating wartime price inflation — running at around 25 per cent per year during the war — which seriously eroded the higher earnings on war work. Furthermore, frustration with restricted mobility, job fragmentation, petty discrimination and the failure of wartime equal pay policies bred bitterness and encouraged militancy.

The pressures and circumstances of wartime thus strengthened independence, confidence, morale and class consciousness amongst working women. At one level, this advanced awareness was illustrated in rapidly rising female membership of trade unions, with Scottish women contributing disproportionately to the doubling of trade union membership between 1914 and 1920. Perhaps the most tangible expressions of this heightened class awareness amongst working women occurred on Clydeside. Witness, for example, the spate of female workers strikes and spiralling demands for inflation-matching wage rises and for recognition of unions recruiting women (especially the National Federation of Women Workers and the Workers Union) during 1910–14, the Clyde rent strikes of 1915, the clothing industry strikes of 1917, the active female participation in the massive 100,000 strong 1917 May Day demonstration in Glasgow and in the anti-war movement.[9] Evidence of female organisation and resistance appears in the other major munitions producing regions in Britain, though perhaps lacking the intensity and breadth of the insurgency on the Clyde.

At one time, the First World War was widely considered to be a major watershed in the position of women within British society. On closer scrutiny, however, the war appears to have had little but a marginal, transitory impact on women in Scotland. The gains that accrued were largely in the political, rather than the socio-economic sphere. Women over thirty gained the vote in 1918 though not full, equal franchise on the same terms as men until a decade later. Post-war legislation also opened new opportunities in the law and professions for middle class women. However, Scottish working class women were rapidly displaced in 1919–20 by demobilised soldiers. As far as possible, the prewar employment situation was restored, including time-honoured sexual divisions of labour. Domestic ideology proved to have been only suspended for the duration of hostilities. The wartime agreements on dilution between the trade unions and the government enshrined in the Treasury Agreement and Munition Act of 1915 meant that the withdrawal of women from specific areas of the labour market was inevitable once peace was restored. By 1921, the pre-1914 patterns had been re-established, hence the occupational profile provided by the 1911 and 1921 Scottish Census are remarkably similar (see Tables 1 and 2). In the event, the emancipating experience of wartime proved to be a transient one for Scottish working class women, raising expectations that were rapidly frustrated in the immediate aftermath of hostilities.

This return to 'normalcy' was backed by the Scottish Trades Union Congress (STUC) and, with some reservations, by the National Federation of Women Workers (NFWW). The organised labour movement in Scotland was divided on strategies to adopt to ease the demobilisation of women and erode inequalities. The STUC adopted a resolution calling for 'equal pay for work of equal value', but did little to implement this in practice. Miss Adams of the National Federation of Women Workers argued at the Scottish Trades Union Congress for the continuation of government factories and the extension of training with maintenance to equip women with the necessary skills for new occupations. But few voices were raised to question the right of returning soldiers to work performed by women during the war and a resolution calling for all occupations to be open on equal terms for men and women was defeated at the STUC Annual Conference late in 1918 by 78 votes to 72. Charles Robinson of Motherwell Trades Council commented that the involvement of women in industry during the war was 'demoralising', had 'a depressing effect upon public morality' and that a woman's 'natural sphere' was 'the home'.[10] It was only really in clerical work and distribution that working class women managed to maintain the ground penetrated during the First World War. Here in the 1920s and 1930s, as Betty Lamont recognised, 'bright blouses were ousting black coats'.[11] The reality for most Scottish working class women between the wars was unemployment, a return to the home to domestic service or to the 'traditional' women's sectors — textiles and clothing.

The largest single sector of female employment in Scotland between the wars remained indoor domestic service, where numbers of women employed rose by 13.4 per cent between 1921 and 1931 (reversing the pre-war trend of decline), reaching almost 140,000, or 21 per cent of all employed females. After 1918, many Scots women were herded back into traditional areas of female employment, such as domestic service, because unemployment benefit would be withheld from those women who refused to take such jobs when offered at the Labour Exchanges. In service, predominantly young women under 25 toiled for a 12–14 hour day, six or six and a half days a week, in virtual bondage to their masters and mistresses. Domestic service was one occupation where conditions and work relationships varied considerably between employers and this makes valid generalisation difficult. Some oral testimonies indicate that women could gain much intrinsic satisfaction, pride and enjoyment from their role as a servant.[12] However, enough evidence exists to suggest that the dominant 'Upstairs Downstairs' image of a large and robust group of uniformed servants operating under a fine division of labour and elaborate hierarchical structure is an erroneous one, such households being rare in Scotland by the 1920s. Most servants worked alone; a solitary existence with a monotonous and physically demanding daily routine of cleaning, washing, serving, caring. One general servant in Stirling described her work thus:

'You were up in the morning — about the back of seven. You would be shouted to and you would be at their beck and call 'til about eight or nine at night. . . . It was hard work there was no hoovers in those days, it was the wee brush and the pan, down on your knees and scrubbing. Scrubbing, blackleading the big ranges and cleaning the flues'.[13] Despite the compensations of relative security and, taking food and lodgings into account, reasonable levels of remuneration (often paid only yearly or half yearly) there is much evidence to suggest that domestic service was becoming more and more unpopular. Increasingly, domestic service became a stepping stone to other work in factories, shops and offices. However, constrained opportunities and poverty drove many young women to accept service as the only available option in the depression years of the 1920s, and 1930s. For some, being so close to ostentatious waste and profligate expenditure was an embittering experience:

And then — I saw it for the first time, but not for the last: butter — and jam, spread thick on the lovely fruit cake — and, to add to my horror, some of it was left on the plates, and, of course, put out to the pigs on the home farm. I nearly choked with anger at the wanton waste. I could remember so many hungry children — and here was good food being contemptuously pushed aside. And I must be allowed to say here and now, that in all of the sixteen years that were to follow, I never met a single domestic servant, male or female, who was at any time satisfied with the food served to them.[14]

During the interwar years almost one in four employed women in Scotland worked in the distribution, food and drink sectors. Employment in a shop, especially a large store, appears to have been regarded by many working class women as rather higher status work than a factory job. 'I've got you a job . . . it's a nice one, not a factory' one Edinburgh women indicated to her daughter in the 1920s. Another recalled how her parents 'thought it was nice to work in Jenner's'.[15] However, higher status needed to be weighed against a series of unsavoury aspects of such employment. The female labour force in distribution had an extremely youthful profile — nearly half of all shop assistants in Scotland were under 20 years of age in the late 1930s. Scarcely surprisingly, therefore, this sector was notorious for its 'blind alley' employment, lack of security, blatant age discrimination, petty rivalries and snobbery between grades, poor wages and lack of trade union penetration. Working hours in distribution were long, varying between 60 (food) and 80 (confectionery) per week and the sector was poorly regulated and marginally protected. Up to the late 1930s, legislation only enforced definite meal times, a weekly half day holiday and a 74 hour maximum working week for workers under 18 years of age. Moreover, these rules, and the minimum wages set by Trades Boards, were often ineffective, argued Miss I. Davidson of the Shop Assistants Union in 1932, because of lack of inspection and policing which had been cut back in the economy drive of 1921–2. The one notable exception to this scenario in interwar Scotland was employment in the Cooperative Wholesale Society, where a trade union closed shop operated.[16]

Manufacturing remained a significant employer of female labour in Scotland between the wars. Clearly, as Table 1 indicates, there was some movement within this sector, with declining opportunities in textiles and

10. Margaret Smith (left) and Lizzie Gillespie, counter staff at Cowlairs Cooperative Society, Springburn, Glasgow, 1934. Courtesy of Springburn Museum Trust.

clothing and some expansion in numbers of women employed in the newer light and electrical engineering, consumer goods industries. The labour process in the latter sections, where conveyor belt techniques and detailed division of labour were increasingly being employed, could be repetitive, monotonous and soul-destroying. According to a government enquiry in 1929 such work was well suited to women because, they argued, 'females were apparently unaffected by the monotony of the work.'[17] However, job satisfaction, pride in the work and an identity with one's machine (often regarded as personal property) was expressed in the recollections of many female textile workers, who could recall intricate details of the work and rarely articulated a feeling of boredom or monotony. The repetitive labour process and close monitoring by predominantly male supervisors could be mediated in what were relatively large textile concerns, by female companionship, camaraderie, and, as Jayne Stephenson has noted, by chatting, joking and singing. 'We had a great time, we had', one textile worker recalled.[18] Weaving was amongst the most skilled of female occupations between the wars and wage payments by piecework placed some women on a par with male workers. Moreover, working conditions in textile factories were subject to stringent, if not always enforced, legislative regulation. Furthermore, a relatively high level of trade unionism amongst female textile workers (at least in Dundee, the Borders and Clydeside, if not in Stirlingshire) helped to maintain standards of health and safety at work.

On the negative side, insecurity of employment savaged the textile industry through the 1920s and 1930s and the constant fear of unemployment undoubtedly had a disciplining effect at the point of production in such sectors. Scottish textile workers were placed under additional pressure as cost-conscious employers responded to the squeeze on profits by increasing working hours, reducing staffing levels and increasing workloads, introducing new technology and speeding up and intensifying work. The Workers Theatre Movement caricatured such trends most effectively in an agit prop skit in 1932:

Speed-up, Speed-up
Worker: We are humans, not machines.
Capitalist: You don't like this fast routine?
Get your pay and get out quick,
You speak like a Bolshevik.
Speed-up, speed-up, watch your step,
Hold on tight and show some pep.
Woman Worker: My head, oh my head! I can't go on.
Capitalist: You want time off, that's your game.
Get your pay and get out quick,

There's no place here for the sick.
Number fifteen, number ten,
I must fire two more men.
Here's a youngster strong and willing,
Will not find the pace so killing.
To do more work for less pay —
That's the problem of the day.[19]

A barrage of newspaper and magazine propaganda after World War One helped to resuscitate and consolidate the Victorian domestic ideology — indeed, the concept that a woman's place was in the home — or 'masculine madness', as the Scottish feminist Eleanor Stewart termed it — may well have been at its most potent during the interwar years. J. D. Young has commented on how deep-rooted patriarchal values were amongst working class males in traditional industrial and mining communities in inter-war Scotland.[20] Typically, women workers in Scotland between the wars terminated their full time employment within the formal economy on marriage (as Table 3 indicates), and usually before the birth of their first child. The Stirling oral testimonies suggest that this was an accepted and rarely challenged norm. Discrimination against married and older women in the labour market abounded in the interwar period. The marriage bar remained firmly in place in teaching and many other occupations exercised an informal bar and, indeed, preference for younger, unmarried workers.[21] Marriage, then, usually meant in the interwar years a reorientation of a woman's working life from outside to inside the home. Reproductive labour replaced productive. The 'marriage poem' which decorated the work bench of one Edinburgh factory worker concluded thus:

May John aye ha'e the money
For his coupon and his beer!
May your St Cuthbert's wedding
Pay a lovely dividend
With bonny bouncing babies
To cheer you to the end.[22]

The work of a married woman within the home included a wide range of labour intensive tasks seven days a week; among them nursing, caring, feeding and minding children, washing and ironing laundry, shopping, food preparation, cooking and washing up for the family, scrubbing, polishing and blackleading equipment (such as the iron and chrome kitchen range), cleaning and sweeping living accommodation, sewing, knitting, making and mending clothes, and responsibility for financial budgeting and household management. Family size was falling between the wars, reducing some of the physical graft involved in domestic labour. Nevertheless, the job remained debilitating. Washing in itself was a heavy physical task which for larger families absorbed a full day and a half a week; soaking, boiling, bleaching, scrubbing, rinsing, 'blueing the whites', starching, hanging up. Moreover, the burden of such domestic work was multiplied by married women taking in paid work to be performed in the home to supplement the family income.

A distinctive, traditional sexual division of labour existed within the interwar Scottish home. Lynn Jamieson has noted how 'all family members took it for granted that a whole range of household tasks were women's work.'[23] Daughters were expected to contribute help with household chores and child-minding very early on in life, whilst evidence suggests that sons and fathers were exempt from all but a few specialised tasks — cleaning and mending shoes; bringing up coal and water; chopping sticks; decorating. Even when girls entered full-time employment they continued to be responsible for many domestic tasks and lacked the privileges conferred on boys on their entry to full-time work.[24] Formal education helped to perpetuate such gender divisions, as Helen Corr has argued, favouring domestic skills for girls; technical skills for boys.[25] Girls were prepared carefully for a life servicing, one way or another, the male 'breadwinner':

Q. And did your father help your mother with any jobs in the house?
A. No. No. No, my father was very well looked after in the house, even to the fact that his tea was poured out for him, and everything was just there for him to sit down. He was the worker o' the house.'[26]

Long habituation and socialisation meant that such sex stereotyping of roles within the working class family could be accepted without question, as simply part of the fabric of everyday life. An Edinburgh woman recalled life for her mother thus: 'She was always working, she never got out anywhere. That was her life.'[27]

Despite some widening of job opportunities and a general improvement in real wages in the 1920s and 1930s, women's work in Scotland was generally of low status; women's labour power was undervalued, and choices of employment remained severely constrained into a small cluster of sex-stereotyped occupations. Whilst limited mobility was possible for women workers through a skill hierarchy in most occupations, the vast majority of women were congregated in the lowest grade, least responsible, least skilled, least independent of jobs. Formal training beyond that obtained by observation and practice on the job was rare for women. Apprenticeships, albeit in decline, remained monopolised by men — a policy tacitly supported by male-dominated trade unions. Male apprentices and articled clerks outnumbered females in Scotland by a ratio of more than 10 to 1. Hence women were denied access to skills outwith the 'female trades' (e.g. needlework). In industry, offices and shops, positions of authority and responsibility remained invariably monopolised by male employees, and chances of promotion and upward mobility for female workers were constrained. Though women constituted 65 per cent of the labour force in the Scottish clothing industry, there were 3273 male employers, managers, overlookers and foremen, compared to just 765 females in 1931. Even more strikingly, in textiles where women constituted 74 per cent of the total labour force, there were only 106 female employers, managers, overlookers and foremen in 1931, compared to 2175 males. As late as 1951, male managers in the Scottish economy outnumbered women in a ratio of almost 6:1. Such structural subordination had important implications, including facilitating sexual harassment in the workplace.

Sexual discrimination and inequalities in the labour market and at work remained endemic in the interwar period. Powerful institutional and social pressures could be exerted to ensure withdrawal in favour of men. Protective state legislation, excluding women from certain trades, restricting working hours and banning nightwork (except under special licence) enabled employers to justify arguments of 'inferiority' and further constrained women's opportunities. The STUC continued to promote the extension of such protective legislation, despite the protests of its feminist members.[28] Gender wage differentials across the British economy hardly eroded through the 1900–1939 period — adult women's earnings remaining on average around 50 per cent of adult male earnings. Even where men and women performed similar work tasks and held jobs involving similar levels of skill, wage differentials remained pervasive — as in teaching at a maximum of 80 per cent of the male rate. This was partly because conventional definitions of skill were saturated with male bias, work performed by women being undervalued and labelled as unskilled, irrespective of objective elements such as task range, discretionary content and training period. Phillips and Taylor noted:

> The perpetuation of sexual hierarchy has been inextricably interwoven with the struggles against the real subordination to capital, as claims to skilled status have come to rely more and more on the sex of the workers and less and less on the nature of the job.[29]

This process has been described appositely by the feminist historian Jill Norris as 'social degradation of skill', the antithesis of the notion of social construction of skill, or skill as a function of bargaining strength, a concept developed by the textile labour historian H. A. Turner.[30] Moreover, the patriarchal notion of 'lesser worth' was firmly enshrined and institutionalised within interwar State welfare policy and the deeply entrenched notion of the 'family wage' for the male earner and 'supplementary wage', or 'pin money', for the female worker. Differentials existed in unemployment benefit and pensions based on gender. The Anomalies Act withdrew benefit from married women if they had no immediate prospects of work 'in their trade', whilst the Trade Boards concocted two separate minimum wage rates within regulated trades for the same occupations, with the female rate averaging 60 per cent of the male. Such undervaluation continued to be justified by employers and managers on the grounds that female workers were physically weaker, more emotionally unstable, less healthy (as reflected in absenteeism), and lacked long-term commitment to work and to developing skills and responsibilities. This had serious implications for women in general and single working women in particular, making it extremely difficult to make ends meet.[31]

The Scottish trade union movement was also, however, deeply committed to patriarchal strategies in the interwar period and patently failed seriously to challenge the prevailing system of gender apartheid. This is not to deny some positive developments. An increasing number of unions recruiting in Scotland opened up membership to female workers between 1914 and the late 1920s. The STUC created a Women's Advisory Committee (WAC) in 1926, which campaigned actively throughout the later 1920s and through the 1930s to raise levels of female membership and awareness within the movement of issues particularly pertinent to women workers, including equal pay, protective legislation, health and nursery provision. The WAC produced its own recruitment leaflets, visited unions, Independent Labour Party and Co-operative branches, organised day and weekend schools to train female officials and established regional women's groups in Glasgow, Edinburgh, Dundee and Aberdeeen. However, in spite of such activities, women's position within Scottish trade unions remained extremely tenuous between the wars. Male workers were more than twice as likely as female workers to be members of a union. According to the STUC's rather crude statistics, female membership fell by 40 per cent between the early 1920s and the early 1930s, from a density of 12 per cent organised to just over 7 per cent, with some recovery in the later 1930s. Such aggregated figures hide, however, significant occupational and regional variations. Female textile workers in Scotland were amongst the most well organised in the 1920s, the textile dominated regions of the Borders and Dundee registering the highest female union densities of 34 per cent and 40 per cent respectively in 1923–4. By contrast, only 14 per cent of women workers in Glasgow and Aberdeen were members of trade unions. Over time, the traditional dominance of textile workers within the female segment of the organised labour movement in Scotland atrophied and by the late 1930s their position was usurped by the growing numbers of female unionists within the services sector.[32]

The relative weakness of female trade unionism in Scotland between the wars can perhaps be explained by reference to five factors. Firstly, women were clustered in occupations which were hardly conducive to collective organisation — in small units, with a high turnover, in domestic service, shops and 'sweated' work. Secondly, employer strategies of fierce anti-unionism and victimisation (as in JP Coats and Singer) worked to dissuade male and female workers from unionisation, especially within the context of mass unemployment, whilst institutionalised welfarist managerial strategies were designed to induce loyalty to the firm and undermine the union. Thirdly, trade unionists recognised that the protections and restrictions conferred by the state on women's employment, especially the minimum wage regulation of the Trade Boards, worked to convince employees that trade unions could fulfil no useful function. Fourthly, low pay created difficulties for many women in actually sustaining union subscriptions. Finally, and perhaps most significantly, women workers continued to be faced with opposition and lack of sympathy from many male trade unionists and union leaderships. Aitken Ferguson, of the Glasgow Trades Council, noted this in 1925: 'The attitude of unions. . . . to the question of women in industry was one of aloofness and disregard of the importance of organising.'[33]

With some notable exceptions, Scottish trade unions remained permeated with chauvinist attitudes and patriarchal strategies, subscribing, in practice, to the concepts of 'separate spheres' and the 'family wage' between the wars. Many unions participated in excluding women from the workplace altogether or segregating and confining women to the lowest paid, most subordinate jobs. Printing provides an example. Female compositors were fairly common in Edinburgh and Aberdeen in the early years of the twentieth century. In 1910, however, the Scottish Typographical Association and the printing employers' association agreed that no new female apprentices would be taken on. By the late 1940s female compositors, as a consequence, had virtually disappeared, thus bringing Scotland in line with England.

Female employment in printing grew through this period, but women — like Annie Davidson in Glasgow — were confined to the 'auxiliary' semi-skilled machine feeding tasks.[34]

Female workers were rarely taken seriously as trade unionists and issues of interest to women members, such as equal pay, welfare benefits, health, creche provision, were rarely taken up by unions or channelled through the STUC. Moreover, the active involvement of women within the labour movement was resisted, partly by a process of denying women representation within decision-making structures. The real influence of the Women's Advisory Committee within the Scottish trade union movement appears to have been minimal in the 1920s and 1930s. For example, when the WAC attempted to establish a women's committee in Edinburgh in the late 1920s, this initiative floundered because of a dearth of trade union support. In 1931 the WAC tried again, this time circularising all affiliated union branches requesting that they agree to meet a deputation to discuss issues and recruitment of female workers. Out of 544 local branches circularised, only forty-five took up the initiative. The 'take-up' by Labour Party sections (40 per cent) and Co-operative Guilds (50 per cent) was significantly better. To a large extent, then, the lines of communication were effectively blocked. Within unions, moreover, female representation in leadership positions and on executive committees was marginal. In an WAC initiated STUC survey in 1938, of twenty-two unions, only five made any special provision for automatic female representation at local and executive level. In the other seventeen, twelve had no female representation whilst five had the following representation:

Union 1. 55 per cent female membership. 24 executive places. 4 females.
Union 2. 41 per cent female membership. 24 executive places. 1 female.
Union 3. 77 per cent female membership. 8 executive places. 2 females.
Union 4. 34 per cent female membership. 12 executive places. 1 female.
Union 5. 17 per cent female membership. 24 executive places. 1 female.

In twelve unions, with a combined density of more than 20 per cent female membership, sixty-eight women held positions of branch chair, secretary and treasurer out of a total of 1281 such positions. In this respect, as in so many others, evidence clearly supports Jane Lewis's maxim that between the wars women were still 'in search of real equality'.[35]

It is perhaps worth reminding ourselves at this point, before we move on to post-1945, that women were active rather than passive players on this historical scene. Examining the objective reality of working women's lives with the benefit of hindsight gives the impression that Scottish women calmly and deferentially accepted their lot and that the female experience of work was a distinctively negative one. This was not entirely the case. Women interacted with their environment and responded vigorously and spontaneously to exploitative, discriminatory working conditions. Though little systematic research has yet been undertaken on female strike propensity between the wars in Scotland, there is perhaps enough evidence to suggest that the prevailing image of a quiescent female labour force is a mythical one. Degradation in relative terms may well have been a marked feature of women's work and home life, but working women rarely articulated a perception of such alienation. Rather, many women undoubtedly derived a great deal of satisfaction, pride and status from their employment and indeed from their domestic role, as good, responsible, caring mothers, keeping a tidy home and carefully and efficiently managing a tight household budget. The latter, key task often involved a very high degree of skill and ingenuity. Clearly, a distinction needs to be drawn between what we can identify as structural elements of subordination, discrimination, segregation and gender inequalities and just how ordinary Scottish women perceived their existence and related to their work. Again, much more research is necessary here. It appears, however, that despite adverse work conditions, women clearly gained much from contact with the labour process — that women's attitude to waged work was a positive one. Oral evidence, in particular, though not without its pitfalls for the historian, provides strong support for the hypothesis that work was a source of identity, camaraderie, job satisfaction, pride and self-respect for Scottish women as well as men. Female shop assistants, clerical workers, domestic servants, seamstresses, teachers, nurses, print and textile workers have all articulated an intense commitment to their jobs. In this sense, the differences in orientation to work between male and female employees may be more apparent than real. Brown and Stevenson's extensive analysis of women's work in Stirling, based on oral testimony, makes this point persuasively: 'The vast majority of working-class women respondents enjoyed their working lives, finding it a positive and rewarding experience combining pride in work and skill, and participation in the collective culture of working-class women'.[36]

Given the nature of female employment in Scotland before World War Two — the immobility, inequalities, ghettoisation, undervaluation — this is a most remarkable illustration of the character and resilience of Scottish working class women.

The 1939–45 war helped to introduce and educate a new generation of working women into the mysteries of male dominated crafts and to expose the contrived, socially constructed barriers between male and female capabilities. Maisie Gordon, who entered the Hyde Park Locomotive works in Springburn during World War Two commented scathingly on this:

> I was at the Hyde Park, in the machine shop, a slinger. It was good. You'd often say to yourself, when I saw a workman coming out of Hyde Park with a dirty face and dirty hands — when I was younger, to me that man grafted. You thought, you know, 'Oh my God, that man's doing a lot of work' and you'd go into it and they're not grafting, you know it's so comical. You know you say to yourself, 'my God, I mind when thae men were like slaves', you know, when they were really hard done by.[37]

The circumstances of wartime production germinated a heightened class consciousness amongst working women, who were drawn into the formal economy in even greater numbers than during World War One. Female trade unionism notably accelerated with rearmament and war and Richard Croucher has argued that during the latter phase of hostilities, 1943–4, British women were more strike-prone than men. A series of industrial strikes were initiated by Scottish women on wage issues, including major confrontations at Rolls Royce, Hillington and at Barr and Strouds. In stark contrast to the coercive, anti-strike strategy of the state on Clydeside during World War One, these disputes were settled by conciliatory means, with the creation of a court of inquiry, and, in 1944, the Royal Commission on Equal Pay (which reported inconclusively two years later). The shedding of female labour from munitions from the Autumn of 1944, long before the termination of hostilities, also helped to contain spiralling industrial militancy.[38]

In many ways the Second World War marked a significant watershed in the relationship of women to waged work. More women maintained their wartime jobs in the formal economy after World War Two than after World War One. One of the most significant changes after World War Two was the universal political commitment to full employment which meant that unlike the 1920s and 1930s, the 30 years to the mid-1970s witnessed a constantly maintained demand for female labour. Thus market circumstances, in conjunction with the inexorable thrust of job-fragmenting technological change and the wider penetration of rationalised work practices, accelerated erosion in occupational segregation and enabled more upward mobility in the postwar period. The permanent disappearance of the marriage bar during wartime played a significant role in this process. In instrument and electrical engineering, insurance and banking, for example, women formed almost 50 per cent of the Scottish labour force by the 1970s compared to less than 20 per cent in the early 1930s. This was a continuation and acceleration of a long-term trend evident throughout the twentieth century. In 1901, of twenty-four major Scottish census occupational groupings thirteen had less than 10 per cent female representation. The same returns for 1931, 1951 and 1971–81 were eight, seven, and three respectively. This translated into a wider choice of occupations for Scottish women.

Women workers undoubtedly shared in the general amelioration of working conditions across the Scottish economy during the war and the post-war period. Environmental conditions were, on balance, considerably better by the 1970s, as were the real rewards for labour, compared to the interwar period. Improved factory sanitation and washing facilities, more frequent rest breaks and more extensive welfare provision introduced during World War Two became permanent features of industry thereafter. Holidays with pay for those in full-time employment became normal rather than an exceptional perk for the privileged elite. Hours of work were shorter, on average, by around 10–20 per cent whilst women benefitted from broad sectoral shifts in the economy with the decline of occupations characterised by long hours — including domestic service, clothing and agriculture — and the growth of ones where shorter hours were the norm — particularly white-collar employment. Arguably, occupational health standards also improved markedly over the post-1945 period in Scotland. Notwithstanding the failure of the long campaign by the Scottish labour movement to include an occupational health service within the NHS, deaths and injuries through industrial accidents and work-related diseases have continued to fall. Although not without its own work-related hazards, the broader shift towards white collar office work, and, within this sector, towards the larger scale office, meant a move towards cleaner, healthier and more congenial work conditions. It has also been suggested that the post-1945 period witnessed a growing awareness of, and reduction in, the incidence of sexual harassment of women at work. Moreover, the proliferation of employment legislation in the post war period, though rarely totally or immediately effective, provided a matrix of protective mechanisms shielding workers against some of the more blatant forms of exploitation in the labour market, not least through the provision of redundancy payments on dismissal. The extension of Wages Councils (replacing the Trade Boards) establishing legal minimum wages across low wage sectors predominantly employing women are also particularly significant in our context.

Work within the home has also altered quite fundamentally in character since World War Two with smaller families, rising real incomes and the penetration of gas, electricity and a range of labour-saving food preservation, cooking, cleaning and laundry appliances and materials into working class homes. Increasingly, traditional domestic tasks, such as the making of clothes, bread and porridge, have been superseded by the availability of cheap goods and services outwith the home. Time spent on the family wash has been drastically slashed. Evidence also suggests that paid work performed in the home (and other forms of casual and seasonal work, including agricultural) has become far less important than in the early twentieth century. This decline in waged work within the home has been influenced partly by improved transport facilities which opened up a wider choice of jobs to women, partly by State intervention which has raised minimum wage rates, thus making such work less attractive to employers, and partly by the continuation of a long, ongoing trend amongst employers to exercise closer, more direct forms of control over their labour. However, homework never entirely disappeared from the Scottish economy and retained some popularity with employers who desired to spread risk and cheapen costs, and with some employees because such work could be integrated relatively easily with child caring and household responsibilities. Racial prejudice and discrimination meant that homework became the resort of growing numbers of immigrant women in Scotland, especially Indians, Pakistanis and Bangladeshis, whose distinct culture and language made it more difficult to obtain work in the formal economy.[39]

Furthermore, the belated extension of trade unionism to a much larger segment of the female labour force in Scotland provided some representation and extended protection at the point of production. As Table 4 indicates, the acceleration in female trade union membership in Scotland came in two spurts. Firstly, during World War Two when circumstances forced extended trade union recognition upon employers. Secondly, from the mid-1960s to the early 1970s, coinciding with and fuelled by an intense phase of industrial militancy. By the late 1970s around 40 per cent of the female labour force in Scotland were unionised. This represented a slightly higher organised density than women in England, a situation explained largely by the fact that Scotland had. a smaller proportion of part-time workers within her economy.

11. The Steamie, Partick, 1955. Courtesy of the People's Palace, Glasgow. 12. Mrs Alf Daniels cleaning the kitchen range, Glasgow, 1955. Courtesy of the People's Palace, Glasgow.

The expansion in union membership meant that more Scottish women were subject to collective bargaining agreements which, in most cases, maintained higher wage levels and work conditions. Unionisation also meant that women could utilise their collective organisation to fight their case regarding unfair dismissal or for accident compensation, two issues which were rarely taken up on behalf of women by Scottish trade unions in the interwar years. Unions could also mediate, through collective bargaining and industrial action, the effects of work restructuring and technological change. Throughout the twentieth century there have been numerous examples of Scottish women — organised and unorganised — actively resisting exploitation in the workplace and challenging the unilateral control of management. Witness, for example, role Scottish women played during the General strike of 1926, the wartime equal pay strikes, the factory occupations by women at Plessey and Lee Jeans and the Women Against Pit Closures campaign.[40] Tighter labour markets and increased collective strength after World War Two undoubtedly raised confidence and encouraged such resistance.

However, it is important not to exaggerate the impact such developments had on the realities of working women's lives in Scotland. Times

Table 4. Female Trade Union Membership in Scotland

	Numbers	% age of total female labour force	% age of total STUC membership
1923–4	78,470	12.3	24.2
1931	48,125	7.2	19.7
1939	57,047	8.5	14.9
1945	136,879	20.5	22.3
1951	140,189	21.0	18.8
1961	155.000	21.8	20.0
1971–2	277,648	34.0	30.4
*1979	353,000	40.3	35.2

Source: STUC, Annual Reports; Census of Scotland; Department of Employment, Interim Report of the Standing Commission on the Scottish Economy (Feb 1988).

Note: *The 1979 figures are taken from E. Breitenbach, 'A Comparative Study of the Women's Trade Union Conference and the Scottish Women's Trade Union Conference', *Feminist Review*, Spring 1981, No. 7, pp. 69–70. Breitenbach calculated that the STUC statistics of 300,000 underrepresented female membership in Scotland by around 53,000 in 1979, or around 17 per cent. Because of the problems in distinguising specifically Scottish membership within British based unions these figures must be regarded as a rough guide to trends, rather than definitive statistics.

changed, the type of work performed altered and employment conditions have undoubtedly improved. However, discrimination and inequality based on gender at the point of production have remained remarkably persistent and have been transmitted by a kind of osmosis into the new 'white blouse' areas of female employment, as the debates around, and the passage of, the Equal Pay and Sex Discrimination legislation of the 1970s indicated. Moreover, the vacuous nature and ineffectiveness of such legislation have proved just how deep-rooted patriarchal values are within British society. Scottish women continued to be confined to less responsible, low status and low paid jobs within almost all sectors, as typists; word processors; secretaries; nurses; waitresses; cleaners; maids; hairdressers; knitters and sewers; charwomen; kitchen and canteen workers. Structural subordination of women in the workplace remained unyielding. The work of Catherine Hakim has shown just how deeply entrenched occupational sex segregation has been in England and Wales since 1945.[41] Stephen Kendrick has produced similar findings for Scotland (*See* Table 5).

What is perhaps the most striking feature of these data is the marginal degree of change over the twenty year period 1961–81, encapsulated in the persistent over-representation of women in the subordinate grade jobs — junior non-manual and personal service — and obdurate under-representation in the employing, managerial and professional categories.

Table 5. Scottish Workers by Socio-Economic Group, 1961 – 1981 (as a percentage of total workforce by gender)

Group	1961		1981	
	male	female	male	female
Employers	3.1	1.5	3.0	1.2
Managers & administrators	4.7	2.1	9.2	3.8
Self-employed professionals	1.0	0.1	1.3	0.2
Professional employees	2.3	0.6	5.3	1.9
Intermediate non-manual	3.5	10.7	7.0	16.6
Junior non-manual	12.3	38.7	10.4	38.2
Personal service	0.9	11.7	1.4	13.7
Foremen & supervisors (manual)	3.4	0.4	4.1	0.7
Skilled manual	36.2	9.4	30.6	4.3
Semi-skilled manual	12.8	14.6	12.3	8.6
Unskilled manual	8.8	7.3	5.9	8.9
Own account workers	2.0	1.2	3.4	1.1
Farmers – employers & managers	1.9	0.3	1.1	0.2
Farmers – own account	1.1	0.2	1.1	0.3
Agricultural workers	4.0	0.9	1.8	0.3
Armed forces	1.4	0.1	1.6	0.1
Total (thousands)	1504	712	1242	862

Source: S. Kendrick, Occupational Change in Modern Scotland, *Scottish Government Yearbook*, 1986, pp.246–7.
Note: 1981 figures are Kendrick's adjusted index, rather than the published statistics.

Numbers of women in the latter categories have, however, multiplied significantly over the course of the twentieth century. In teaching the marriage bar has been removed, whilst women have entered the law and medicine in increasing numbers. By 1981, 25 per cent of all female professionals in Scotland were doctors. In total, 70 per cent of all professionals in the education, welfare and health sector were women in 1981 and between 1961 and 1981 the number of female managers doubled. However, this was also a period of upward mobility for Scottish male workers. Fundamentally, the socio-economic status profiles of male and female workers registered little change between 1961 and 1981. In 1961, the seven higher status job categories accounted for 18.4 per cent of male and 6.2 per cent of the female labour force. By 1981, the figures were 27.4 and 9.1 per cent respectively. A mere 8 per cent of professionals in 1981 in science, engineering and technology in Scotland were women, leading Kendrick to conclude that: 'the most important aspect of occupational gender segregation is the relative exclusion of women from the professions as a whole'.[42]

Developments in the manual sector in Scotland post-1945 suggest a shift from skilled to unskilled work. The proportion of skilled female manual workers was almost halved between 1961 and 1981, whilst the number of women classified as unskilled manual rose. The dissemination of flow production, assembly line techniques of production and the growth of multinational companies in Scotland undoubtedly played a role here, as Watt has argued, whilst in the distribution sector, skill content of jobs has eroded with the advent of the giant store and self-service techniques. Whether one can reasonably extrapolate from such evidence to suggest a general deskilling dynamic, with reference to female work in Scotland throughout the course of the twentieth century, is, however, a much more contentious proposition. The main difficulty here lies in the impossibility of measuring changes in genuine skill content through the transition from manual to non-manual work. This

13. Helen Camley, domestic assistant, Stobhill Hospital, Glasgow, 1988. Courtesy of Springburn Museum Trust.

is not to deny, however, that women have remained confined towards the bottom end of skill, status and pay hierarchies within all sectors of the economy.[43]

The position of part-time female workers perhaps best reflects the continuing undervaluation and discrimination exercised against women in the post-war labour market in Scotland. In 1951, when 668,000 women and 1.5 million men were engaged in the Scottish economy, there were only 43,752 part-time workers recorded in Scotland, 93 per cent of whom were women. In 1976, there were 555,000 Scottish women working full-time and 306,000 part-time, whereas by 1985, 407,000 women in Scotland worked on a part-time basis (viz. under thirty hours per week) against 492,000 full-time. As the depression of the early 1980s deepened, full-time jobs for women and men contracted whilst part-time jobs — predominantly filled by female workers — proliferated. Such a strong association between female labour and part-time employment in Britain is almost unique in Europe. Motives for taking part-time work varied: poverty or inadequate family income were most important. Other women took such work for companionship, job satisfaction or because they were bored at home. For other Scottish women, the maintenance of rising living standards and satisfaction of growing expectations in an increasingly consumerist society were critical stimulants. To employers operating increasingly in more difficult economic circumstances, such labour was especially advantageous because part-timers provided flexibility at a low cost. Part-time workers remained, however, amongst the least organised and most exploited sections of the postwar Scottish labour force — low paid; low status; often working unsocial hours; with few of the employment rights enjoyed by full-timers. Married women found it more difficult to utilise their skills and qualifications fully when returning to the labour market, in a full or part-time capacity, after child rearing. Deskilling through the characteristically truncated female work cycle occurred, exacerbated by the fact that married women were more geographically immobile and hindered, as the WAC noted, by age discrimination. Moreover, the customary double burden of child care and household duties with paid work remained pervasive. Whilst British husbands in the 1970s and 1980s appear to have devoted more time to their children and performed some limited household chores — most notably washing-up and tidying — the evidence overwhelmingly indicates that despite the media hype about the existence of the 'new man', husbands have not significantly altered their role within the family and that the traditional sexual division of labour within the home has persisted. As

Shirley Dex noted: 'women have gone out to work despite the lack of adequate child care provision . . . and despite the lack of husband's participation in domestic work.'[44]

The ghettoisation of women to the bottom of the employment hierarchy and the proliferation of part-time employment from the 1950s limited the erosion of gender wage differentials, which remained virtually unaltered from the 1930s to the 1960s, and only markedly narrowed in the late 1960s and the 1970s. In 1981, women's average earnings in Scotland had reached 60–62 per cent of male average earnings, a somewhat wider gap than existed in England. This situation has continued to drive one parent families (around one in ten in Scotland) deeper into the poverty trap.[45] Equal pay has been difficult to achieve because of the persistence of sexual discrimination working at a number of levels, including skills acquisition. Sex-typing in education has eroded painfully slowly. Child care facilities remain inadequate. Incomes policies restraining wage rises militated against fundamental alteration of wage differentials. Employers have proved to be reluctant to promote women or to train women for skilled and responsible positions because of a traditional belief in the inferiority, lower efficiency and poorer commitment of female workers. The classic example would be teaching, a profession dominated by women, but with very few women in senior grades or headships. Many trade unions recognised in the 1970s that this was the crucial issue, not the principle of equal pay. 'Without equal opportunities, equal pay is only a partial success' commented the Scottish Schoolmasters Association. At the same conference the Association of Broadcasting Staff reported: 'Frankly, what concerns the ABS much more is the apparent discrimination against women in the filling of posts, particularly higher graded posts'.[46]

Gender discrimination continued to exist, however, at the very core of the organised labour movement in Scotland. In this respect, the Scottish trade unions simply reflected and accepted the dominant male chauvinism of a patriarchal capitalist society. Over seventy-three years, 1897–1970, only ten women compared to 166 men served on the Parliamentary Committee (later General Council) of the STUC and surprisingly the majority of these were clustered in the earlier rather than later part of this period. Sheila Lewenhak commented in 1973 that:

> the situation of women vis a vis the governing body of the Scottish Trade Union Congress has scarely altered since 1899 when both Margaret Irwin and Isabella Blacklock were members of the Parliamentary Committee and Miss Irwin was its Secretary.[47]

Evidence suggests that slowly changes were taking place, the movement was becoming less chauvinistic and that particularly in the 1970s and 1980s trade unions in Scotland became more sensitive to the needs and aspirations of the female segment of their membership. Arguably, this was partly in response to growing female membership of unions and the crisis many trade unions in Scotland suffered from the erosion of their traditional base as coal and heavy industry contracted. Perhaps most significantly, however, such changes were a consequence of the pressure and educative role of the revived civil rights and feminist movements. Many unions thus initiated positive action programmes to facilitate change, attempted to improve female representation, created Women's Committees and special conferences. Changes have been evident in recruitment policy, for example, with reduced subscription rates for part-time workers and maternity. Moreover, issues particularly pertinent to women workers have been increasingly taken up, such as child-care, sexual harrassment, employment rights of part-time workers, health issues, access to education, parental leave and equal pay. The Women's Committee of the STUC has also become more influential and, symbolic perhaps of the winds of change, the term 'advisory' has been dropped from its title.

Such changes have not, however fed through into any really fundamental alteration in female representation in decision-making structures within the unions at local, region, executive and leadership levels. In 1982, there was only one female member of the twenty-one strong

Table 6. Representation of Women Within a Sample of Unions in Scotland, 1985–6

Union	Total members	Female members	% age of women	Total FTO	Female FTO	
TGWU	132,564	30,416	23	54	3	(10)
GMB	115,941	44,750	39	29	3	(11)
AEU	95,000	15,000	16	19	0	(3)
NUPE	71,443	48,581	68	16	2	(11)
USDAW	45,396	29,103	64	20	1	(13)
EIS	45,559	29,150	64	14	3	(9)
COHSE	24,600	20,172	82	5	0	(4)
BIFU	22,000	11,500	52	4	1	(2)

Source: Sutherland and Strachan, in *Scottish Government Yearbook*, 1989, p. 234.
Note: FTO denotes full time officers. The numbers in brackets indicate the amount of female FTO posts which should exist in proportion to the number of women members.

STUC General Council and of 549 delegates to the STUC Congress, only thirty-nine were women.

Patriarchal values within the labour movement and the traditional view that trade unionism was a man's world proved extremely difficult to eradicate. In this sphere, as in so many others, recent years have witnessed long overdue and, on balance, only somewhat limited, marginal progress. As Rosalind Mitchison commented in 1935:

'It is perfectly possible to hear Scottish trade union leaders referring to the women they are supposed to represent as "bloody nuisances". The long-established unions have not much changed their view of society from the days when they killed the Women's Emancipation Bill in 1919 by insisting on the Restoration of Pre-war Practices Act. They still think that the status of labour as a whole is sustained by the protection of the position of the male workers, and these male workers are expected to earn enough to support their women folk.'[48]

IV

Women have always worked and work has always been a central feature of Scottish women's lives, more important, perhaps, than many commentators have given credit for. Valid generalisation is difficult, because work assumed a wide variety of forms and meant different things to different individuals, depending partly on social class, age, race and the region in which they resided. Dissecting the work experience suggests, however, that at certain levels quite marked change has occurred. The patterns of employment and the conditions and environment in which Scottish women toiled have been quite radically transformed through the course of the twentieth century. By the end of our period a significantly larger proportion of married women participated in the formal economy. Changes in the structure of the Scottish economy, technological and demographic factors have all played a role here. The traditional manual occupations, notably domestic service, textiles, clothing and agriculture, where 65 per cent of the Scottish female labour force were employed in 1901, had dwindled to insignificance by the 1980s. At this point female workers in Scotland were clustered predominantly in offices, shops, hospitals and schools. Paid work undertaken within the home declined in incidence, whilst smaller families and, to a lesser degree, the penetration of labour saving technology into the home have altered the nature of unpaid domestic work, reducing much of the physical drudgery and debilitating toil which previously characterised such tasks. Occupational segregation eroded somewhat, a process accelerated by the impact of two world wars. The locus of employment has altered, hours of work have been considerably reduced, working lives — within the formal economy at least — have been radically shortened and real wages for female labour in Scotland have substantially risen. State intervention extended significantly into new realms, attacking sexual discrimination, bolstering employment rights, eroding gender wage differentials and maintaining, at least until very recently, minimum wages. Trade unionism, which touched few women at the turn of the century, became an accepted part of the fabric of industrial relations, hence extending a broad, protective matrix and the benefits of collective bargaining across a much larger segment of the female labour force.

Women themselves, it should be stressed, played a pivotal part in this process of transition, through organisation, resistance to blatant exploitation and campaigning for change. The myth of female quiescence needs to be laid finally to rest. The attitudes and perceptions of British women towards work differed widely, as Zweig, Dex and others have shown, though the weight of evidence indicates that attitudes towards women working in the formal economy have become significantly more positive between the 1930s and the 1980s, amongst both women and men.[49] Oral evidence strongly suggests, moreover, that Scottish women gained self-respect, pride, identity, satisfaction and much enjoyment from the labour process and the cameraderie of the workplace. This was not, in other words, an entirely negative experience. Women have not had any lower commitment to work than men, just fewer advantages and less opportunities.

Women's lives were undoubtedly less constrained, less restricted by the 1980s compared to 1900. Nevertheless, despite notable change in many areas it remains the case that fundamental inequalities based on gender continued to persist within Scottish society, that gender discrimination in the labour market and the workplace proved impossible to eradicate throughout the course of the twentieth century. The structural subordination and vertical segregation of women in the workplace was transferred from one set of occupations (largely manual) to another (predominantly white-blouse). A marked sexual division of labour continued to persist both within the Scottish home and the formal economy, with women clustered into the lowest status, menial, poorest paid, part-time, undervalued and under-protected jobs. Change has been superficial, at the margin, rather than of any fundamental nature. Male workers continued to monopolise top jobs. Women continued to be perceived within an intensely patriarchal society as 'naturally' responsible for child rearing, housework and servicing a husband's needs, hence women's increased participation in part-time, rather than full-time employment. In this sense the Victorian concept of 'separate spheres' — discussed in detail by Eleanor Gordon in Volume Two of this series — remained pervasive and immune to any but marginal dilution.

Women's position within the labour market, moreover, has been very much at the whim of broader economic forces. The female 'reserve army of labour' was drawn into formal participation during wartime and buoyant conditions, and forcibly thrust out when circumstances altered. Evidence suggests that the 1980s recession witnessed the resuscitation of domestic ideology and more blatant discrimination as competition for jobs in an overstocked labour market intensified. This occurred within a decade when wage councils were abandoned, cuts in the public sector hit women more severely than men and when the penetration of the microchip further deskilled and fragmented work tasks and placed female labour in the clerical and distribution sector under threat. Women, in other words, proved to be more vulnerable than men to job loss. Wide differences in the economic activity rates of married women in different regions of Scotland suggests that there exists a very large pool of potentially active female workers awaiting the opportunity to enter the formal labour market.[50] There is every chance, it appears, that demographic changes working through the 1990s will provide such an opportunity.

In the final analysis, it is the continuities in the work experience of women in Scotland throughout the course of the twentieth century which are really striking — the lack of fundamental change. Women have been allowed to enter the formal economy, but only in a subordinate capacity, on terms dictated by men. Patriarchal values and sexual discrimination proved to be tenaciously persistent, too deeply ingrained within Scottish society to suffer serious erosion. Despite legislative change designed to remove gender inequalities, women remained critically disadvantaged in the labour market and the workplace. At least at one level, this represents a failure on the part of the organised labour movement in Scotland to break with its own patriarchal strategies, a tendency to accept rather than to challenge vigorously custom and traditional values and, at least until quite recently, a reluctance to take the offensive against this all-pervasive, ugly system of gender apartheid within Scottish society.

NOTES

I would like to thank Eleanor Gordon, Liz Tuach, Isobel Lindsay, Callum Brown and Jim Treble for reading and commenting on this chapter. Also thanks to Jayne Stevenson for providing access to the Stirling Women's History transcripts, to Ronnie MacDonald at the Scottish Trades Union Congress and Audrey Canning at the Willie Gallagher Library who provided invaluable help with sources and references.

1. S. Kendrick, 'Occupational Change in Modern Scotland', *Scottish Government Yearbook*, 1986, p. 251. See also R. Mitchison, 'The Hidden Labour Force: Women in the Scottish Economy Since 1945', in R. Saville (ed), *The Economic Development of Modern Scotland, 1950–1980* (Edinburgh, 1985), pp. 183–94.

2. For a general discussion see G. Anderson (ed), *The White Blouse Revolution: Female Office Workers Since 1870 (1988)*; L. Davidoff and B. Westover (eds), *Our Work, Our Lives, Our Words: Women's History and Women's Work* (1986).

3. S. Kendrick, 'Social Change in Scotland', in G. Brown and R. Cook (eds), *Scotland: The Real Divide* (1983), p. 52. According to other sources, female participation rates peak at 50 per cent in 1979 and fall through the 1980s. See the Standing Commission on the Scottish Economy, *Interim Report*, Feb. 1988, p. 18.

4. R. S. Cowan, 'A Case Study of Technological and Social Change: The Washing Machine and the Working Wife', in M. S. Hartmann and L. Banner, *Clio's Consciousness Raised* (New York, 1974). See also R. S. Cowan, *More Work For Mother* (1989). For a general discussion of the impact of household technology in Britain see C. Davidson, *A Woman's Work is Never Done: A History of Housework in the British Isles, 1650–1950* (1982).

5. G. Joseph, *Women at Work: The British Experience* (1983), pp. 163–4. Increasingly this pattern is becoming modified as more women choose to return to work between childbirths. See also S. Dex, *Women's Work Histories* (1984). For criticism of the under-representation of female employment in the census see S. Alexander, A. Davin, E. Hostettler, 'Labouring Women: A Reply to Eric Hobsbawm', *History Workshop*, 8, Autumn 1979; Using oral evidence, Elizabeth Roberts has estimated that 40 per cent of married women worked part-time in North-West England at some point in their married lives before 1939. See E. Roberts, *Women's Work, 1840–1940* (1988), p. 49; E. Roberts, *A Woman's Place: An Oral History of Working Class Women, 1890–1940* (1984).

6. I. Watt, 'Occupational Stratification and the Sexual Division of Labour: Scotland Since 1945', in T. Dickson (ed), *Capital and Class in Scotland* (1982), pp. 213–7.

7. E. Gordon, 'Women, Work and Collective Action: Dundee Jute Workers, 1870–1906', *Journal of Social History*, 21, 1987; B. Kay, 'They Fairly Mak Ye Work: Dundee and the Jute Industry', in B. Kay (ed), *Odyssey* (1980), pp. 36–45; W. Walker, *Juteopolis* (1979). For more detailed discussion of differences in regional economic activity rates in 1971 and 1981 see R. Mitchison, op. cit., pp. 190–3. Dundee continued to sustain one of the highest activity rates at 66–67 per cent, whilst the Highlands and Islands registered relatively low rates, at around 48 per cent.

8. G. Braybon and P. Summerfield, *Out of the Cage* (1987), p. 131.

9. J. D. Young, *Women and Popular Struggles* (1985), pp. 146–8; J. Melling, *Rent Strikes: People's Struggle for Housing in West Scotland, 1890–1916* (1983); J. Liddington, *The Long Road to Greenham: Feminism and Anti-Militarism in Britain Since 1820* (1989).

For the biographies of two Women's Peace Crusade activists — Helen Crawfurd and Agnes Doolan see W. Knox, *Scottish Labour Leaders, 1918–1939* (1984) pp. 81–6; 89–92.

10. Scottish Trades Union Congress, Annual Report (hereafter referred to as STUC, AR), 1919, pp. 83–6. See also STUC, AR, 1918, pp. 50–1; 1916, pp. 76–7.

11. STUC, AR, 1934, p. 72; see also STUC, AR, 1925, pp. 123–4. In Scotland, the number of male clerks and typists stagnated between the 1920s and 1950, whilst the number of female clerks and typists rose from 77,451 in 1931 to 138,699 in 1951. See G. Anderson, op. cit., p. 11.

12. M. Harrison, 'Domestic Service Between the Wars', *Oral History*, vol 16, No. 1, Spring 1988, pp. 48–54.

13. Stirling Women's Oral History Project (hereafter cited as Stirling WOHP), Transcript X3.1.

14. Jean Rennie, in J. Burnett (ed), *Useful Toil*, p. 237. For a discusson of working conditions in domestic service see T. McBride, *The Domestic Revolution* (1976); P. Taylor, 'Daughters and Mothers — Maids and Mistresses: Domestic Service Between the Wars' in T. Clarke, C. Critcher and R. Johnson (eds), *Working Class Culture* (1979); E. Higgs, 'Domestic Service and Household Production', in A. V. John (ed), *Unequal Opportunities* (1986).

15. Pentland and Calton Reminiscence Group, *Friday Night Was Brasso Night* (1987), pp. 19–20.

16. STUC, AR, 1938, pp. 84–7; STUC, AR, 1934, pp. 73–5; Annie Davidson, in J. McCrindle and S. Rowbotham (eds), *Dutiful Daughters* (1979), pp. 68–9;

17. *A Study of the Factors which have Operated in the Past and those which are Operating now to Determine the Distribution of Women in Industry*, Cmd. 3508, 1930, p. 30.

18. Stirling WOHP, Transcript A1. See also Transcripts H1, L1 and E1: Jayne Stephenson (ed), *Five Bob a Week: Stirling Women's Work 1900–1950*, p. 5. See also G. Hutchison and M. O'Neill, *The Springburn Experience: An Oral History of Work in a Railway Community* (1989), pp. 71–2.

19. *Redstage: Journal of the Workers' Theatre Movement*, Sept. 1932, p. 7. For a comment on such developments in Scottish textiles see A. Tuckett, *The Scottish Trades Union Congress: The First Eighty Years, 1897–1977* (1986), pp. 237–8.

20. J. D. Young, *Socialism and the English Working Class* (1989), p. 181; 183–4.

21. STUC, AR, 1931, pp. 69–71; STUC, AR, 1934, p. 73.

22. Pentland and Calton, op. cit., p. 16.

23. L. Jamieson, 'Limited Resources and Limiting Conventions: Working Class Mothers and Daughters in Urban Scotland c1890–1925' in J. Lewis (ed), *Labour and Love: Women's Experience of Home and Family, 1850–1940* (1986), p. 66.

24. Ibid., pp. 66–7; Stirling WOHP, Transcripts D2, P2.1, G1, B4, X3.1, L.1, V2.1.

25. H. Corr, 'The Schoolgirls Curriculum and the Ideology of the Home, 1870–1914' in Glasgow Women's Studies Group, *Uncharted Lives: Extracts From Scottish Women's Experiences, 1850–1982* (1983). See also H. Corr, 'An Exploration into Scottish Education' in W. Hamish Fraser and R. J. Morris (eds), *People and Society in Scotland, vol II, 1830–1914* (1990).

26. Stirling WOHP, Transcript G1.

27. Pentland and Calton, op. cit., p. 10.

28. STUC, AR, 1921, p. 98; STUC, AR, 1935, pp. 68–9; The Open Door International for the Economic Emancipation of the Woman Worker, *Report of Conference*, 25–9 July, 1938, p. 6.

29. A. Phillips and B. Taylor, 'Sex and Skill', *Feminist Review*, 6, 1980, p. 26. See also S. O. Rose, 'Gender at Work: Sex, Class and Industrial Capitalism', *History Workshop Journal*, 21, Spring 1986, pp. 120–22.

30. J. Norris, '"Well Fitted for Females". Women in the Macclesfield Silk Industry', in J. A. Jowitt and A. J. McIvor (eds), *Employers and Labour in the English Textile Industries, 1850–1939* (1988), pp. 187–202; H. A. Turner, *Trade Union Growth, Structure and Policy* (1962). See also D. Busfield, 'Skill and the Sexual Division of Labour' in Jowitt and McIvor, op. cit., pp. 153–70.

31. STUC, AR, 1935, p. 67; STUC, AR, 1931, p. 71; 1933, p. 70. For a discussion of the family wage in the Scottish context see E. Gordon, 'The Scottish Trade Union Movement, Class and Gender, 1850–1914', *Journal of the Scottish Labour History Society*, 23, 1988, pp. 32–4.

32. STUC, AR, 1931, p. 60. A detailed account of the work of the Women's Advisory Committee appears in the STUC, AR, 1949, pp. 81–86. See also A. Tuckett, op. cit., pp. 271–4. Bella Jobson, one of the foremost WAC activists, became president of the STUC in the late 1930s.

33. STUC, AR, 1925, pp. 131–2; 1928, pp. 75–7, 81–2. On the weakness of female trade unionism in Scotland see STUC, Minutes of the Organisation of Women Committee, 7 April 1930 and the STUC, AR, 1931, pp. 62–4.

34. S. Gillespie, *A Hundred Years of Progress, 1853–1952: The Scottish Typographical Association* (1953), pp. 199–207; A. Davidson, op. cit., pp. 68–9. For more detail see S. Reynolds, *Britannica's Typesetters* (1989).

35. STUC, AR, 1939, pp. 101–4; 1931, p. 61; 1932, p. 60; 1928, p. 84; Jane Lewis, 'In Search of Real Equality' in F. Gloversmith (ed), *Class, Culture and Social Change* (1980).

36. C. Brown and J. Stevenson, 'The View from the Workplace: Women's Memories of Work in Stirling, c1910–1950' in E. Gordon and E. Breitenbach (eds), *The World is Ill-Divided: Women's Work in Scotland in the Nineteenth and Early Twentieth Centuries* (forthcoming). See also S. Reynolds, op. cit. It is worth making the point, perhaps, that the workplace camaraderie noted by women interviewed in their 70s and 80s is likely to be exaggerated somewhat because of the isolation and increasingly housebound nature of old age. Oral history, as Angela John has noted in this context, can distort, as well as reflect reality. See A. John, 'Scratching the Surface: Women, Work and Coalmining in England and Wales', *Oral History*, vol 10, no. 2, Autumn 1982.

37. G. Hutchison and M. O'Neill, op. cit., p. 69.

38. R. Croucher, 'Women and Militancy in the Munitions Industries, 1935–45', *Bulletin of the Society for the Study of Labour History*, 38, Spring 1979, p. 8; R. Croucher, *Engineers At War, 1939–45* (1982), p. 285.

39. R. Arshad and M. McCrum, 'Black Woman, White Scotland', *Scottish Government Yearbook*, 1989, pp. 207–227; S. Pennington and B. Westover, *A Hidden Labour Force (1989), pp. 160–2*; E. Breitenbach, *Women Workers in Scotland* (1982), pp. 18–20.

40. Y. Strachan and L. Sutherland, 'Women in Trade Unions in Scotland', *Scottish Government Yearbook*, 1989, pp. 228–245. E. Breitenbach (1982), op. cit., pp. 30–31; Lothian Women's Support Group, *Women Living the Strike* (1986); D. Elson and R. Pearson (eds), *Women in Multinationals* (1987). For an example of organised response to work restructuring see STUC, Women's Advisory Committee Minutes, 7 Sept 1959.

41. C. Hakim, *Occupational Segregation* (1979).

42. S. Kendrick, *Scottish Government Yearbook*, 1986, op. cit., p. 249.

43. I. Watt, op. cit., pp. 213–219. For a general discussion of the deskilling hypothesis related to female workers see V. Beechey, 'The Sexual Division of Labour and the Labour Process: A Critical Assessment of Braverman', in S. Wood (ed), *The Degradation of Work?* (1982), pp. 54–73.

44. S. Dex, *Women's Attitudes Towards Work* (1988), p. 43. This section is based largely on F. Nelson, 'Part-Time Women Workers in Glasgow', in Glasgow Women's Studies Group, *Uncharted Lives*, op. cit., pp. 186–193. See also STUC, AR, 1966, p. 166; 1969, p. 212–3.

45. I. Watt, op. cit., pp. 227–8. See also E. Hunter, 'Women and Poverty' in G. Brown and R. Cook (eds), op. cit., 152–161 and J. Lewis and D. Piachaud, 'Women and Poverty in the Twentieth Century', in C. Glendinning and J. Millar (eds), *Women and Poverty in Britain* (1987).

46. STUC, Women's Advisory Committee Agenda and Report, 18 Nov. 1972.

47. S. Lewenhak, 'Women in the Leadership of the Scottish Trades Union Congress, 1897–1970', *Journal of the Scottish Labour History Society*, No. 7, 1973, pp. 3–23.

48. R. Mitchison, p. 187. For a full discussion of the changing nature of patriarchal relations at work see S. Walby, *Patriarchy at Work* (1986). Ester Breitenbach has suggested that the British TUC has been notably less chauvinist in its strategies than the Scottish TUC, arguing that 'the cultural traditions of Scotland reinforce male bias and sexism, and create more difficult conditions for women struggling for equality and liberation.' See E. Breitenbach, 'A Comparative Study of the Women's Trade Union Conference and the Scottish Women's Trade Union Conference', *Feminist Review*, no. 7, Spring 1981.

49. S. Dex, op. cit., pp. 30–32, 43–4. See also F. Zweig, *Women's Life and Labour* (1952).

50. See R. Mitchison, op. cit., pp. 189–94, for an attempt to calculate the dimensions of this 'hidden' labour force.

CHAPTER 6

Towards a Principled Society: Scottish Elites in the Twentieth Century

David McCrone

Like other advanced industrial countries, Scotland has undergone massive economic restructuring in the course of the 20th century. As a consequence, its class structure has become more complex and opaque, reflecting changes in the nature of occupations, and in forms of ownership and control of material assets. The purpose of this chapter is to chart how the character of Scotland's elites has changed under economic, political and social pressures. In particular, the chapter will argue that the elites have become more diverse, diffuse and defensive in the course of this century; that traditional forms of power based on land and local property have declined in favour of forms of ownership and control which are more impersonal, less concrete and more distant; that, nevertheless, Scottish 'civil society' has survived the centralising influences of both business and government to create a distinctive Scottish social and political agenda in the 1980s and 1990s; and that as Scotland approaches the 21st century, key groups in the Scottish class structure have dissented from the values of the Anglo-British state and of market liberalism to the extent that new political arrangements within the British state seem likely.

The key players in this drama are the gentry or landed aristocracy, the industrial and commercial bourgeoisie, the professional classes, the petite bourgeoisie, and the 'service class' — managers and administrators in both the public and private sectors. We will not treat these groups as a 'ruling class' because their material and cultural interests have usually been quite diverse and unintegrated. Their rulership has been partial rather than hegemonic, relating to special spheres of influence and power which have waxed and waned over the course of the century. Neither is it possible to chart their changing fortunes in a rigorous statistical way, because the available data are not precise enough, even in occupational terms, over the course of the century. Quite apart from the fundamental assumptions which have to be made about how social class is operationalised, there are considerable difficulties and risks in using what appear to be straightforward statistical data. The

Table 1: Classes of Occupations, 1901

		All	Males	Females
I	'professional class'	2.93%	4.10%	1.86%
II	'domestic class'	5.84	1.61	9.75
III	'commercial class'	7.13	13.38	1.35
IV	'agricultural &			
	fishing class'	6.88	11.87	2.27
V	'industrial class'	34.75	53.24	17.82
VI	'unoccupied &			
	non-productive'	42.47	16.00	66.95

Source: table IV, p.xxxiii, *Census of Scotland, 1901*, vol.III

problems of constructing, for example, time-series based on the Census showing shifts in occupations are considerable. It is not until 1961 that occupations are shaped into 'socio-economic groups' by the Registrar-General, and previous to that 'classes' refer to simple classifications of occupations. Similarly, even if we know how an occupational title was classified in, say 1921, we cannot assume that it has the same social meaning and economic rewards in 1981.

At the turn of the century, the Census of 1901 acknowledged six 'classes of occupations', which even in their crude state, showed up the class and gender inequalities of Edwardian Scotland. Clearly, we cannot use these classifications as representing 'social classes' in any sociological sense of the term, but they do give a clue as to how livings were made in early 20th century Scotland. And in this respect, Scotland was a highly developed society.

Class and Power In Twentieth-century Scotland

The turn of the century marked a new maturity in the Scottish economy, one which sought new commercial opportunities overseas and in England. At home, the Forth Bridge, completed in 1890, stood as a monument to technological progress and the industrial bourgeoisie which had made it, much as the Eiffel Tower, completed one year previously, did for its French equivalent. Overseas investment was also important. In 1900 it stood at £300m and by the outbreak of the Great War it had reached £500m. Scottish money found its way into Australia, Canada and New Zealand, into the rebuilding of Chicago, into American ranches and real estate. The jute masters of Dundee had helped to

create the investment trust as a vehicle for surplus profit, and lawyers
channelled small and large funds into overseas opportunities. None of
this was deemed unpatriotic, and as Lenman says[1]:

> It was a commonplace of late Victorian comment that Scotland invested abroad on
> a scale per head with no parallel among the other nations of the United Kingdom.

By the outbreak of the Great War, Scotland was firmly locked into the
international division of labour. It is commonplace to describe Scotland's
economy as 'over-specialised' at this time, too dependent on the staple
trades of textiles, coal mining, shipbuilding and heavy engineering. If
this were so, it was because Britain's industrial and trade structure itself
had adapted to international opportunities. The above trades accounted
for approximately 50 per cent of net industrial output and employed 25
per cent of the working population. Continental Europe remained a key
market for Scottish as for British goods; other important export markets
were to be found in the British Empire, South America and Asia[2]. In
this regard, Scottish entrepreneurs were no different from their British
counterparts. In Marquand's words[3]:

> British entrepreneurs failed to compete with the Germans and Americans in the
> new technologies of the late 19th and early 20th century because, in the short term,
> they could survive and prosper by selling more of their existing products in their
> traditional markets in Latin America and the Colonies. Meanwhile, capital which
> might have been invested in modernising British industry flowed abroad instead.

The Landed Gentry

While Scotland in 1900 continued to share in the prosperity of imperial
Britain, so also could its elites afford to assert their power and influence
in most spheres of Scottish life. At the top of the Scottish social hierarchy
in the early years of this century stood, in the Checklands' apposite
phrase[4], the 'mighty magnates' — men (rarely women) heading the great
houses of Buccleuch, Argyll, Bute, Atholl, Sutherland, who owned huge
tracts of the Scottish countryside (and not a little urban space as well).
This was a 'rentier' class which made its money from its substantial
stake in land, and which retained control over key social institutions.
As the *Scots Pictorial* of 1897[5] pointed out:

> The administration of nineteenth-century welfare in Scotland was dominated not by
> new forces, the new wealth, the industrial capitalist that ruthlessly exploited the
> natural and labour resources around them, but by an older set, one that looked back
> to an earlier, seemingly golden period. Scottish government meant the laird, who as
> was said by Skelton, sought the quietness of country life, but instead lamented the
> encroachment of Morningside suburbia. (*Scots Pictorial*, 1897, p. 434).

The gentry were marked off from the industrial and commercial bourgeoisie by their commitment to the country rather than the city. In cultural terms, too, they were distinct. These lairds and nobles had for long diluted their Scottishness by sending their sons to English Public Schools, a feature which marked them apart from the Scottish bourgeoisie which, by and large, spoke with Scottish accents and affected such manners and life styles as were compatible with their new-won wealth.

In religious terms too the classes were divided. Many of the gentry had retained a commitment to Episcopalianism, and a few, like the Marquess of Lothian, were Catholics. Many probably retained an attachment to the aristocratic ethos of the 'old society', and its social ideal of harmonious, organic values. Those who had access to the trappings of a more ancient Highland culture could play the clan chief, with its patina of tradition and romantic noblesse oblige. As late as the 1960s, for example, the Duchess of Erroll could write:

> In too many countries the great historic families are separated from the mass of the people, but in Scotland we have been fortunate in that pride of Name has never depended on wealth and rank, and in that the clan tradition has always prevented class barriers from arising to divide our proud nation . . . We are all one family of Scots, the branches of that family being the clans and Names, and the Chief of Chiefs our Queen.[6]

The possession of country estates, or access to those of friends or family, allowed the Scottish gentry to forge a distinctive life-style with its pastoral and sporting pursuits. Hunting and shooting were the pastimes of the great magnates like Buccleuch, the largest landowner in Britain, and Roxburghe, his near neighbour.

The Bourgeoisie

Alongside these landed families, stood the industrial and commercial bourgeoisie. The owners of both land and capital in Scotland were powerful and self-confident, and as a result, in the words of Sidney and Olive Checkland:

> Scotland became endowed with great commercial and industrial families, taking their place alongside the landed nobility, and to some extent linked together by marriage.[7]

It would be a mistake, however, to imply that the industrialists and the gentry were separate and competing elites, because the new commercial dynasties assimilated to the older landed ones, often by marriage. Some indication of this intercourse can be gauged from the patterns

14. Keeping the land, c. 1930. Scottish Ethnological Archive, National Museums of Scotland.

15. Gentlemanly pursuits. Scottish Ethnological Archive, National Museums of Scotland.

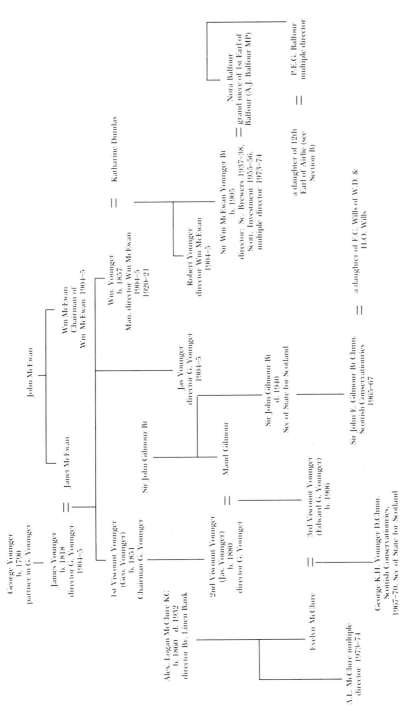

Figure 1. Intermarriage in Scottish industry and finance. The Younger and Balfour families.

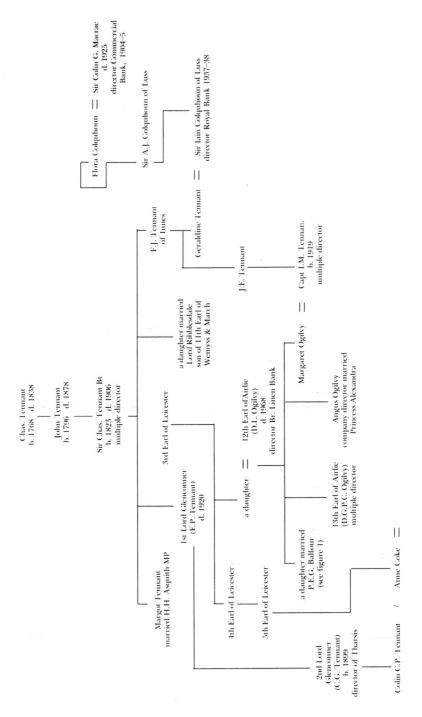

Figure 2. Intermarriage in Scottish industry and finance. The Tennant and Ogilvy families.

of intermarriage of the Younger and Balfour families, centred around brewing and banking, and for the Tennant and Ogilvy families which fused landed interests with new wealth extracted from chemicals[8]. (See Figures 1 and 2). This 'gentrification' of the Scottish elite is reflected in these dynastic trees, much along the lines described by the historians, Martin Wiener, and W. D. Rubinstein for the English elite[9].

The alliance was also political. The lords and lairds had provided leadership for the Conservative Party in Scotland, and indeed, helped to give it its somewhat reactionary image right down to the 1890s. In the intake of MPs following the 1895 election, nine 'Conservative' MPs were landowners, seven were businessmen and one came from the professions. This was in contrast to the Liberal-Unionists who had broken away from the Liberal Party over Irish Home Rule in the 1880s. Nine Liberal-Unionists were businessmen, two were professionals, and only three described themselves as landowners. Such was the power of this Unionism that it was, unlike the English case, able to absorb the ideologically weaker Conservatism. It drew its strength from the burgeoning, imperialist-inclined capitalist class concentrated in west-central Scotland. As Michael Fry[10] points out, 'It was Unionist because imperialist; it was imperialist because its prosperity was bound up with Empire.'

This Unionism was assertive and resilient, and carried all before it in the general election of 1990 making a clean sweep of Glasgow's seats, and although its fortunes ebbed in 1906 and 1910, it retained the capacity to mobilise its coalition of bourgeoisie and Protestant workers. As a result of this burgeoning power, Toryism, hitherto regarded, as Hutchison points out, as the creed of 'lairds and law agents'[11]. had to accommodate to this new Unionism. Gradually, Conservatism moved from its reactionary position in the 1890s to a degree of commitment to progressive reform. Above all, however, as the Checklands observe, the Liberal-Unionists acted as 'a bridge over which middle class man could pass from Liberalism to Toryism without suffering any sense of betrayal'[12].

The 'Calvinistic inheritance', as the Checklands put it, of Scottish capitalists generated an image of 'Presbyterian reserve' coupled with tightfistedness, sanctimoniousness 'and a liking for whisky'[13]. This new elite were not averse to criticising the landed interest for its inefficiency and laxity, such a critique drawing upon 'the harsh realism of political economy'[14]. The Checklands provide a neat summary:

> By 1900, Scotland had produced a breed of major industrialists whose actions and prestige dominated the economic scene. They included such names as Colville, Baird,

Yarrow, Tennant, Lorimer, Elder, Pearce, Neilson and Beardmore. These were the
magnates of shipbuilding, heavy engineering, iron and steel and coal. They were
autocrats, their decisions were made, conveyed and not discussed. They had a strong
desire to keep everything in their hands.[15]

The cousins and the brothers of these industrialists entered the
professions, to become the lawyers, doctors and churchmen of
Edwardian Scotland. Crucially, the professionals were Scottish, educated at fee-paying and Merchant Company schools in Edinburgh and
Glasgow, and at Scottish universities. Even a university like Aberdeen
which, at the turn of the century, prided itself on admitting large
numbers from its rural hinterland, found that:

the majority of those who went to the university from a parish school were not poor
boys but the sons of the rural middle class — of the minister, of the schoolmaster
himself, of farmers, often described as prosperous, although this category could cover
different levels of wealth.[16]

The traditional bourgeoisie, big as well as small, was nothing if not
Scottish. Since the Treaty of Union in 1707, it had dominated Scottish
civil society, its institutions and its mores. This was not some pliant
agent of southern power, but a class with its roots deep in Scottish
culture and tradition[17]. Not only did it speak with a Scottish accent,
it immersed itself in the folklore and literature of its native land. It
spoke the poetry of Burns, it knew (usually at second hand) the novels
of Scott, and it took pride in the folk memories of Wallace, Bruce and
the Covenant. Its Kirk had long seen itself as one of the few institutions
left to speak for Scotland, although its capacity to do so had been fatally
weakened in the Disruption of 1843. It celebrated its distinctive values
of thrift, hard work and personal achievement. 'Getting on' was an
unspoken but vital aim in life, and a moral duty.

It cultivated its own myths to powerful effect. None was more
significant than the 'lad o' pairts' — that mythical male figure who had
the brains but not the material means to 'get on' through education[18].
In the late 19th century, a new strain of literature emerged in lowland
Scotland — the Kailyard — which celebrated the way of life associated
with this mythical figure. Scotland, self-evidently, was an egalitarian
country — at least compared with England. Here, so it was said, if you
have the brains and work hard, then there is little you cannot achieve.

Such a set of expectations was encouraged by Presbyterianism itself.
Did it not celebrate the 'democracy of the elect'? Was it not based on
an ideology of individualism — the soul standing unadorned before
God? The Kirk had established a system of parish schools after the

Reformation which generated a degree of literacy, albeit limited, which stood Scotland in good stead when it came to providing a literate, and compliant, labour force. At heart, this 'egalitarianism' indicated an equality of the elect (the Godless, and the Catholic were not included), in a spiritual as well as a material manner, a religious and moral equality borne of a commitment to the Kirk, and, naturally enough, to Godliness. The locus of this egalitarianism was the 'parish', religious as well as secular, usually in the small town or village community.

Now this egalitarianism did not imply equality. As Allan MacLaren has pointed out:

> The egalitarianism so often portrayed is not that emerging from an economic, social or even political equality; it is equality of **opportunity** which is exemplified. All men are not equal. What is implied is that all men are given an opportunity to be equal. Whatever the values attached to such a belief, if expressed today, it would be termed elitist not egalitarian.[19]

In these respects, egalitarianism was a key element in a conservative ideology which congratulated itself on the openness of Scottish society and its social institutions. In more recent times, such a set of values was pressed into the service of the campaign in the 1960s to defend local authority fee-paying schools. Only these, it was argued, would give the 'lad o'pairts' the educational and social opportunity to 'get on'. This, manifestly, was a far cry from the notion of socialist equality. Ultimately, this set of values was celebratory rather than analytical. It was enough to claim it as a feature of traditional Scotland. This inherent egalitarianism overrode social distinctions, by arguing that these did not matter; rather than that they should be swept away. MacLaren again:

> It is important to remember that the belief in a specific Scottish egalitarianism never implied that Scotland was in any sense a classless society. It held that the social gap between classes was never important, and through societal encouragement and institutional means the 'lad o' pairts' with ability and resolution could easily effect a crossing.[20]

Such an ideology of social opportunity helped to unite the Scottish middle class, its haute bourgeoisie with its reliance on substantial capital, its professions with their hold on credentials allowing them to dominate much of Scottish life, and at the margins of this class, the petite bourgeoisie whose hold on middle class status was so much more fragile.

The Petite Bourgeoisie

Much as in the rest of Britain, Scotland's small business class owed their position to the ownership of petty property, small parcels of houses, flats and shops[21]. Out of these a modest living could be had as long as economic and political conditions remained stable. In the late 19th and early 20th centuries, the petite bourgeoisie came to dominate much of the economy and polity of Scotland's towns and cities. In late 19th Edinburgh, for example, the lawyers and professional men withdrew from local political affairs, leaving the Town Council to be run by small landlords and shopkeepers. The kind of politics they indulged in were largely negative and defensive. Because local revenues were raised by property taxes — 'the rates' — many small property owners got themselves elected to the local council in order to control the level of public spending. Landlordism provided for many a modest means of livelihood, particularly as some insurance against business failure and to provide for women and children should they outlive the owner himself. These petty property owners were classical 'rentiers', depending on letting out a few modest flats to working class tenants. Often they themselves lived close by, in 'superior' tenements built to a higher standard than those they let out, or in villas in the growing suburbs of the cities.

In both political as well as geographical terms, the small business stratum had limited horizons. Rarely did they own property outwith their communities, seeing it as 'stone and lime, something we can go and see'. Above all, they dominated town politics for much of the 20th century. By the 1920s, the challenge from Labour persuaded them out of their 'Independent' labels and into loose coalitions variously described as 'Progressive' (in Edinburgh, Aberdeen, and Dundee) and 'Moderate' in Glasgow. Claiming that 'politics had nothing to do with local government', that local men were the best guardians of the public purse, they maintained their hold on politics until the 1930s (in Glasgow), until the 1950s in Aberdeen and Dundee, and in Edinburgh, right down until the 1970s. If bigger capital and the professions were content to let small capitalists run the towns and cities, they did so as long as no serious challenge came from Labour.

Elsewhere, in the countryside, the lairds kept a firm grasp of local politics until the reorganisation of local government in 1974[22]. The Duke of Buccleuch and the Duke of Roxburghe between them held the convenorship of Roxburgh County Council for 43 years between 1900 and 1975. The great Border landowners were able to exercise influence directly in this way, but also indirectly through the offices of Sheriff Depute, and Commissioners of Supply. They were, in addition, Lord-Lieutenants of the counties, and Commissioners of Peace. In 1918, the convener of Roxburgh County Council was the Duke of Roxburghe; his vice-convener was the Duke of Buccleuch; and Lord Ellesmere was a fellow council member. In 1975, before the County Council was abolished, the convener was the Duke of Roxburghe; the Duke of Buccleuch and Baroness Elliot were also on the council. Nothing much had apparently changed.

For much of the century, the traditional elites of Scotland continued to dominate the economic, social and political life of the country. Only the small business stratum was marginalised as the state, following the social unrest in 1915, placed restrictions on the rent levels of 'small dwelling houses' or tenement flats. The divide between this stratum and the skilled artisans had always been a weak one, and after this defeat, the petite bourgeoisie became steadily detached from its more secure bourgeois neighbours.

At its upper reaches, the industrial and commercial bourgeoisie merged into the ranks of the gentry, marrying into their families, and purchasing landed estates on the fringes of Glasgow and Edinburgh. Those who remained in the cities symbolised in stone their superior status. As Smout has put it:

> Their finest monuments were their own homes — the sweeping terraces of Glasgow's West End, with gleaming stained glass and art nouveau decoration, and the stolid villas, with their ample gardens of lilac and laburnum, in Edinburgh's southern suburbs.[23]

In cultural terms, the gentry and the bourgeoisie were divided by education and patterns of speech. While the former finished its education at English public schools and at Oxbridge, the bourgeoisie and the professions remained culturally Scottish in speech, education and temperament. They were Presbyterian by religion and individualistic by inclination. In their heyday before the Great War, they maintained a firm hold over their fellow-countrymen and women. In Lenman's words:

> The main achievement of the great self-confident Victorian bourgeoisie which dominated Scotland before 1914 was to maintain their own ascendancy within a society which tolerated, nay, positively encouraged enormous inequalities of income, without provoking any serious challenge to their position.[24]

What went wrong?

The Changing Structure of Scottish Business

The first, and perhaps most important, reason is that Scottish capitalism altered significantly. In a remarkable but neglected piece of research,

16. Liberating the small man: the role of the car. Scottish Ethnological Archive, National Museums of Scotland.

17. Respectable streets, c. 1900. Scottish Ethnological Archive, National Museums of Scotland.

John Scott and Michael Hughes produced an 'Anatomy of Scottish Capital'[25] for specific time-points: 1904/5, 1920/1, 1937/8, 1955/6, and 1973/4. They chart the radical transformations in Scottish business this century — from a self-confident, locally controlled economy, to a weakened, externally dependent one. The structure of business in 1904/5, for example, reveals the importance of the railway companies, and their inter-connections with coal, steel and engineering.

Regional clusters were important, no more so than in Dundee where the jute barons of Cox, Baxter and the Flemings held sway. Similarly, there appeared to be a clear distinction between Edinburgh clusters — centred on the banks and the North British railway — and the Glasgow segment, focused on Tennants' companies, the Caledonian railway, and the Clydesdale bank. Central to the business inter-connections were the banks and the financial system generally, a system in which the landed gentry played a leading part. The Marquess of Linlithgow, for example, was a director of the Bank of Scotland, and Standard Life; The Duke of Buccleuch, of the Royal Bank, Standard Life, and Scottish Equitable; The Earl of Mansfield, of the National Bank, and Scottish Equitable; and The Marquess of Tweeddale, of the Commercial Bank, Edinburgh Life, and Scottish Widows.

This complex web of interlocking ownerships and directorates within Scottish dynasties helped the Scottish economy to remain fairly independent from England, although the take-over of indigenous companies by those from the south had been noticeable as early as 1900. That Scottish business by the outbreak of war in 1914 still bore the signs of its origins as family concerns was both its strength and weakness. There had been few attempts at financial or technical reorganisation on the lines of American or German business, and little signs of a managerial revolution in this period. The capacity of Scottish business leaders to wield personal control and autocracy did not bode well for the future. Following the Great War, the expansion of the Scottish banks and the development of insurance companies led not only to a more interlocked system, but one in which Scottish capital had less autonomy. Family control remained relatively strong, despite the fact that more resources and power had flowed outwith Scotland in the inter-war period, a feature which was to become even more marked after the Second World War.

Just as Scotland had benefited from being part of 'the world island' — 'the centre of an informal network of trading relationships and capital movements, of which her formal empire was merely a part'[26], so it suffered from general British decline. Marquand comments:

> What is special about Britain . . . is not that she abandoned market-led adjustment.
> It is that, after abandoning it, she failed to become a developmental state on the
> pattern of her more successful competitors on the European mainland and in the
> Far East.[27]

While Scotland, as part of this unitary British state, could not escape
its downturn, moves were afoot in the 1930s to restructure its economy,
moves which were not to come to fruition until after 1945 when economic
diversification became even more necessary. In the inter-war period,
the regrouping of the civil service, the designation of Scotland as
a separate area for industrial development, and the creation of the
Scottish Economic Committee seemed to indicate the makings of a
corporate state. Foster and Woolfson comment:

> State planning was now presented as a key vehicle for the fulfilment of national
> development. The character of the planning was statist, corporativist (sic) and
> paternalist, owing at least something to the Presbyterian heritage of previous
> centuries.[28]

Foster and Woolfson point out that the eclipse of the old-style Tories in
1940 ushered in new corporatist initiatives, and as a result 'the wedding
of pre-war directive statism with the mixed economy concepts of Keynes,
left a lasting legacy within the Scottish establishment'[29]. While the old
dynastic families retained their hold on traditional industry, foreign and
English capital began to play a much greater role in Scottish economic
affairs. Scotland's earlier prosperity had reflected its rapid adaptation to
the market opportunities of Empire, a pattern which was to prove very
difficult to break in the 20th century. If the fortunes of the Colvilles,
the Tennants, the Beardmores and others like them had rested upon the
earlier opportunities of steel, coal, and engineering, then the cold winds
of economic change in the 1920s and 1930s left the social and political
order which they had built up cruelly exposed. The Second World War
had given a belated boost to those Unionist interests which remained
on condition they accepted an extension of state power. Nevertheless,
demise was not far off, and as Fry has put it, post-war saw the 'decline
of the Scottish capitalist class, from the self-made local businessmen, to
the dynasties of the Clyde'[30].

What had happened to the structure of Scottish business in this
period? The dominant force in Scottish heavy industry in the 1930s,
the Colville/Lithgow/Nimmo complex based on coal, iron and steel
had disappeared with nationalisation, and the links between financial
companies became a more pronounced part of business network which,
according to Scott and Hughes:

was a mixture of family firms and firms controlled by financial interests. It was the financiers and members of the dominant families who welded these companies together into a densely connected system in which, nevertheless, certain spheres of influence could be identified.[31]

By the mid 1950s, there was still little evidence of a 'managerial revolution', although new family dynasties were created which shared control with older interests. The late 1960s, however, 'seem to mark a period in which Scottish capital, the traditionally dominant dynastic families, were encountering a major crisis of confidence and direction'[32]. By the 1970s, while companies subject to family control had a predominantly Scottish character, those companies — growing in importance — which were controlled by corporate interests had much lower levels of Scottish participation. The network of Scottish business interests was increasingly held together by the three banks, the Bank of Scotland, the Royal Bank of Scotland, and the Clydesdale Bank, each with their own clusters of related companies and spheres of influence. In spite of the fact that Scottish companies formed less and less of a distinct and autonomous entity in the face of external takeovers and amalgamations, 'family control remained a potent element in Scottish capital'. 'The major characteristic of the period studied [1904/5 to 1973/4]', they conclude, 'has not been a managerial revolution, but a managerial reorganisation of the propertied class'[33]. Hence, there emerged a small corps of multiple directors who manage the business system as a whole in Scotland. The same names, said one critic, crop up again and again. In the summer of 1989, the Secretary of State for Defence in the Conservative Government, George Younger, announced that he was resigning from politics to take up a directorship with the Royal Bank of Scotland. His family name is indeed one of those which 'crops up again and again' in the upper echelons of Scottish business.

The surviving importance of kinship in Scottish business has to be set alongside the growing significance of foreign and English capital in Scottish business. Scottish dynasties may continue to wield influence but in a diminishing sector of Scottish business. The problems of rapid industrial decline in the last fifty years forced the state, both national and local, to play a more active role in diversifying the Scottish economy. Hence, government induced merchant capital to fund the building of a steel strip mill at Ravenscraig in the late 1950s, the Rootes Car Company to relocate at Linwood, and new timber and aluminium plants to be set up at Fort William and Invergordon. The influx of foreign-owned plants began to generate concern over Scotland becoming a 'branch-plant economy'[34]. Since the mid 1980s, the following major Scottish companies have been subject to takeover: Distillers (by Guinness), Coats Paton (by Viyella), House of Fraser, Yarrow (Trafalgar House), Bell's (by Guinness). Further unsuccessful raids were carried out on the Royal Bank of Scotland (by Standard Chartered Bank) and on Scottish and Newcastle Brewers (by Elders of Australia).

Creating a Scottish Agenda

What are the implications of these major transformations in Scottish business for the structuring of power and control in Scottish society? First, it is plain that an indigenous business elite continues to exist around the financial sector, although in recent years it has found its control of these key institutions under attack. Second, the state at different levels has played a significant role in economic affairs, and state officials are a larger and more important part of Scotland's bourgeoisie. Third, the phenomenon of the 'branch plant economy' has reduced the number of native capitalists and swollen the number of officials and managers in key sectors. Fourth, Scotland is more of a 'corporate society' given the role of what the late John P. Mackintosh described as the 'non-democratic elite' — bureaucrats, businessmen, politicians — who have, in the absence of devolved political power, had the task of 'modernising' Scotland's economy. The structure of economic power in Scotland, then, is a curious amalgam of old and new wealth, the individual and the corporate, the indigenous and the foreign, the private and the public. One journalist was drawn to comment in the late 1970s that Scotland's elites 'all know each other — a tight circle of politicians, businessmen, civil servants, lawyers, trade unionists, churchmen, academics, and a nostalgic sprinkling of titled gentry. They fix the nation's agenda'[35].

At a more academic level, research by Moore and Booth[36] suggests that, while in strict terms Scotland cannot be called a 'corporatist state', if only because it is not a separate political system, it does contain a 'pattern of policy networks' in which the values and culture of decision-making elites sustain a distinctive set of institutions and relationships which influence bargaining and policy outcomes. Scotland, say Moore and Booth, is a 'close-knit community where a high level of individual contact is possible'[37]. Central to this policy network are bodies such as the CBI in Scotland, the STUC, the Scottish Council (Development & Industry), and the Scottish Development Agency. They argue that Scotland represents a 'negotiated order' operating somewhere between corporatism and free-market pluralism, that the 'Scottish policy community' mediated through the Scottish Office represents a 'meso-level of the British state'[38].

In this context, we can begin to see the underlying political and economic reasons for the divergence between the Scottish and English political agendas which has been so striking in the 1980s. To employ Marquand's thesis again, Britain's adjustment problems have as much to do with politics as with economics, notably the intellectual and moral vacuum at the heart of the political economy. The emergence of a distinctive political economic agenda in Scotland over the past 30 years seems in large part to reflect the fact that Scotland has moved significantly towards such economic developmentalism. The curious character of the British state adds to this growing divergence. In Marquand's (anglocentric) words:

> We cannot speak of a 'British state' in the way that one speaks of a 'French state' or, in modern times, of a 'German state'. The UK is not a state in the Continental sense. It is a bundle of lands . . . acquired at different times by the English crown [sic], and governed in different ways. Its inhabitants are not citizens of a state, with defined rights of citizenship. They are subjects of a monarch, enjoying 'liberties' which their ancestors won from previous monarchs.[39]

If large numbers of Scottish 'subjects' of the 'English crown' express a desire to become citizens of their own state, then we should not be at all surprised, particularly as the economic agendas and sets of moral principles which underlie them have diverged in recent years.

The Changing Class Structure

These shifting agendas are underpinned by the changing profile of the class structure in Scotland. Here we are dependent upon census data, which carry risks as well as opportunities. Be that as it may, we are indebted to the researchers who carried out the Scottish Mobility Study in the 1970s for reclassifying occupational titles between 1921 to 1971 to provide a valid time series (see Table 2)[40].

These series show a continuing decline in the proportion of skilled manual workers in the labour force, and second, a continuous rise in non-manual employment. The major proportional increases over this fifty year period are among professional employees, intermediate non-manual workers (occupations ancillary to professions), and junior non-manual workers (eg clerical, sales). The major decreases are to be found among skilled and semi-skilled manual workers. In general terms, the percentage of manual workers (categories 9, 10 & 11) has fallen from 62.4 per cent in 1921 to 51.1 in 1971.

*Table 2. Socio-Economic Groups 1 to 12 (Non-Farm, Non-Armed Forces) as
a Percentage of Total in SEGs 1 to 12, 1921–1971*

Socio-Economic Groups	1921	1931	1951	1961	1971
1 & 2 Employers & Managers	6.1%	5.6	6.2	6.8	8.0
3 Professional self-employed	0.6	0.4	0.4	0.7	0.7
4. Professional employees	1.3	1.1	1.6	1.8	2.8
5. Intermediate non-manual	3.1	3.1	4.4	6.1	8.2
6. Junior non-manual	14.7	15.9	19.5	21.9	21.6
7. Personal service	7.7	8.9	5.7	4.7	5.7
8. Foremen & Supervisors	1.4	1.5	1.9	2.5	2.6
9. Skilled manual	35.3	31.3	29.0	28.2	24.3
10. Semi-skilled manual	15.4	14.1	14.9	15.8	13.9
11. Unskilled manual	10.3	13.9	13.8	9.6	10.3
12. Own account workers	3.9	4.2	2.5	1.9	2.0

Major revisions of occupational categories make it very difficult to
compare 1981 data with the above, but the general distributions are
similar[41]. For the purposes of this paper, the categories have been
grouped together (see Table 3).

In general terms, between 1961 and 1981, there have been major
proportional increases among managers and administrators, professional
employees, and intermediate non-manual workers. On the other hand,
the biggest proportional fall has occurred among skilled manual workers.
There are, of course, major gender differences in employment patterns.
Whereas skilled and semi-skilled manual occupations account for 43
per cent of men's employment, most women are to be found in junior

Table 3. Social Class in Modern Scotland, 1981

'Propertied' Class (employers, self-employed professionals, farmers, own account workers)	6.5%
'Service' Class (1) upper (managers & administrators, professional employees, intermediate non-manual)	21.9%
'Service' Class (2) lower (junior non-manual, personal service)	27.3%
Manual 'Working Class' (foremen & supervisors, skilled, semi-skilled, unskilled, & agricultural workers)	42.4%
Other	1.7%

(*Source:* adapted from Census 1981, Scotland, Economic Activity (10% sample) Table 18b)

non-manual jobs (38.2 per cent), followed by intermediate non-manual (16.6 per cent) and personal service work (13.7 per cent)[42].

What evidence is there that Scotland's historical trajectory has affected the distribution of its occupations? Traditionally, Scotland has had more manual workers than the UK as a whole, and fewer non-manual workers. Scotland shows a shortfall among non-manual workers compared with England and Wales, but this is almost all accounted for by the shortfall of managers and administrators in the private sector, suggesting that Scotland's status as a 'branch-plant' economy has eroded the apparatus of decision-making within its boundaries. Similarly, there is a proportional shortfall in own-account workers in Scotland — broadly speaking, the self-employed. Scotland's dependence on the state since the 1960s shows up insofar as the rapid expansion of the state service sector almost wholly explains the increase in intermediate non-manual workers. Thus the expansion in employment in the state sector virtually accounts for the boom among non-manual employment right up until the 1980s.

We can conclude, therefore, that Scotland's recent economic history has given a peculiar profile to its occupational structure, even although the broad trends — the decline in the proportion of manual workers, and the increase in non-manual — reflect those of the UK as a whole (and, of course, other advanced industrial countries). The broad shaping of its occupational structure reveals that there are now more workers in the 'service class' than in the manual working class, for the first time in Scotland's history. However, as the percentage of people doing non-manual work has grown, so it is likely that Scotland's 'middle class' (however we choose to define it) has grown too, and in the process has become more fragmentary and diverse.

Social Mobility in Scotland

Such a conclusion is reinforced by findings from studies of intergenerational social mobility carried out in the mid 1970s[43]. Looking at the extent to which sons ended up in occupational categories similar to their fathers (ignoring women has been one of the key problems in these studies), researchers concluded that while there was a high degree of self-recruitment (sons ending up in the same category) among manual workers as well as among the higher social groups, there was considerable upward mobility from below into the top echelons of society. Hence, fully one third of respondents in Class 1 (professionals, managers, administrators) had, by the 1970s, come from manual working class backgrounds. These data for Scotland mirrored those for the UK as a whole, with the exception that the sons of small proprietors (mainly small farmers and crofters) were less likely to upwardly mobile than those in England. Although the Scottish and English researchers chose to use slightly different occupational classifications, the results of both studies are remarkably similar.

Such has been the rate of occupational and social change in Britain, especially since the war, that social classes are fluid and open insofar as, in the words of Payne 'at all levels a majority of sons enter other classes, and in all classes, the incomers outnumber those whose fathers were in the same class'[44]. The implication of these findings for this chapter is far-reaching, namely, that Scotland's middle classes have not only grown in size, but have become much more diverse in terms of social origins, and hence life styles, social values and even political attitudes. Far less than before are we able to read off the politics of class interests from occupational position. Compared with the turn of the century when it was possible to identify a fairly self-contained professional class, a class of bourgeois owners of capital, together with a miniscule but powerful landed aristocracy, as Scotland's 'ruling class', in the late 20th century, such an exercise becomes much more difficult. While we cannot deny that there are significant and self-contained centres of power in Scotland, it seems the case that the operations of this power has become much more opaque, and that forms of ownership and control have become more impersonal, distant and less concrete.

Towards a 'Principled Society'

At this stage we can gather together some of the strands which are woven into Scotland's class structure, and see how they sustain the argument that in terms of its moral economy, Scotland is, (to borrow Marquand's phrase) a 'principled society'. Thus, we might argue that Scotland's traditional upper class — its aristocracy and gentry — while educated at English public schools, retain a degree of commitment to 'Scottish' values if only because they have taken on the patina of their historic culture. Further, we might surmise that they retain a commitment to the aristocratic ethos of the 'old society', and its ideal of harmonious, organic values. Secondly, the most likely social carriers of neo-liberal, free-market values — the indigenous bourgeoisie — were not only caught up in neo-corporatist activity from the 1930s, but they were also the class which has suffered most from the process of economic restructuring which has occurred since 1945.

Scotland's professional classes — lawyers, doctors, teachers, churchmen — while socially conservative, embody the survival of a distinctive Scottish 'civil society', and can be considered as keepers of native institutions, and hence incipient 'nationalists', resistant to further anglicisation. The 'service class', in broad terms, the managers and administrators especially those working in public institutions, who operate within a managerial ethos, are likely to be supportive of a proto-corporatist, interventionist political economy.

At the same time, Scotland's working class is thirled to a 'labourist' tradition, at least since the 1930s, which places high value on corporatist activities in its quest for economic prosperity. The close links between organised labour and a Scottish economic agenda which encompasses collectivist or community values have a long pedigree north of the border[45].

Political change

These shifts in the social agenda were both mirrored in, and reinforced by, political changes. The electoral rise of the Labour Party, the extension of the franchise, and the granting of Home Rule to Ireland in 1922 allowed the bulk of the Scottish Catholic working class to support Labour. Partly as a response, the middle class vote swung increasingly behind the Conservatives. By the 1920s, the Conservatives and their allies had overtaken the Liberals in Scotland, and while they never managed to perform as well as their counterparts in England, they were, until the mid 1950s, the most successful party in Scotland in electoral terms. It is clear that as late as the 1960s part of the Conservative's strength in Scotland lay in its appeal to section of the Protestant working class through the complex associations of Protestantism, Orangeism, Unionism, and British patriotism[46]. Such a complex required the leadership of a self-confident, indigenous bourgeoisie able to mobilise electoral support for the Right on the basis of Protestant patriotism.

Throughout the inter-war period, militant Protestantism had been a feature of municipal politics in Scotland, notably in Edinburgh where Protestant Action operated an informal electoral pact with the right-wing Progressive Association[47]. In Glasgow, there is irony in the fact that the intervention of the Scottish Protestant League in 1933 gave Labour control of the city for the first time.

What is particularly noticeable about the Progressives and Moderates who fought the right-wing cause at the local level was that their principal appeal was to the petit bourgeois, the small, local businessmen who believed in what they saw as a-political administration by knowledgeable

— essentially local — people. By 1935, in Edinburgh the Progressives had incorporated virtually all the anti-socialist forces, and Conservatism had disappeared[48]. In the city, the tighter organisation of those committed to 'non-partisan' and strictly 'local' politics had the effect of squeezing the Tories out of the council, and as the Progressive Party grew in strength, so it became more thoroughly petit bourgeois in character. Above all, small capital was mobilised over taxation on rented housing which, until the 1950s, was largely provided by this stratum. Theirs was a defensive politics, geared to restricting rates increases which fell overwhelmingly on these men and women of property.

This was not the first time that small property interests had come into conflict with the bigger bourgeois[49]. The sequence of rents strikes and industrial militancy before, during and after the First World War, especially but not exclusively in the West of Scotland, had faced the government of the day with a dilemma, which they resolved by imposing rent restrictions on urban landlords who were overwhelmingly drawn from the ranks of the petit bourgeois. Largely at the instigation of bigger, industrial capital, the government was able to detach unrest over rents from issues of pay and conditions, leaving a sense of betrayal among small house-capitalists. The rise of these 'non-political' groupings like the Progressives and Moderates at the expense of Conservatives in the 1920s and 1930s was much easier to achieve as a result.

By the 1970s, a bitter struggle had broken out between the defenders of the ideology of 'economy', 'localism' and 'non-partisanship' — the Progressives — and a new group of aggressive, young politicians who saw the necessity of making local government more 'professional', more sophisticated, and who insisted that a specifically Conservative Party was required in City Chambers. Ultimately, the latter group won out, not least because at a national level the Conservative Party came to see that it needed a presence in the council chambers, and not simply every four or five years at national elections. Nevertheless, this split in municipal politics which stretched back to the early years of this century reflects one potential weakness of Conservative politics in Scotland, namely, a division within the ranks of capital itself.

In the post-war period, as the indigenous leaders of Scottish capital — the local businessmen and the great Clydeside dynasties — found their influence slipping away, leadership of the Unionist Party fell once more into the hands of the 'lairds and law agents' as it had in the 19th century, and the party began to select MPs from among the anglicised upper class equipped with Public School English manners[50]. Partly as a result, but also because of wider secular changes, Protestant working class support ebbed away, and by 1964 the 'Unionist' label was dropped in favour of the 'Conservative' one. The native social base of Scottish Unionism collapsed, derived as it had been from local industrial and business interests allied to Protestant working class support. This peculiar form of Scottish identity centred on religion and patriotism was relegated to history.

By the 1970s, wider changes were sweeping through Scottish society and politics. Rapid rates of social change, coupled with increased social and geographical mobility, were detaching many people, especially the young, from their traditional allegiances. The Scottish National Party became one of the main beneficiaries of this change, and successfully appealed to the young and to all social classes[51]. At the high point of its electoral success in 1974, the SNP was able to capture substantial sections of non-manual workers, above all the young, and those who had become upwardly socially mobile across the manual/non-manual divide. It did especially well among intermediate non-manual workers (teachers, for example) in the October 1974 election, and while its electoral fortunes fluctuated thereafter, the capacity of the SNP to destabilise party politics in Scotland in large part reflected an increasingly volatile electorate. As new forms of social cleavage emerged — housing tenure and occupational sector, in particular — the Conservative Party found it difficult to mobilise the electorally semi-detached in the way it had done south of the border. Above all, it seemed that Scottish Conservatism had lost its traditional social leadership among Scotland's bourgeoisie at a time when national differences between Scotland and England became more salient. There simply was not a sufficient social base in Scotland left in which to 'naturalise' the Conservative message. The old values, which set the social agenda for much of last century, have largely failed in the late 20th century. Cultural change has gone hand in hand with political and economic change to refashion Scotland's social geography, and to allow its old social rulers less scope for exercising control.

Conclusion

In a decade short of the century, the role of the Scottish elites has changed significantly. At the turn of the century, they were more self-confident in their own economic abilities and capacity to map out a new direction for Scotland. The political leaders of this society saw their future and that of their country firmly within the United Kingdom. That was what it meant to be Unionist. It meant economic self-confidence and social control, linked by imperial interests, and cemented by a robust Protestantism which brought many working class Scots into the Unionist fold. By the late 1980s, Unionism as a political creed had grown thrawn and defensive, and reduced to its most simple meaning of doing Westminster's bidding. It no longer provided a game-plan for a country and its leading classes.

The argument of this chapter has been that Scotland has moved steadily away from the ethos of market liberalism, and the reductionist model of human nature which underpinned it. This shift has occurred, firstly, for economic reasons insofar as the collapse of the Scottish economy from the 1930s ushered in a more 'developmentalist' strategy for the state in Scotland. Secondly, Scotland has developed a political 'negotiated order' of decision-making, which has sought to establish a consensus. This order was in place by the time Thatcherism, with its neo-liberal, anti-state ethos, emerged. The attack on the state in Scotland came to be viewed in large part as an attack on the country itself. Finally, changes in the composition of Scotland's class structure weakened the social carriers of neo-liberalism, and strengthened social strata sympathetic to collectivist and 'organic' principles. Diverse social groups, from the aristocratic upper class through to organised labour were not hostile to the 'developmental' state. There is irony in the fact that the culture which spawned Adam Smith has, in the 1980s, decisively rejected the crude reworking by the New Right of his views. The diverse agencies of the state, together with sections of Scotland's industrial and commercial elite have framed a set of principles, albeit incomplete, for the development of modern Scotland. Such principles were founded on a growing sense of common purpose, a vision of society, and a set of moral precepts, reinforced by nationalism, which were deeply at odds with the tenets of Thatcherism and the Anglo-British state.

NOTES

1. B. Lenman *An Economic History of Modern Scotland* (London, 1977), p. 192.

2. M. W. Kirby *The Decline of British Economic Power since 1870* (London, 1981).

3. D. Marquand *The Principled Society: new demands and old politics*, (London, 1988), p. 9.

4. S. and O. Checkland *Industry and Ethos: Scotland 1832–1914* (London, 1984).

5. I. Levitt 'Welfare, Government and the Working Class: Scotland, 1845–1894', in D. McCrone et al. (eds.) *The Making of Scotland* (Edinburgh, 1989), p. 121.

6. Foreward by the Countess of Erroll, to R. Bain *The Clans and Tartans of Scotland*, (London & Glasgow, 1968). p. 7.

7. S. & O. Checkland *op. cit.*, p. 175

8. This diagram is reproduced with the kind permission of John Scott, from J. Scott & M. Hughes *The Anatomy of Scottish Capital*, (London, 1980), fig.4.7.

9. M. Wiener *English Culture and The Decline of the Industrial Spirit, 1850–1980* (Harmondsworth, 1981); and W. D. Rubinstein *Men of Property: the very wealthy in Britain since the Industrial Revolution*, (London 1981).

10. M. Fry *Patronage and Principle: A Political History of Modern Scotland* (Aberdeen, 1987), p. 110.

11. I. G. C. Hutchison *A Political History of Scotland, 1832–1924* (Edinburgh, 1986), p. 200.

12. S. & O. Checkland *op. cit.*, p. 85.

13. *ibid.*, p. 4.

14. *ibid.*, p. 85.

15. *ibid.*, pp. 178–9.

16. R. Anderson *Educational Opportunity in Victorian Scotland*, (Oxford, 1983), p. 124.

17. E. Hobsbawm *Industry & Empire*, (London, 1969), ch. 15.

18. For a discussion of the 'egalitarian myth', see D. McCrone, F. Bechhofer and S. Kendrick 'Egalitarianism and Social Inequality in Scotland', in D. Robbins (ed.) *Rethinking Social Inequality* (Farnborough, 1982).

19. A. A. MacLaren (ed.) *Social Class in Scotland* (Edinburgh, 1976), p. 2.

20. ibid., p. 9.

21. D. McCrone & B. Elliott *Property and Power in a City: the sociological significance of Landlordism*, (London, 1989).

22. A. Morris *Patrimony and Power: a study of lairds and landownership in the Scottish Borders*, (Ph.D., Edinburgh University, 1989).

23. T. C. Smout *A Century of the Scottish People, 1830–1950*, (London, 1986), p. 112.

24. B. Lenman *op. cit.*, p. 203.

25. J. Scott & M. Hughes *op. cit.*

26. D. Marquand *op. cit.*, p. 8.

27. *ibid.*, p. 113.

28. J. Foster & C. Woolfson *The Politics of the UCS Work-In: class alliances & the right to work*, (London, 1986), p. 92.

29. *ibid.*, p. 97.

30. M. Fry *op. cit.*, p. 193.

31. J. Scott & M. Hughes *op. cit.*, p. 153.

32. J. Foster & C. Woolfson *op. cit.*, p. 114.

33. J. Scott & M. Hughes *op. cit.*, p. 223.

34. See, for example, J. Firn 'External Control and Regional Policy', in G. Brown (ed.) *The Red Paper on Scotland* (Edinburgh, 1975); and S. Young 'The Foreign-Owned Manufacturing Sector', in N. Hood and S. Young (eds.) *Industry, Policy and The Scottish Economy* (Edinburgh, 1984)

35. C. Baur *The Scotsman*, 18th September 1978.

36. C. Moore & S. Booth *Managing Competition: meso-corporatism, pluralism & the negotiated order in Scotland*, (Oxford, 1989).

37. *ibid.*, p. 29.

38. *ibid.*, p. 150.

39. D. Marquand *op. cit.*, p. 152.

40. G. Payne 'Understanding Occupational Transition', *Sociological Review* 25, 1977.

41. S. Kendrick 'Occupational Change in Modern Scotland', in D. McCrone (ed.) *The Scottish Government Yearbook 1986* (Edinburgh, 1987).

42. *ibid.*, pp. 246–7.

43. J. Goldthorpe *Social Mobility and Class Structure in Modern Britain* (London, 1980); and G. Payne *Employment and Opportunity* (London, 1987).

44. G. Payne (1987) *op. cit.*, pp. 89–90.

45. M. Keating & D. Bleiman *Labour and Scottish Nationalism*, (London, 1979).

46. I. Budge and Urwin *Scottish Political Behaviour* (London, 1966); and J. Bochel and D. Denver 'Religion and Voting: a critical review and a new analysis', in *Political Studies*, 18, 1970; For an extended discussion of the declining fortunes of the Conservatives in Scotland, see S. Kendrick & D. McCrone 'Politics in a Cold Climate: the Conservative Decline in Scotland', in *Political Studies*, XXXVII, 1989.

47. See, for example, T. Gallagher *Edinburgh Divided: John Cormack and No Popery in the 1930s* (Edinburgh, 1987); and *Glasgow: The Uneasy Peace* (Manchester University Press, 1987).

48. The role of the petite bourgeoisie in Edinburgh's politics is discussed at length in D. McCrone and B. Elliott *op. cit.*

49. See, for example, J. Melling *Rent Strikes: People's Struggle for Housing in the West of Scotland, 1890–1916* (Edinburgh, 1983).

50. M. Fry *op. cit.*, p. 224.

51. S .Kendrick *Social Change and Nationalism in Modern Scotland*, Ph.D. Edinburgh University, 1983.

CHAPTER 7

A Proletarian Nation? Occupation and Class Since 1914

John Foster

Gowans and Gloag made metal containers, bolts and girders and metal trestles, fine castings for sections of engine casings, a thousand men working in great rattling sheds built to hold the labour of three times that number in a rattle and roar of prosperity. Even Tavendale would think of that now and then, Gowans had flourished just after the war, high wages and bonuses dished out to all, pap for the proletariats. Wonder what they did with the high money then? — Spent it on the usual keelie things, dogs and horse racing and sleeping with whores, poor devils — it had nothing to do with him.

Lewis Grassic Gibbon, *Grey Granite*, 1934[1]:

> Simply by visiting Glasgow one can see life as it will be through the country if the trend to council house ownership continues. Housing in industrial Scotland has much in common with that in many Iron Curtain countries . . . more than any other part of Britain Scotland is divided into middle class and working class housing areas . . . In this way housing has frozen class divisions leaving the socially deprived to feel they are out in the cold and to resent it . . .'

Conservative Political Centre, *The Eclipse of the Private Landlord*, August 1974.

First, a comment on general approach. The places where Scots worked, and the type of jobs they did, are reasonably well recorded. But class, and its social signifiance, is another matter. Historians have no direct way of discovering how Scots placed themselves socially in relation to others, how they gave meaning to the way they spent their income or how they related their position at work to their understanding of their political interests. On this it is only possible to test *presumed* relations using evidence that is indirect and usually incomplete. Did draughtsmen see themselves as middle class or working class — or was this classification irrelevant? There can be no direct answer. We might be able to look at how far draughtsmen were unionised, how often they took strike action, where they lived and how they voted. All this information, if it were available, would be relevant. But presumption would remain. This chapter will therefore be somewhat untidy. It will seek to be be as clear as possibly about its initial assumptions. But it

201

will then have to set off on a ragged course in search of information that will take it across the normal borders of politics, family life and industrial relations.

1. A Proletarian Nation?

The material on industrial and occupational structure given in Figures 1 to 3 provides us with some useful starting points. Occupationally, it shows that Scotland was not, in terms of the types of job people did, very different from England[2]. On this front, the two countries developed roughly in parallel.

In terms of sectors, mining and agriculture have been in slow decline since the 1920s (Figure 1). Manufacturing, on the other hand, remained stable until the 1970s but then declined sharply — with some of the slack being taken up by the service sector. Taking particular industries Scotland, like England, has seen the decline of its older trades, especially textiles and heavy engineering. The rise of new industries took place somewhat later than in England but by the 1970s production in consumer durables and electrical and electronic goods again reflects the average pattern for Britain (Figure 2). In terms of the types of job people do, there has been a steady decline in the number of manual workers, particularly skilled manual workers, a large increase in the number of junior and intermediate non-manual jobs and a slight decrease in the number of self-employed workers. This also matches the British pattern (Figure 3).

So, while there are indeed some significant differences, which we will explore later, the broad picture is the same. At the end of the first world war the economy depended on heavy manual labour. In Scotland, as in Britain, one in six of all male workers laboured below ground as miners. One in four were either engaged in producing metal or turning it into manufactured commodities. Almost a quarter of all female workers were employed in the exhausting, dirty and often dangerous labour involved in the various divisions of the textile and clothing industries. Sixty years later the situation was transformed. There were virtually no miners left in Scotland, only five thousand shipyard workers and less than 15,000 textile workers. Most women now work in social services and distributive trades. Only a minority of men are employed in manual grades.

Yet if we look at attitudes, particularly perhaps political attitudes, a quite reverse process seems to have been at work. Far more people now support the political party identified with the trade union movement.

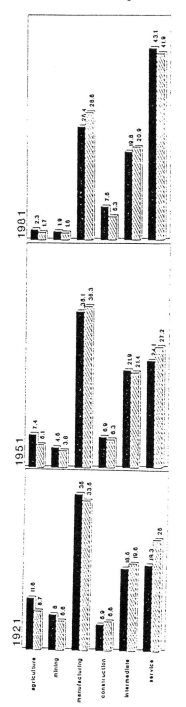

Figure 1. Employment sectors: Scotland and Britain.

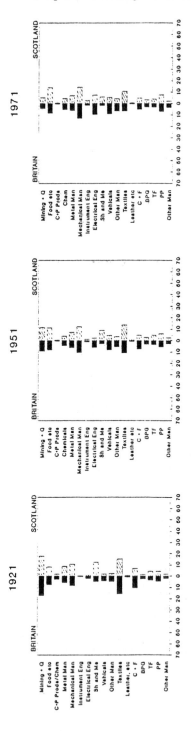

% of total industrial employment

Figure 2. Industrial orders: Britain and Scotland.

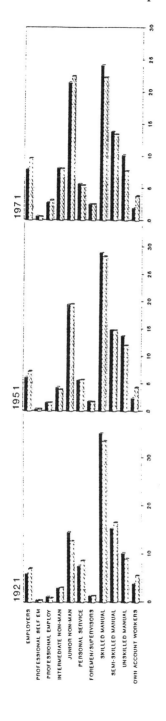

Figure 3. Socio-economic groups: Scotland and England and Wales.

Up to 50 per cent of Scots were voting Labour in the 1980s as against 30 per cent half a century before[3]. Similarly, in terms of trade union membership. In 1927 only 30 per cent of those eligible were in unions. By the begining of the 1980s over 50 per cent were[4]. In terms of housing, another indication of class orientation, 52 per cent of Scots were living in council or other publc sector housing by 1980[5].

One obvious explanation might be that this shift in attitude is the result of proletarianisation. In the strict sense orginally used by Marx, class position is not defined by whether or not the work is of *manual* character but by people's relationship to the means of production. On this definition it is indeed true that by the 1980s more Scots were proletarians. Fewer owned and controlled their own conditions of employment. More were employees. But as an explanation this itself will not do. The decline in the number of farmers, tradesmen, self-employed professionals is far too small. It only amounts to a 3.5 per cent shift. On the other hand, 89 per cent of economically-active Scots were already employees in 1921 — and most of them, manual workers as well as clerks and teachers, did not vote Labour or belong to a trade union. It is change *within* the ranks of employees that has been the crucial factor.

It might therefore be suggested that what we are dealing with is a more general shift in political and social alignments that has occurred as a result of events at British level. In general, it can be argued that people's subjective social identities do not follow class positions in any spontaneous way. Employees will not automatically see themselves as having interests that are opposed to those of their employers. The emergence of positive *class* identities requires social action, that is, mobilisation on issues that highlight conflicts of class interest, and particularly perhaps action that focuses this mobilisation at the level of the political system. This would point to a British level of explanation. Two world wars, the political battles for full employment and the welfare state, major conflicts over the legal status of the trade union movement, all these were experienced across the political system as a whole. But again, as an explanation, this in fact is not enough. Despite all the problems with evidence, it is clear that on *class* identity the pattern in Scotland deviates quite sharply from the British norm. In the 1970s, which is the first period for which we have anything definite, Scottish responses to direct questioning show that far fewer tended to classify themselves spontaneously as 'middle class' than their counterparts in England. 39 per cent of English did so but only 24 per cent of Scots — despite almost identical occupational structures in the two countries[6]. This is also paralleled politically. From the 1960s at least there has been a consistent trend away from the Conservative Party and, almost as consistently, towards Labour. Moreover, this appears to have been a characteristic that has developed quite recently. In the interwar period there does not appear to have been much difference between England and Scotland, and temporarily in the mid 1950s more people voted Tory than in England. But since then there has been a major transformation in political allegiances, and by the late 1980s the political geography of Scotland was strikingly different from that south of the border.

This brings us, therefore, to the question posed in the title of this chapter. If we are looking for what is distinctively new and Scottish about developments over the last half century, it would seem to lie in this area *between* occupation and class. Scots now see themselves as 'more' working class and 'more' Labour than might be expected. Indeed, this class orientation would seem to be extending to nationality itself — with Scots not just increasingly identifying as a separate nation but as a nation which they perceive to be somehow more exploited, more embattled and, in terms of composition and interests, more proletarian than that of their English fellow citizens south of the border. Why, then, should this be? What has changed the self-image of the Scots over the past half century?

This chapter will seek to review the evidence. It will ask whether this apparent Scots peculiarity is in fact simply a function of the wider North-South divide; whether, on the contrary, there were already, even at the beginning of the twentieth century, elements within the experience of the Scottish nation which would lead to this outcome — or whether we are indeed dealing with new factors, not present before, which have a specifically Scottish dimension. We will start with a slightly more detailed look at trends in occupational composition — which will remind us that regional diversity *within* Scotland is more marked than that of any other part of these islands — and then focus on some of the more important motors of fast social change: the two world wars, the two slumps and the long period of post-war modernisation.

2. Nation within a Nation

Figures 1 to 3 demonstrate what has already been noted about Scotland's occupational development: its *general* conformity with that of England. This should need no further emphasis. The main objective of this section is to identify significant divergences, both in comparison with England and within Scotland itself, and to begin to assess their importance.

Beveridge's famous contrast between the fates of Scotland and London in the twentieth century was made in 1942. He noted that Scotland — with 2 per cent unemployment in 1913 — had over 15 per cent of its workforce unemployed through most of the 1920s and 1930s. In London, on the other hand, there was 8.7 per cent unemployment in 1913 and 8.2 per cent in 1937[7]. Beveridge's contrast is — to some extent — an illuminating one. Although Scotland's population had been growing slightly less strongly than England's in the three decades before 1914, it had still been growing. After 1921 this expansion stopped, emigration increased and the number of Scots living in their own country remained static at 5 million for the remainder of the century.

If Scots had not emigrated on this scale, and the population continued to grow at the same rate as that of England and Wales, there would have been another million and a half people living in Scotland by the 1980s. The number of working age would have been 25 per cent higher. It is this missing labour force which goes a long way to invalidate the arguments of those who seek to use similarity of industrial and occupational structure to claim that Scotland's development is no different from the English average. Naturally, unless levels of technology are very different, the industrial and occupational profile of any relatively large and dispersed region (and Scotland included 10 per cent of the British population) is likely to be roughly similar to the norm. But similarity at this level does not of itself establish that there is, or is not, the same level of economic health or competitiveness. The size and composition of the working population will in the long run, and from economic necessity, tend to move into line with the jobs that are available. The key issue in Scotland's case is the number of new jobs which did not get created, investments which were not made and the industries which as a result failed to expand as soon or as fast as those in Britain as a whole. Indeed, if the 'missing Scots', the million who emigrated, had remained in Scotland, then the contrast of unemployment rates would have been quite dramatically worse by the end of the twentieth century.[8]

Yet, if Beveridge's contrast does highlight differences in the twentieth century, it has also tended to mask some of the underlying structural differences which existed before the First World War. It is more than a little misleading to suggest that the period to 1914 was simply one of parallel growth between the two countries — or even, as some have claimed, that before 1914 Scottish workers were better off than those in the south-east of England. To start with, 1913 was at a point in the trade cycle when there was exceptionally high activity in heavy industry and shipbuilding and when the service-based economy of the London region faced severe depression. More fundamentally, there is now a great deal of evidence to suggest that the Scottish economy was more sharply cyclical than the English, and that even in the normally cyclical capital goods industries the severity and length of depressions was worse. Across those areas of northern Britain outside what has been described as the 'industrial heartland' of Lancashire and Yorkshire *all* workers, skilled and unskilled, had from the 1860s suffered significantly higher levels of cyclical unemployment than their colleagues further south[9].

The performance of the Scottish economy is reviewed elsewhere in this volume. But it is relevant to note R. H. Campbell's well-known contention that the rise of Scotland's heavy industry economy from the middle of the 19th century was based upon a quite different investment strategy to its counterpart industries in England. Scottish employers in general invested less in plant and equipment. The shipbuilding industry in particular, despite its transcendent size, was less productive per employee, and invested less in research and design, than that elsewhere in Britain[10]. This drive to keep overheads to a minimum was, Campbell suggests, a structural feature of the Scottish economy: the product of its perceived weakness within the British market and the consequent attempt to reduce exposure to cyclical downturn. Instead, Scottish employers competed not through the level of investment and equipment but through their control over the workforce. Wages were lower. Managerial direction was tighter. It was on this basis, claims Campbell, that the Scottish economy was able to maintain the momentum of its development up to the end of the 19th century.

We will examine later the way in which Scotland's employers sought to use their inheritance of separate Scottish civil institutions to sustain quite distinct, and far more coercive, patterns of industrial relations. For the moment it is important to note the consequences for industrial and occupational structure. Scotish labour had to be cheap. It also had to be plentiful. This was not just because Scotish industry was itself more labour-intensive, but because its methods of labour control required the maintenance of a significant unemployed reserve. Authoritarian, hire and fire management depended on it.

Yet, this *expanded* labour requirement had to be sustained in face of a wider British labour market which generally offered better wages and status and where the industrial trade cycle was considerably less volatile. This inevitably generated large-scale emigration, particularly among the skilled trades, during periods of cyclical downturn, and, whenever demand revived, led on to short-term labour shortages and sharp, destabilising wage pressures. A vicious circle established itself. The conservative investment strategy of Scottish employers was reinforced. New investment was restricted, profits invested elsewhere — increasingly abroad through investment trusts — and the competitiveness of Scottish industry further reduced. So, even in the late nineteenth century when Scottish industry was still expanding, we can see many of the occupational features which would continue to characterise it in the twentieth century: high internal and external migration, the net loss of skilled workers, immigration into Scotland of unskilled workers from Ireland (then at double the English rate), a higher level of unskilled labour within occupational profiles — but also higher levels of bank saving, industrial disinvestment and a consistently larger segment of national income going to rentiers[11].

Scottish wage levels reveal these contradictions quite clearly. Up to 1914 *most* wages remained well below the English level — even though the scale of the dfferential had been falling steadily since the mid-19th century. On the other hand, by the outbreak of war the sustained boom in heavy industry had produced a substantial island of skilled wage rates, mainly in the West of Scotland, which had pushed *above* the UK average. These were in shipbuilding, coal, engineering (Clyde only), cotton (men only), jute, building and clothing[12]. These gains had almost all been won over the previous two decades. They were further consolidated during the first world war and probably gave rise to the belief that Scottish wages were *generally* higher than the English. By the 1930s, however, even these islands of high wages had been wiped out. Under the impact of prolonged mass unemployment heavy industry wages lost their privileged position, and Scottish wage levels fell back to between 5 and 10 per cent lower than the UK average. Public sector wages moved up a bit relative to industrial wages, but even here Scottish wage levels were lower than the UK average. The Second World War saw a slight recovery, though not to the same relative level as in the First, followed by a return to substantial differentials for the 1950s and 1960s. These two decades, during which 400,000 Scots emigrated, saw Scottish wages about 5 per cent below the British. Significantly for what we know of occupational composition, salaried jobs fared slightly worse than manual and women slightly worse than men. It was only at the end of the 1960s and through the 1970s that the differential was again challenged and new islands of high wages emerged. These appeared first among the metal working trades on the Clyde and later for all workers in the oil areas of the north east. In part this resulted from the bargaining strength of workers within these markets but partly also from the sharply decreased bargaining strength of English workers under the impact of much higher levels of unemployment from the mid-1970s. Once more, however, by the end of the 1980s it is the differentials against Scotland which become more obvious — with a disproportionately fast growth in the number of part-time female workers and the highest proportion of low paid workers of any British region[13].

The little we know about the scale of unionisation broadly corroborates this pattern — although also indicating some interesting variations. There have been three fairly reliable surveys. The first, by the Webbs in 1892, suggested a level of organisation well below the British average[14]. Union membership expressed as a percentage of the population came to only 3.7 per cent as against 4.6 per cent for the UK — something like 20 per cent lower overall. Moreover, it was also geographically very limited. 'Nearly all' the trade unionists identified by the Webbs were in the 'narrow industrial belt between the Clyde and the Forth', and one third of these (as against a sixth in England and Wales) were in engineering and metal trades. The second survey by the STUC in 1924 showed 11 per cent unionised compared with 12.6 per cent for the UK. This indicates that at least a good part of the leeway had been made up by 1924. By the time of the next survey in 1947 the differential still remained — at 17.7 per cent for Scotland and 18.2 for the UK — but was now quite small[15]. Since then there has been no survey, but calculations made in the mid 1980s confirm the persistence of a very slight differential against Scotland. At the same time they also show that the *fall* in union membership in Scotland under the impact of mass unemployment in the 1980s was less marked than it was in England and Wales. Between 1980 and 1983 the decline amounted to just over 1 per cent of the population (from 20.9 per cent to 19.7 per cent) as against a fall of over 2 per cent at UK level[16].

This picture — of persistently high unemployment and of a workforce having to struggle against its consequences — becomes even sharper when we turn to the regions *within* Scotland (Figure 4). As Kendrick, Bechhofer and McCrone have demonstrated, industrial specialisation has both been highly developed *within* Scotland at sub-regional level and this specialisation has itself been subject to quite dramatic changes[17]. There was the original distinction between the crofting counties of the north and west and the counties, in east, central and south Scotland, which combined textiles with larger-scale tenant farming. This was followed from the mid 19th century by a further distinction between those areas which maintained their textile specialisation (the Borders, Paisley and Perth-Angus) and those which transferred to either coal or heavy engineering and shipbuilding. It was during this period that West Central Scotland emerged with its phenomenal concentration of heavy industry occupations. The quarter of a million jobs in coal, steel and heavy engineering drew on a continuing stream of immigrants from Ireland and elsewhere in Scotland. By the end of the First World War this relatively small area of Scotland contained something like double the average British proportion of such occupations[18]. This pattern, with its particularly high levels of sub-regional concentration in mining and shipbuilding, persisted beyond the Second World War. The switch to 'new' industries post-war also tended to be highly localised. The new consumer durable plants tended not to be sited in the old heavy industry areas but in New Towns and semi-rural locations on the periphery of the central belt. Electronics in Glenrothes, Livingston and Stirling, motor manufacturing plants in Renfrewshire an l in West Lothian, would be typical examples. Finally, throughout the period Edinburgh tended to hold the same anomalous position — in terms of services and financial occupations — as London did in England.

One conclusion sometimes drawn from this subregional diversity is that Scotland possesses a truly 'national' economy, a microcosm of the British, with its own internal specialisation and division of labour. In a sense this was true. But it would be a mistake to take it as an automatic mark of national strength. Such internal specialisation occurs fairly routinely in the process of industrial location. If, however, it has in Scotland's case been especially marked, it would seem to derive from those particular features of the country's economy by which, as we noted earlier, Scotland's employers were more than usually dependent on labour as a factor of production. For any given operation they generally needed more labour and labour that was also cheaper and more pliable. This required the maintenance not so much of high general levels of unemployment but labour reserves that were geographically concentrated and occupationally specific. Scotland's particularly internal diversification appears to be the consequence of this: a whole series of geographically distinct and occupationally narrow labour markets.

The sub-regional variations in wages and unionisation provide plenty of evidence for this. Wages in the Borders have been well over 10 per cent lower than those of central Scotland throughout this century. It is here that the remnants of the textile and knitwear industry have localised themselves and done so with wages up to 20 per cent below those in the English knitwear industry[19]. In North Ayrshire the lace

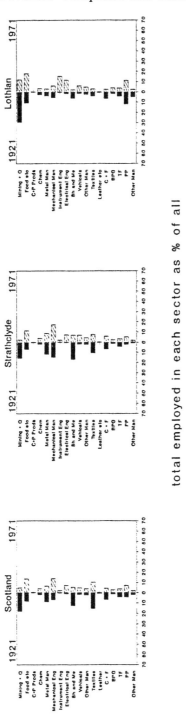

Figure 4. Industrial sectors by regions.

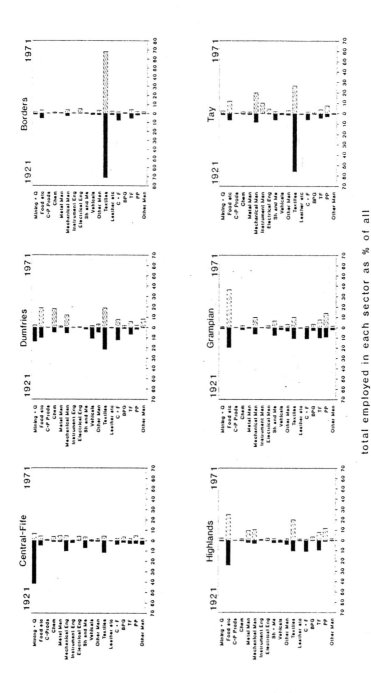

Figure 4. Industrial sectors by regions (continued).

industry survived into the late twentieth century on the basis of a poorly unionised, localised labour pool[20]. Even in heavy industry employers sought to sustain tight, socially dependent local fiefdoms, and dominant local firms have often exerted considerable political pressure to steer new industries — in the creation of industrial estates in the 1930s and New Towns in the 1950s — away from direct competition for existing pools of labour[21]. Equally with unionisation. While the surveys of 1924 and 1947 show a spread out of West Central Scotland into other areas, the geographically localised and patchy character of organisation has remained a strong feature of the Scottish trade union movement into the late twentieth century and largely explains why the overall level of unionisation continues to remain, despite the tradition of Clydeside activism,, slightly below the British average.

This, then, seems to have been the inherited pattern in Scotland: restricted, localised labour markets, each dependent on maintaining their own reserves of unemployed labour, which — as Southall has demonstrated — serviced unstable, cyclical and undercapitalised industries. This, in turn, generated that other particularly Scots occupational trait: high internal and external migration. The narrow prospects and fluctuating local demands for labour sustained what has been called a culture of migration. The well-documented flow of emigrants out of Scotland was, it seems, itself based upon a historically high level of *internal* migration. In a labour force disproportionately composed of immigrants — from Ireland or the Highlands — and without quite the same experience of stabilised rural proto-industrialisation as in England further migration came much more easily.[22] Indeed, without continued immigration *into* Scotland from Ireland and Eastern Europe, Scotland's population increase would have ceased long before 1920. The migrant Scot was in many ways the direct product of this particular experience of proletarianisation.

This returns us to our original question. Occupationally, as much as any part of the British isles, Scots have long been proletarianised. As a population they have been overwhelmingly dependent on selling their professional and trade skills. Indeed, in order to do so they have been compelled to move, considerably more than others, wherever employment could be found. Yet in terms of class identity it is only in the last thirty years that Scots have, organisationally and politically, begun to identify more — rather than less — with the institutions and objectives of the labour movement. The statistics do not themselves seem to solve this riddle of what happened in the 1960s and 1970s. Apart perhaps from the cumulative effects of high external migration, they do not show much that is qualitatively new or different for these later years. Next therefore we will turn to a more concrete examination of particular sequences in the story.

3. War and the Red Clyde

The years 1914–20 have a special significance because they produced that most famous symbol of Scottish proletarianisation, the Red Clyde. If, moreover, unemployment did play a special economic and social role in Scotland, it was during these five years that it virtually disappeared. Did the coming of wartime full-employment and the consequent rupturing of local labour market disciplines also cause a rapid transformation of class perceptions? A number of recent commentators have tended to deny that this happened. McLean and Reid, for instance, claim that Clydeside workers simply used their new labour market strength to defend sectional interests. It was for this reason, they argue, that the authorities were able to isolate doctrinally socialist strike leaders in 1916 and deport them from the Clyde. The mass of workers were not interested[23]. How strong, therefore, were such sectional identities? Let us start by looking at some studies of class cohesion and stratification at the outset of the war.

It was to the douce, grey city of Edinburgh that the authorities deported the Glasgow shop stewards leaders in April 1916, and it is for this city that we have the most effective studies of social structure. Robert Gray has shown just how far Edinburgh's working people were themselves divided by the physical experience of poverty. Edinburgh's non-skilled workforce had to contend with the usual casual employment combined with wages below the British average and housing that was desperately bad and overcrowded. Their stunted, malnourished children were more than two inches shorter than those of white collar workers going to school a mile away[24]. For such families, with little or no social security provision, unemployment or illness inevitably meant going hungry. This difference in physical circumstance was matched by quite distinct cultures. The skilled workers, while not necessarily identifying with the middle class establishment, valued their own standing and respectability as tradesmen and considered trade unionism in the same self-regarding light. They intermarried to some extent with white collar workers and foremen, and ensured their children were able maintain their positions by formal and informal controls over the skilled job market. In the years immediately before 1914 Gray finds signs of greater social interlinkage with the unskilled.

He also notes that the Trades Council, which of course only represented a minority of even the skilled workforce, took some political initiatives of a labourist kind designed to meet the needs of all workers. But the overwhelming impression is of the abyss of poverty which was the fate of the majority of workers who provided the light and heat, transport and docking, cleaning and cooking for Edinburgh's polite society.

John Holford's more recent study reminds us how different Edinburgh was from Glasgow — less than half the size with no heavy industry and little engineering — and the degree to which its small industrial workforce was dominated by printing, railways and rubber manufacture[25]. Within these industries labour remained relatively passive both before and during the war. In printing and on the railways, where there was a mainly male labour force, management was by delegating authority to skilled workers and maintaining a modus vivendi with their unions. Rubber was non-union and used mainly female and semi-skilled labour.

This stratified, contained and regulated workforce is very different from what we know of Clydeside. The million workers congregated in the West of Scotland were also sharply divided — by skill, trade and religion. But employment relations were also far more fraught and conflictual. Joseph Melling and Hamish Fraser have both emphasised the degree to which the rebuilding of Clydeside's economy after the collapse of cotton textiles was on a non-union basis[26]. The economic and political crisis of the 1830s and early 1840s left the new heavy industry employers determined not to allow the trade union movement to re-establish itself in their industries. They sought to buttress their control over local labour markets and particularly in coal and iron made active use of religious divisions and the selective employment of immigrant Irish labour in opening new mining areas. In shipbuilding, with its new iron and steel technology, the detailed management control of labour was seen as crucial, and several Thames shipbuilders came to the Clyde at least in part to escape union control. The repertoire of employer tactics in the 1860s and 1870s included anti-union lockouts, tied housing and, especially, the maximum exploitation of labour market fluctuations. The privilege of permanent employment would be given only to a core of loyalists who would then subcontract labour as required[27]. It was only after a prolonged struggle lasting a generation and a half that wage parity was achieved with England. During the intervening years earnings remained up to 15 per cent lower than those south of the border[28].

Industrial relations in the West of Scotland were, therefore, quite different to those in England (and also probably Edinburgh with its English-administered railway employment). Still in 1914 most employers were non-union — or would like to be if they could get away with it. Unlike England, regulated collective bargaining and the moderating hand of official trade unionism was not seen as an aid to management. The key battles for skilled unionisation came a generation later than they did in England and directly overlapped with those of the unskilled. This made for a major difference in attitude which was reinforced by the high level of continuing informal workplace struggle. The principle of trade unionism always remained in dispute. Even after conceding union recognition shipyard and steelworks managements preferred to rely, like their close associates in Belfast, on autocratic styles of control which were buttressed by informal structures of patronage, loyalism and discrimination. In the bitter guerilla battles fought out, section by section, on the shop floor, both sides sought to exploit the highly cyclical character of demand, and wages and rights won during periods of boom would be rolled back during the following depression. The balance of market power and its legal and economic determinants remained matters of particularly intense concern for Clydeside trade unionists[29].

This meant that the sectionalism of Clydeside's workforce was always qualified and limited by a basic 'us and them' identity against the employers. Each skilled group fought to maximise its area of legitimate control. There were high levels of ethnic exclusiveness and discrimination. The gulf in material experience between skilled and unskilled was no smaller, especially in terms of housing, than that in Edinburgh. Yet there was also embedded in these occupational identities a collectivism which found expression in the perpetual battle against management, and which demanded a fierce rank and file loyalty. Unlike England, and perhaps Edinburgh, shop stewards and yard and pit representatives carried an authority which often outweighed that of formal trade union structures. This difference in emphasis was also carried over into the field of formal politics. In Scotland there was much less scope for Lib-Lab electoralism. On the one hand, *direct* identity with employer politics, whether Orange or Liberal, lasted longer as a mass phenomenon than in England, and was fed by a mixture of paternalism, patronage and sectarianism. On the other, *organised* labour found it much more difficult to develop alliances with a political establishment which remained basically anti-union. So, although Labour was electorally less successful, it was also more class-oriented, and there was no counterpart in Scotland to the electoral pact negotiated in England with the Liberal Party in 1903[30].

   The Board of Trade statistics used in Figure 5 make two things quite clear about the eruption of industrial action which took place in the virtual full employment conditions of the war[31]. First, they show that the bulk of strike activity was concentrated in heavy industry, coal, steel and shipbuilding, and that the 1916 anti-dilution strikes in engineering comprised only a very small fraction of the total. Second, they show the *generality* of strike action. It included many previously unorganised occupations in which women took the leading part. Even more revealing are the figures for arbitration and conciliation hearings (Figure 6)[32]. The number rose dramatically through the war, and nowhere faster than in the West of Scotland. By the first half of 1916 approximately a sixth of the British total were taking place in the West of Scotland — between two or three times more per worker than might be expected. It is this massive scale of state intervention which is the clearest indicator of the prior absence of established collective bargaining on the Clyde and the degree to which backward, authoritarian managements now found themselves pushed on to the defensive. Politically and socially, the drastic change in the balance of industrial power also transformed politics within the industrial communities of the Clydeside. The blow struck against profiteering landlords in 1915 was one which involved both workers and housewives (and also probably quite a number of working housewives). Subsequent action on prices, rationing and food supply drew into activity many sections of the working population which had been previously been excluded.

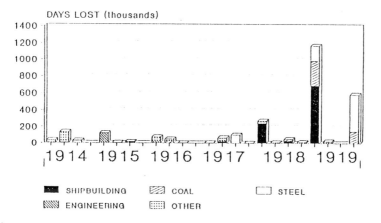

Figure 5. Days lost each quarter: West of Scotland.

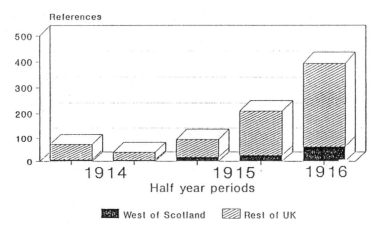

Figure 6. Arbitration.

The final point to stress about industrial relations in these years is the quite exceptional character of the 1919 general strike[33]. There was nothing like it elsewhere in Britain — the nearest equivalent was in Belfast. It was not just much bigger than anything before. It was also far more politicised. What initially made it so successful, and why the authorities saw it as such a threat, was the active use of mass pickets.

These included in their ranks significant numbers of unemployed. Both the recently demobilised solders and the women who had been laid off in their thousands from the munitions industries in December 1918. The strike's central demand for a 40 hour week was argued explicitly in terms of class power in the labour market. The mobilising force of this demand — in the West of Scotland (and Belfast) but not elsewhere in Britain — would seem to underline the understanding which workers had of the special dependence of labour relations in these two areas on the manipulation of unemployment. They were not willing to see their wartime gains lost as the balance of power once more turned against them.

In terms of its objectives the 1919 strike achieved neither shorter hours nor the maintenance of full employment conditions. But it did represent a definitive expression of the new occupational relations which had emerged during the war and it seems to have been this that gave it such a potent force in popular memory. The strike involved large numbers of women. Leadership was exercised by shop stewards and unofficial work place-based committees. It encompassed a breadth of activity which spanned different industries (coal, steel, shipbuilding as well as virtually all Glasgow employment) and both skilled and unskilled workers. Through the participation of women and demobilised soldiers, it sustained the new links with the working class communities which had been forged during the wartime struggles on rents and rationing.

The strike also underlined the differences between the class politics of England and the West of Scotland. In January 1919 the Scottish Trade Union Congress effectively followed the lead of the unofficial strike committee[34]. In the subsequent months the relative weakness of constitutionalist labourism was amply demonstrated by the decision of the Scottish ILP to seek affiliation to the Third International. This was repeated in 1920. Scotland's biggest union, the miners' federation, split over the same issue in the years that followed. Finally, and again in contrast to England, Communists and supporters of the Third International were able to win official Labour Party nominations in key centres of heavy industry, Motherwell (steel and coal), Greenock (shipbuilding) and the shipbuilding communities of of Glasgow (Govan and Anderston/Kelvingrove)[35].

The Red Clyde was, therefore, no mirage. At the same time, because it depended so much on labour market conditions which were exceptional and temporary, this level of class mobilisation could not easily be **stabilised in post-war conditions**. Unemployment after the war was still more disabling than it had been before. In looking at this return to 'normality' it is difficult to know how much weight to attribute to simple market forces and how much to employer deliberation and government intervention. Within two years employment in shipbuilding had fallen from 60,000 to 18,000[36]. Not for another twenty years did the level of activity on the Clyde again reach that of 1913. In coal and steel there were similar reductions in employment. The collapse in world trade, the demotion of sterling as the world banking currency and the new policy priorities of government all contributed to making this the moment when the relative positions of the English and Scottish economies sharply diverge.

In terms of class orientation, however, there could be no simple return to the status quo. While the balance of occupations remained roughly the same, it was never possible to reassemble the group loyalties and identities of the pe-war period. Sharp and only partially reversible shifts had occurred which offset the far more disadvantageous economic conditions and the often ferocious attacks on working class organisation. It is here, in this untidy process of partial reversal and partial transformation, that we can perhaps find the best explanation for the continuing riddle of Scottish class formation: how, despite roughly the same occupational profile and more heavy industry, despite the rawness of Scottish industrial relations and, above all, the experience of wartime mobilisation, still in the 1920s and 1930s class identities among workers remained less coherently developed than in England.

4. The Long Depression

John Boyd Orr in his report on infant mortality, commissioned by the Scottish Health Department in 1943, exposed the gulf that separated most working class families in Scotland from their middle class fellow citizens[37]. At the same time he also underlined the growing gulf between Scotland and England. In the 1930s infant mortality in Scotland was the worst in Western Europe apart from Spain and Portugal. Seventy seven

18. Part of the women's contingent of the Scottish Hunger March to London, February 1934, near Barnet in Hertfordshire. Courtesy of the Picture Library of the Communist Party of Great Britain.

babies out of every thousand died in their first year compared with fifty five in England and Wales. In Social Class Five 98 out of every thousand babies died — three times the rate for Social Class 1[38]. These appalling rates were closely matched to poor nutrition and bad housing. In Boyd Orr's categorisation of nutritional sufficiency Group I included those families that were deficient all areas: protein, fat, calories, vitamins and minerals. In Britain as a whole 10 per cent of families came within this group[39]. In Scotland it was 20 per cent. In housing the contrast was even sharper. 23 per cent of Scots families lived in overcrowded accommodation as against 4 per cent for England and Wales[40].

Boyd Orr's research focused on the years 1934-8 and reflected the cumulative effects of a depression which lasted in most parts of Scotland from 1921 to 1939. Heavy industry went down immediately after the war and stayed down. Scotland shared little of England's temporary prosperity in the later twenties. Nor, after the further collapse of 1931-3, did it benefit from the boom in middle class purchasing power which stimulated consumer industries in the south. Scotland saw no significant surge in suburban house building[41]. Even rearmament was late and limited[42]. During the two decades 450,000 Scots emigrated, unemployment never fell below 10 per cent and a decisive gap emerged between the growth rate of Scotland and England[43].

The sheer scale of this deprivation provides at least part of the answer to our question. Immediately after the ceasefire unemployment was, as we have noted, concentrated among women and ex-soldiers — the soldiers disproportionately recruited from among the unskilled and pre-war unemployed in both city and countryside. But for most of the interwar period unemployment was characteristically male and industrial — although, unlike the 1980s, there was not quite the same impact on the juvenile labour market[44] There remained a quite bouyant demand for girls and young women in distribution and services. Boys were taken into industry as apprentices, but typically discharged as soon as they were eligible for adult wages. It was the adult male with skills in traditional industrial occupations who made up the bulk of the unemployed. In mining, steel, shipbuilding and most branches of engineering up to 30 per cent, and in some cases over 50 per cent, of the available workforce remained unemployed for periods of two or three years at a time. Some emigrated. A very few were 'transferred' to other occupations, and generally out of Scotland, under state schemes. But most remained. James Barke's *Major Operation* paints a vivid picture of the socially segregated Glasgow which resulted[45]. In Kelvindale and along Great Western Road the complacency of the middle class was maintained by the polite evasion of bankrupts and mortgage defaultors. The teacher in his deck chair in the garden of his corporation house in Mosspark now enjoyed the fruits of the wartime housing struggles — for it was predictably those in permanent and well-paid employment who were disporportionately allocated the houses built under the 1919 and 1923 housing acts. Dividing the densely packed working class tenements of Partick were the tramlines of Dumbarton Road. 'They might have been a barbed wire entanglement'. To the north were those families who had managed to maintain employment and who could afford the relatively well repaired red sandstone. To the south were the grey sandstone slums, in worse condition and more overcrowded than before 1914, and housing a significant number of now unemployed skilled shipyard and engineering workers.

It was in these circumstances that the informal structures of patronage and control, so important before 1914, could reassert their influence. With many industrial firms cutting their work forces to half the previous level there was every opportunity for weeding out militants and reinstating the authority of often masonic charge hands and foremen. Which school you attended, Catholic or Protestant, would still make a considerable difference to employability. Even the very largest employers, such as the shipbuilder James Lithgow and Thomas Craig of the steel firm Colvilles, would pride themselves on being able to know by name a significant proportion of their work force[45]. Lithgow did his best to maintain Port Glasgow as a town under the direct administration of his own family. Loyal employees were enrolled in the Territorial Army. Boundaries were redrawn to enable the firm to maintain a proprietorial grip on infrastructure. On a less grand but much wider scale the dense network of smaller businesses and subcontractors also sought to promote relations of material dependence and cultural deference between employers and workers[47]. Indeed, even from within the working class itself somewhat similar structures of employment-based patronage started to emerge. This was perhaps particularly so within the still partly distinct and segregated Catholic population. Pubs and illegal betting houses, small-scale operations in carting and jobbing building, even some areas of corporation employment after Labour started to win control of councils in the 1930s, provided a ready basis for patronage of another kind — but one no less incompatible with class consciousness and organisation[48].

It was during the first upsurge of large-scale unemployment in the early to mid 1920s that Glasgow witnessed the rise of the razor gangs described in *No Mean City*. Associated with this was a certain amount of sectarian conflict. The second, more massive upturn in unemployment between 1931 and 1933 witnessed a far more politicised expression of Protestant extremism. During these years the Scottish Protestant League won six seats on Glasgow Corporation and in 1933 polled an aggregate vote of 67,000 across 22 seats as against Labour's 63,000 and the Moderates 53,000[49]. Traditionally, it had been the Moderates, the municipal face of the Unionist Conservatism, which had gained the votes of the Orange element within the working class. The significance of the SPL was that its temporary success was based on a direct attack on both the Moderate Party and the Orange Order from a populist standpoint. It accused these bodies of not taking a hard enough line against Catholics and at the same time of not defending the interests of the working class Scot in terms of employment and social welfare. The SPL's main bases of support were in the largely skilled working class and white collar areas of Dennistoun, Cathcart, Camphill, Kinning Park and Govanhill. In Edinburgh Protestant Action enjoyed a somewhat similar burst of electoral success.

There was, therefore, much that was corrupt, bigoted and craven in Scottish life between the wars. But it would be quite misleading to make this the complete picture. Glasgow did not become another Belfast. Nor was all resistance smothered by mass unemployment. It is the argument here that while the reality of unemployment did result in the recrystallisation of many of the old informal controls and identities of the pre-war period, this did not happen in quite the old way. The culture of class resistance, though contained, was stronger and more mature. Organisationally it provided far more effective links between industry and the community than before 1914 and indeed compared to most parts of England. This was in part because of the continuing vigour of workplace collectivism, even if often as much sectional as anti-management in its immediate expression, and in part because of the weakness of those forces within the wider Labour Movement which elsewhere provided the foundation for reformist politics.

The Labour Party as such was not notably effective, and the new legitimacy the party enjoyed largely derived from events at British level. It twice controlled the Scottish Office, and electorally made up the leeway of its pre-war weakness compared to England. In Wheatley it had a parliamentarian and administrator who did much to lay the basis for socialised housing in both Scotland and England. But it was effectively a different party from what had existed in Scotland before the war. The 1918 constitution removed a large part of the party's local autonomy. In particular it terminated the directing role of the trades councils, which in Scotland had a power and status not matched in England, and ended the political non-exclusive and federal character of Scottish level organisation as it had existed in the pre-war Scottish Workers' Representation Committee. This was now replaced by centralised control from the British executive — a control exercised with a particularly heavy hand in the interwar period in Scotland to eliminate challenges from the Left of the party. Moreover, the reformed party's new allies in Scotland were perilous ones for a nominally socialist organisation. After the upsurge of rank and file mobilisation in 1919–20 the Catholic hierarchy effectively decided to throw its weight behind the right-wing of the Labour Party and to open a major organisational offensive, through Catholic Action, against the Left[50]. The immediate concern was mainly to ensure Labour support for the continuation of separate Catholic schools, but the new alignment also profoundly influenced the methods and assumptions of local Labour Party organisation. On the industrial front there was a similarly compromising rapprochement. Clydeside employers were now far keener to promote the authority of the official trade union movement, and while union leaders in Scotland were not directly represented on the party's leadership, the power-broking barons of the transport workers, engineers and municipal workers unions were closely associated both in practice and the public mind with the direction of the Labour Party.

One clear sign of the response within the politicised section of the working class was the disaffiliation of the ILP from the Labour Party in 1931–2[51]. This move was largely led from Scotland. Maxton, McGovern and the Glasgow ILP councillors had to confront constituents from the poverty-ridden slums of Glasgow's East End who could find little to convince them that the Labour Party was a vehicle for socialist change. The ILP now declared itself as a party of class struggle and moved into a fraught alliance with the Communist Party. A still more dramatic indication of this mood was the 1926 General Strike. The strike revealed just how quickly the dynamism of the wartime shop stewards movement could be reborn even in quite adverse industrial circumstances. Within a matter of days the Left was in control of virtually all the major strike committees including the biggest at Glasgow Trades Council. Elaborate structures of dual control emerged. These often included food and fuel distribution, transport control, recreation and entertainment, social service provision and in a number of mining areas Workers Defence Corps.[52] This experience left a number of important legacies of which the most significant was the consolidation of the community base of active class organisation. Wider community involvement had been a crucial development during the war and been sustained in many areas by the post-war struggles on rents and unemployment. In the 1930s the Little Moscows of Fife, Ayrshire and the Vale of Leven were only extreme examples of a community activism which persisted, even as a minority phenomenon, in most areas of working class Scotland.[53]

Hence, the superficial appearance of interwar class relations is a little misleading. It is true that despite the size of the working population, and all its experience of poverty and deprivation, it was no more, and sometimes less, disposed to vote Labour than in England. The culture of industrial loyalism undoubtedly played a part here. So did sectarian politics. But there was also a distinctively different structure to working class political organisation. In Scotland it was fractured in a way it was not in England. The ILP and the Communist Party together represented a real force on the ground — and more important still were able to involve large numbers of people in quite different styles of class activity to that offered by the Labour Party. This may have represented a major electoral liability for the Labour Party as it existed in 1929 or 1935. But it also represented a potential strength for any future movement that might seek to mobilise a class challenge to existing social relations.

5. Modernisation

During the six years of the 1939–45 war the *average* height of Glasgow children (aged 13) increased by just under 2 inches[54]. The number of Scotish children dying in their first year fell by 27 per cent — the biggest fall anywhere in Europe[55]. As overcrowding and overall food supplies actually worsened during these years, the improvement can only be attributed to the better distribution of food to those Scots, probably a near majority, who were previously denied adequate nutrition[56]. The statistics provide a vivid rebuttal to those who argued that poverty-based malnutrition either did not exist or was cultural and self-induced. The transformation in consumption itself was directly related to the implementation of previously rejected schemes for free milk and other foods for school age children and, ultimately, to the shift in the balance · of class power in wartime. Within a matter of months, as the demand for labour tightened, the influence of the shop stewards movement and of work place collectives was restored. The first group to utilise this new power were the apprentices. As soon rearmament began on Clyde side, in 1938, they sought to reduce the wage differential with the skilled adult which had been so ruthlessly exploited over previous years[57]. This was swiftly followed by other actions to retrieve previous work place rights.

The biggest single industrial dispute in Scotland during the last war took place in the giant Rolls Royce aircraft factory on the Hillingdon industrial estate south west of Glasgow. Employing 20,000 workers, and with a mass of subsiduary factories, it had been shifted north just before the war. The demand was for equal pay for equal work. The workers involved were women[58].

War had meant the re-assemblage of Scotland's heavy industry work force. It drew back into employment those excluded, and demanded the industrial mobilisation of women. The radical class attitudes which had been sustained in the community struggles interwar now returned, reinforced, to industry. The official historians of the Second World War single out the Clydeside for the strength of its shop stewards' movement, and for the vigour with which the Left sought to turn the Joint Production Committees in the shipyards, factories and mines against the ideology of competitive capitalism[59]. Planning, it was argued on the basis of wartime experience, represented the way forward. Social ownership was the only real guarantee for the gains of wartime. Similar conclusions were in fact drawn by those such as Boyd Orr and Sir William Whyte who had chronicled the pre-war deprivation[60]. Now in documents like *Planning Our New Homes*, from the Scottish Health Department, and in *The Clyde Valley Plan* Scots were offered the vision of a country healthy, clean and fully employed in which new towns and garden cities replaced the old slums[61].

The following thirty years did indeed see a process of modernisation which transformed occupational structures and patterns of residence. Its character, by no means what was envisaged in 1945, also brought unforeseen transformations in class attitudes. New industries arrived. New towns were built. Enough houses had been constructed by the mid 1970s to eradicate, at least on paper, the problems of overcrowding and hygiene. But, though state directed, these changes were uncoordinated, insufficiently funded and, in outcome, unable to ensure either sustained economic growth or prepare the country for slump of the 1980s. Emigration continued. Population stuck at the five million mark, and for the first two decades unemployment remained at double the British figure[62].

The new industries arrived in two major waves. The first, in the late forties and early fifties, initially created something like 30,000 new jobs largely in consumer durables, mechanical engineering and electronics[63]. This was very largely overseas investment, almost entirely American. However, compared with the size of the existing industrial work force of 600,000, this first wave of new industrial investment was relatively insignificant. It was mainly accommodated on the periphery of the old industrial belt in Lanarkshire, Renfrewshire, Dunbartonshire and Fife and provided employment for the only two new towns, East Kilbride (1947) and Glenrothes (1948) actually built in the decade after the war. All this was far short of the original plans for comprehensive redevelopment involving a combination of publicly owned utilities and firms relocated from the south. The major physical change of this period came a bit later in the early 1950s: the creation of housing schemes within the existing major conurbations of Dundee, Edinburgh and Glasgow. It was the new Conservative government which enabled local authorities to enter the field of mass housing construction. In the 1950s 500,000 houses, almost double the interwar total, were built — but to a lower standard and without any planned link to employment. The housing acts of 1952 and 1957 reduced the level of subsidy, and local authorities, intent on meeting the political pressures for more housing, were left with little or no funds with which to provide public amenities or transport systems. Worse, from 1957 considerable pressure was exterted by central government for still cheaper system building methods which were quite unsuitable for the Scottish climate[64].

The real transformation in the occupational and residential base of Scottish society came in the 1960s and early 1970s. This was ultimately not so much a consequence of much that was new as of the destruction of what was old. The second wave of external investment, that between 1960 and 1970, brought — initially — only 37,000 new jobs. The big change came in the massive contraction of employment in the traditional industries and in the simultaneous demolition of the inner cities. This development was in fact planned comprehensively and in detail. The Toothill report of 1961 and even more the White Papers of 1963 and 1966 argued that further government assistance for traditional heavy industry should be ended[65]. Instead, its labour should be released to permit Scotland to play its part in the overall economic development of the British economy, and in particular to act as a buffer to the inflationary pressures being generated in England. Labour reserves within Scotland were identified as amounting to a fifth of the estimated British labour deficit. The following years saw a stream of British as well as American branch plants being moved into Scotland starting with the Rootes car plant at Linwood. Detailed attention was given to the modernisation of infrastructure[66]. New technical colleges were developed. Transport was dramatically improved. Motorways were built across Central Scotland and the blue train network created fast rail transport down both sides of the Clyde, and did much to unify previously localised regional labour markets[67].

In the event the arrival of new factories faltered in the late sixties and was reversed in the 1970s. The haemorrage of heavy industry jobs, on the other hand, continued. In the ten years to 1967 119 of Scotland's 166 coalmines were closed. The number of miners was halved to 38,000, and halved again in the following decade. The shipyard labour force went down from 70,000 to 47,000 by 1967 and down again to 20,000 by the later 1970s[68]. Combined with the relocation of population from the inner city tenements, these closures throughout heavy industry and its mass of subcontracting trades effectively broke up what was left of the old industrial social structures. Where previously the Drumchapels, Easterhouses and Polloks had family links running back to Maryhill, Bridgeton and Govan, these base areas of working class Clydeside (and their equivalents on the east coast) were themselves bulldozed and their factories closed.

What is remarkable, however, (though not perhaps surprising) is the degree to which this dispersed population retained and strengthened its *class* allegiance while the cultures of industrial deference and sectarian division, so much part of the old urban Scotand, largely disintegrated. It was the decade *after* the 1963 White Paper which marked the decisive turning point for the Conservative Party. Where it had previously been able to match Labour, it now lost its considerable share of the working class vote[69]. Conversely, the same years marked a rapid increase in unionisation despite absolute levels of unemployment in the 1970s higher than those in the 1960s. Perhaps still more surprising was the increase in support for Labour. This continued to rise, against the national trend, through the 1970s and into the 1980s.

Given the quite massive decline in the size of the industrial working class (manufacturing employment was almost halved to 380,000) and the proportionate increase in the size of the service sector, it might have been expected, at least by 'post-industrial' commentators, that a non-class party would have been able to draw the benefit. But this was not the case. Even the Scottish National Party, which was also able to exploit demand for national self-determination, failed to consolidate a firm voting base.

6. Occupation and Class

Earlier we argued that in terms of occupational composition there was little to choose between England and Scotland, and hence industrial

19. Office staff, Lothian Coal Company, c. 1930. B. Kay (ed.) *Odessey Two* (1982).

20. Darvel Lace Queen, Jean Murdoch (Paton) with procession, 1953. B. Kay (ed.) *Odessey Two* (1982).

structure itself could not explain very much. If there was a major difference between the two countries, it was rather in the occupational *dynamics* of employment, in the way labour markets were structured. Scottish employers, highly dependent on labour as a factor of production, placed much more emphasis on the maintenance of distinct, localised labour markets which both incorporated strong elements of social control and retained their own internal reserves of unemployed and under-employed labour. Correspondingly, Scottish labour tended to be less unionised and more ruled by convention, deference and fear than any agreed framework of collective bargaining. We also noted that these somewhat adverse conditions generated high levels of migration and emigration and, whenever labour market conditions changed, a tendency to use radical action to turn the tables on the employers.

Our first area of historical review examined what happened when full employment conditions occurred during the first world war. This showed how quickly existing patterns of social behaviour changed in these circumstances. Where previously Scottish workers had been somewhat less well organised in class terms than those in England, they now overtook them and, at least in the heavy industries of the Clyde and coalfields of Fife, adopted far more advanced forms of political action. The second area of review looked at what happened when these abnormal labour market conditions ended. In two decades during which the growth of the Scottish population ceased — and whole communities emigrated — many of the old patterns of deference and control were reconstructed. And while some legacy of wartime radicalism remained it was no longer able to present a mass challenge to the old order.

How, then, do we explain what happened in our final area of review, the years since the beginning of the last war? While the first two decades saw no decisive departure and, if anything, a modified return to the pre-war status quo in the 1950s, it is the period since the mid-1960s which has seen Scottish politics sharply diverge from those of England. It is in Scotland that the intensifying regionalisation of British politics has been most marked. Scots are now more prone, not less, to support the Labour Party. Even taking into account the higher unemployment, the growing differences in occupational structure and the cumulative effects of 'big' working class encircling a smaller middle class, neither William Miller nor more recently Johnston and Pattie find these factors themselves sufficient to explain the deviation of Scottish politics from the British norm[70]. In fact, if we bear in mind the consequences of mass unemployment in the 1920s and 1930s, we might expect it to have had a sharply depressive effect on the strengthening of working class and Labour allegiances. Yet this has not been the case.

The initial stage of our answer points to the process of industrial and social modernisation. On this front the 1960s do seem to have marked a turning-point. There had been external investment before. There had also been a certain amount of urban redevelopment. But it was during the sixties that Scottish-controlled employment actually became a minority sector in industry, and that the rebuilding of infrastructures — particularly transport — seems to have significantly eroded the remaining localised labour markets in Central Scotland[71]. Bearing in mind our earlier analysis of what was distinctive about Scottish employment relations, these developments seem to have been particularly important and precipitated change in two crucial areas.

First, they sharpened and developed trade union organisation. Incoming industry, like Scots industry before it, sought to benefit from Scotland's higher unemployment and labour's weaker bargaining position. But they did so in quite different ways. Almost all the American firms came in with the expectation of being able to enforce non-union employment. Instead, however, of lower wages, their objective was to secure a much fuller control over the labour process, to exploit their higher levels of technology, and they were willing to pay significantly over the Scots wage rate to do so[72]. British firms, like Rootes, came north with the objective of maintaining the lower Scottish wage rates and, while recognising Scottish trade union structures, to negotiate local wage deals[73]. Neither strategy was successful, and the competition between American and British firms for skilled labour in the later 1960s and early 1970s largely explains the ending of wage differential against Scotland. But it did not happen spontaneously. It required difficult and protracted struggles, largely focussed at shop floor and shop stewards level, which raised issues of basic class principle. In American firms it involved the right to trade union membership. In British firms the creation and maintenance of all-British bargaining structures. The result was a much strengthened shop stewards movement, often with Left leadership, and, no less important, a generalisation of the class issues within each work place which now penetrated the non-manual strata. The draughtsmen's union DATA, now part of MSF, played a crucial role here, and this period saw a major spread of unionisation among white collar industrial staff[74]. The development and consolidation of the public sector, both nationalised industries and local government services, also provided the basis for all-British organisation among grades of employee who were previously outside the trade union movement.

The other impact of these changes was on the Scottish employers themselves. They now found themselves no longer masters in their own house, relegated to smaller-scale employment in the technologically less advanced industries. Their tight local fiefdoms were things of the past, and they were without a significant voice in the development of new industrial infrastructures[75]. Even under Conservative administrations modernisation and planning were now seen to be directed to the interests of growth industries and external capital. And where the old indigenous industries had sustained complex local structures of subcontract and servicing, this was much less the case with the incoming branch plants[76]. Hence, at the very time that the organised boundaries of proletarianisation were being rapidly extended, the cohesion of those in the *opposite* class position was starting to disintegrate. The small business and localist base of the Conservative Party in Scotland began its long process of political desertion[77].

However, to leave the explanation at this level would be to make the transformation in class loyalties largely reflexive. There was also another factor at work which brings us back to Scotland's legacy of working class activism: the organised political intervention of those who saw themselves as proponents of a new socialist social order. Without this, it is unlikely that the Scottish labour movement would have had the toughness and clarity, particularly important at the shop stewards level, to win the factory-level struggles of the 1960s and 1970s. More important still, it is unlikely that the Scottish labour movement would have been able to seize the political initiative at national level. Of key significance here was its success in projecting and popularising a radical, indeed basically Marxist, critique of how the existing mode of production was harming specifically Scottish development. Uneven development and the stagnation of Scottish industry, were, it was argued, the consequence of monopoly concentration, of big business domination of state power and the activities of its Scottish quislings. In 1971–2 these quite sophisticated arguments gained a mass response during the fifteen month work-in at the Upper Clyde Shipyards. Increasingly they also became the focus of the long series of battles over industrial closure which followed. Why, asked the stewards at Fort William, Kilmarnock and Inchinnan, at Linwood, Bathgate, Greenock and Uddingston, at Gartcosh and Polmaise, should capital, especially perhaps external capital, have the right to rob communities of their employment and thereby halt the wider development of the Scottish economy?[78]

As taken up and developed by the Scottish Trades Union Congress, this theme became a central one for the entire Scottish political community in the 1980s. Amid the desperate struggle to halt the slaughter of industrial jobs, all Scots employees, managers and scientists as well as manual workers, increasingly came to see the survival of their national economy as linked to the balance of power between capital and labour at British level. Indeed, it would seem to be the ability of the Scottish Trades Union Congress to build on this perspective that enabled it to take possession of the issue of devolution and, temporarily at least, marginalise the SNP.

This scale of politicisation is confirmed by recent comparative reseach on the phenomena of one day political strikes in Britain[79]. The fifty national and regional political protest strikes which took place between 1969 and 1985 provide an important test for the differing levels of class activism in the regions and nations of Britain — particularly so because they were *general* calls and because all of them in essence challenged the legitimacy of the government. The response in Scotland reveals three significant characteristics. First, that against the national trend in terms of Scotland's higher unemployment, political strike action was strongly supported from 1969 onwards. Second, also against the trend in terms of unemployment, the support for such action was far better sustained into the mid-1980s than in any other part of Britain. The strike of 14 May 1980 received more support in Scotland than any previous strikes, even those during UCS, and far more than elsewhere in Britain. Third, that in the 1980s a large part of the support was, for the first time, drawn from the public sector and from white collar employment. The mass of low paid and mainly female workers in health, local government and the civil service now emerged on to the stage for the first time.

Such strikes, and most others, were made illegal by the Conservative government between 1985 and 1988. But neither such legislative intervention in industrial relations nor the attempts at large scale social engineering — through housing provision, health, education and the privatisation of public sector industry — appear to have halted, let alone reversed, the process of class formation in Scotland. In light of went before it is unlikely that it would have done so.

NOTES

1. Lewis Grassic Gibbon, *Grey Granite*, in *A Scots Quair*, (London, 1950 edition,) p. 372.
   2. Stephen Kendrick, Frank Bechhofer and David McCrone, 'Is Scotland Different?

Industrial and Occupational Change in Scotland and Britain', *Restructuring Capital: recession and reorganisation in industrial society*, ed. H Newby et al, (London, 1985.) Most of the statistical information used here is derived from this research report and from Clive Lee, *British Regional Employment Statistics*, (Cambridge 1979.)

3. William Miller, *The End of British Politics?: Scots and English political behaviour in the Seventies*, (Oxford, 1981)

4. Laurie Hunter, 'The Scottish Labour Market', *The Economic Development of Modern Scotland*, ed. R Saville, (Edinburgh, 1985)

5. Andrew Gibb and Duncan Maclennan, 'Policy and Process in Scottish Housing, 1950–1980', in Saville, op cit.

6. William Miller, op cit. p. 80

7. William Beveridge, *Full Employment in a Free Society*, (London, 1944,) p. 74.

8. Isobel Lindsay, 'Out migration and the Scottish Economy', paper for the Standing Commission on the Scottish Economy, 1989, and 'Scotland and its migratory tradition: twentieth century social and economic implications', paper presented to the Social History conference (Manchester 1988). I am grateful for being allowed to see this material before publication.

9. Humphrey Southall, 'The origins of the depressed areas: unemployment, growth and regional economic structure before 1914', *Economic History Review*, XLI, 2 (1988). Ron Martin, 'The Political economy of the North South divide' in *The North–South Divide*. Jim Lewis and Alan Townsend, eds. (London, 1989.)

10. R. H. Campbell, *The Rise and Fall of Scottish Industry, 1707–1939*, (Edinburgh, 1980)

11. Geoff Payne, 'Occupational transition in advanced industrial societies', *Sociological Review*, Volume 25 (1), 1977 from whom the materials in Figure 3 are derived; T. W. Jones, 'Occupational transition in advanced societies — a reply', *Sociological Review*, Volume 25 (2), 1977.

12. D. J. Robertson, 'Wages' in *The Scottish Economy*, ed. A. K. Cairncross, (Cambridge, 1954.)

13. Laurie Hunter, op cit.

14. Sidney and Beatrice Webb, *The History of Trade Unionism*, (London, 1920 edition,) p. 428–440.

15. J. D. M. Bell, 'Trade Unions', in *The Scottish Economy*, ed. A. K. Cairncross. (Cambridge 1954)

16. John McInnes, 'Economic Restructuring reledvant to Industrial Relations in Scotland', Centre for Urban and Regional Research, Glasgow University, Discussion Paper No. 26, 1987.

17. Kendrick, Bechhofer and McCrone, op cit. pp. 85 ff. Unlike this text, however, Figure 4 uses the 1921 census as a basis for comparison with 1971 — not 1931. In terms of classification there was no change over the period 1921 to 1931, and the 1921 census has the advantage of showing Scotland's industrial structure as it existed at its most expanded form and before the mass unemployment of the 1930s. When this census is used the index of industrial differentiation used by Kendrick et al does in fact reach a level higher than that for any other British region — while the internal levels of differentiation, between those areas with little heavy industry and the West of Scotland, also show up particularly starkly.

18. Board of Trade, *An Industrial Survey of the South West of Scotland*, ed. W. R. Scott, (HMSO, London, 1932.)

19. Laurie Hunter, op cit, and Kendrick, Bechhofer and McCrone, op cit; D. F. Macdonald, *Scotland's Shifting Population, 1770–1850*, (Glasgow, 1937;) E. H. Hunt, *Regional Wage Variations in Britain, 1850–1914*, Clarendon, (Oxford, 1973) p. 50.

20. Billy Kay, 'Up the Valley: the lace industry in Irvine Valley' in B. Kay (ed), *Odessey Two: voices from Scotland's recent past*, (Edinburgh, 1982).

21. John Foster and Charles Woolfson, *The Politics of the Upper Clyde Shipbuilders Work-in: class alliances and the right to work*, (London, 1986) pp. 98 ff.

22. H Southall, 'Origins' as cited previously and Ron Martin, 'The Political Economy of Britain's North–South Divide' in J. Lewis, ed., *North–South Divide*; D. F. Macdonald, op cit.

23. Iain McLean, *The Legend of the Red Clydeside*, (Edinburgh, 1983;) Alastair Reid, 'Dilution, trade unionism and the state in Britain during the first world war', in S. Tolliday and J. Zeitlin eds. *Shopfloor Bargaining and the State*, (Cambridge 1985.) James Hinton, *The First Shop Stewards Movement*, (London, 1973) provides a more balanced appraisal; additional statistics can be found in J. Foster, 'Strike action and working class politics on Clydeside 1914–1919', *International Review of Social History*, XXXV (1), 1990.

24. Robert Gray, *The Labour Aristocracy in Victorian Edinburgh*, (Oxford, 1975,) p. 85.

25. John Holford, *Reshaping Labour: organisation, work and politics in Edinburgh in the Great War and After*, (London, 1988).

26. Joseph Melling, 'Scottish industrialists and the changing character of class relations in the Clyde Region', in Tony Dickson ed. *Capital and Class in Scotland*, (Edinburgh, 1982;) Hamish Fraser.

27. Calum Campbell, 'The Making of a Clydeside Working Class: shipbuilding and working class organisation in Govan', *Our History*, No. 78, July 1986; Alan B. Campbell, *The Lanarkshire Miners, 1775–1974*, (Edinburgh, 1979) and 'From Independent Collier to Militant Miner: tradition and change in the trade union consciousness of the Scottish miners, 1874–1929', *Scottish Labour History Society Journal*, No 24, 1989.

28. R. H. Campbell, op cit.

29. Sylvia Price, 'Clydeside riveters earnings, 1889–1913' in J. Kuuse and A Slaven eds. *Scottish and Scandanavian Shipbuilding seminar*, mimeo, Glasgow, September 1980; J. Mortimer, *History of the Boilermaker's Society*, (London, 1973.)

30. Christopher Harvie, 'Before the Breakthrough, 1888–1922' in *Forward! Labour Politics in Scotland 1888–1988*, eds. I Donnachie, C. Harvie and Ian Wood, (Edinburgh, 1989.)

31. *Board of Trade Labour Gazette*, monthly 1914 to 1919. These figures cover the Lanarkshire, Ayrshire, Dunbartonshire and Renfrewshire county areas and include all disputes lasting more than a day and involving more than 20 workers.

32. These figures are calculated from the listings of Conciliation and Arbitration and Committee on Production hearings in the monthly *Board of Trade Labour Gazette*.

33. This account is based on *Forward*, the *Glasgow Herald*, the minute books of the Clyde Shipbuilders Association (Strathclyde Region RO TD 241/1/18) and Ministry of Munitions reports (PRO MUN 1/17 31 January 1919 and MUN 5/18, 1 February 1919).

34. Angela Tuckett, *The Scottish Trade Union Congress: the first 80 years, 1897–1977*, (Edinburgh, 1986), p. 157.

35. Alan McKinlay, 'Doubtful wisdom and uncertain promise' in *The Independent Labour Party in Scotland: foundation to disintegration*, eds. A Mckinlay and R. Morris,

(Manchester, 1990), Ian Wood, 'Hope Deferred: Labour in Scotland in the 1920s' in Donnachie, Harvie and Wood, op cit.

36. Alan Mckinlay, 'The Inter-war Depression and the Effort Bargain: Shipyard Riveters and the Workman's Foreman', *Scottish Economic and Social History*, No. 9, 1989.

37. *Infant Mortality in Scotland*, Department of Health (Scotland), HMSO 1943 (compiled by John Boyd Orr).

38. *Ninetieth Annual Report of the Registrar General for Scotland.*

39. John Boyd Orr, *Food, Health and Income: a report on a survey of adequacy of diet in relation to income*, (London, 1936)

40. *Distribution of new houses in Scotland*, Cmd. 6552

41. Robert Baird, 'Housing', in A.K. Cairncross ed., op cit. p. 205 showing proportionately less than half the amount of private house building in Scotland compared to Scotland between the wars.

42. Still in 1941 90 per cent of the factories taken out of production for war purposes were unused: cited in Christopher Harvie, 'Labour and Scottish government: the age of Tom Johnston', *Bulletin of Scottish Politics*, No 2, Spring 1981

43. D. J. Robertson, 'Population growth and movement' in A. K. Cairncross, op cit.

44. *Board of Trade Industrial Survey of South West Scotland*, W. R. Scott ed., HMSO, 1932 pp. 183–191; George Rawlinson, 'Organisation by the Unemployed: similarities from the 1920s to the 1980s', in *Unemployed Workers Centres in Scotland, 1988*, (Local Government Centre, Paisley College, 1988); Richard Croucher, *We refuse to starve in silence: a history of the National Unemployed Workers Movement*, (London, 1987.)

45. James Barke, *Major Operation*, (Glasgow, 1936,) p. 85.

46. J. M. Reid, *James Lithgow*, (London, 1964,) esp. p. 89 and pp. 113–122; Peter Payne, *Colvilles and the Scottish Steel Industry*, (Oxford, 1979.)

47. Ian MacDougall, 'Mungo McKay and the Green Table: one man's rule in the mining villages of Midlothian', in *Odyssey: voices from Scotland's recent past*, Billy Kay ed., (Edinburgh, 1982)

48. Tom Gallagher, *The Uneasy Peace: religious tension in modern Scotland*, (Manchester, 1987.)

49. Steve Bruce, *No Pope of Rome: anti-Catholicism in Modern Scotland*, (Edinburgh, 1985,) p. 52

50. Ian Donnachie, 'Scottish Labour in the Depression: the 1930s' in Donnachie, Harvie and Wood, op cit. Tom Gallagher, op cit. reviews the evidence on Catholic attitudes to Labour. The distegration of the Liberal Party from 1918 faced the Catholic Church with a particularly severe problems in Scotland where education now threatened to fall under the control of often pro-Orange Unionists. This seems to have brought the hierarchy towards the position of generalised support for Labour already held by Irish nationalists such as Charles Diamond. Quickly, however, this support was qualified, and from 1922–23 there was a sharp organisational offensive against the Marxist Left within the Labour Party both by the Church and by Diamond and the newspapers he controlled.

51. R Dowse, *Left in the Centre*, London, 1966; Robert Morris and Alan Mckinlay (ed), *The Independent Labour Party in Scotland 1893–1932*, (Manchester, 1990;) Alan Mackinnon, 'Communist electoral strategy', *Marxism Today*, August 1980 shows the jump in Glasgow's East End Communist vote in 1931 and the threat this seemed to pose to the ILP.

52. Paul Carter, 'The West of Scotland' and Ian MacDougall, 'Edinburgh' in Jeff Skelley, ed., *The General Strike, 1926*, (London, 1976); John McLean, 'The General Strike in Lanarkshire', *Our History*, No 65, 1976; Ian MacDougall, ed. *Militant Miners: recollections of John MacArthur*, (Edinburgh, 1981.)

53. Stuart Macintyre, *Little Moscows*, (London, 1980); Sean Damer, *State, Local State and Local Struggle: the Clydebank Rent Strike of the 1920s*, (Discussion Paper Centre for Urban and Regional Research, Glasgow University, No. 22, 1985.)

54. John Gollan, *Scottish Prospect*, (Glasgow, 1948) p. 198 citing the report from the Glasgow Education Department in *Glasgow Herald*, 2 March 1946.

55. Ibid p. 253 from *Ninety-First Annual Report of the Registrar General for Scotland* (1947).

56. John Boyd Orr, *As I Remember*, (London, 1966,) p. 120

57. Alan McKinlay, 'Apprentice strikes on Clydeside', *International Review of Social History*, vol XX1, 1986

58. P. Inman, *Labour in the Munitions Industry*, (HMSO, London, 1957) p. 364

59. Ibid, p. 376 and 401; interview with Arnold Henderson, wartime convener of the John Brown yard, Clydebank, 1970 (in STUC Archive).

60. John Boyd Orr and Frank Webb, *Housing and Health*, (London, 1944) Sir William Whyte, *Scotland's Housing and Planning Problems*, (London, 1944.)

61. *Planning Our New Homes*, Department of Health for Scotland, HMSO, 1944; *Clyde Valley Regional Plan 1946*.

62. Laurie Hunter, 'The Scottish Labour Market', in Saville ed., op cit.

63. Joan Cawdery and A. C. C. Taylor, 'Branch plant performance in Scotland', *Scottish Economic Bulletin*, December 1985; R. Pounce, *Industrial Movement in the UK, 1956–1975*, (HMSO, London, 1981); Duncan Maclellan and John Parr (eds.), *Regional Policy: past experience and new directions*, (Oxford, 1979.)

64. Andrew Gibb and Duncan Maclennan, 'Policy and process in Scottish Housing', in Saville ed., op cit.

65. Scottish Council (Development and Industry,) *Inquiry into the Scottish Economy 1960–61*, (Paisley, 1961) (Toothill Report); Scottish Development Department, *Central Scotland: A Programme for Development and Growth*, HMSO, Edinburgh, 1963, Cmnd. 2188; *The Scottish Economy, 1965–1970: a Plan for Expansion*, HMSO, Edinburgh, 1966, Cmnd. 2864.

66. David Sims and Michael Wood, *Car Manufacturing at Linwood: the regional policy issues*, Clyde Valley Industrial Policy Archive, Paisley College, 1984 examines the wider background.

67. The 1966 White Paper made a particular close examination of labour markets and how greater mobility could be achieved by developing the transport system.

68. John Foster and Charles Woolfson, op cit, pp. 107 ff.

69. William Miller, op cit. p. 37; James Kellas, *The Scottish Political System*, (Cambridge, 1976.)

70. William Miller, op cit. pp. 75 ff; Ron Johnston and Charles Pattie, 'Voting in Britain since 1979: a growing north-south divide?' in *The North-South Divide: regional change in Britain in the 1980s*, Jim Lewis and Alan Townsend, eds. (London, 1989.)

71. John Firn, 'External Control and Regional Policy', *Red Paper on Scotland*, ed. G. Brown (Edinburgh, 1975,); M. Cross, *New Firm Foundation and Regional Development*, (Farnborough, Gower, 1981) S. Boyle and others, *Claiming the Future: The Scottish Economy – Ownership, Control and Development*, (London, 1989.)

72. David Forsyth, *US Investment in Scotland*, (New York, 1972,) pp. 195–207.

73. Sims and Wood, op cit.

74. Peter B. Smith, 'The development of DATA 1920–1975', MPhil, Glasgow University, 1981

75. Foster and Woolfson, op cit. pp. 105ff.

76. Brian Ashcroft, James Love and James Scouller, *The Economic Effects of Inward Acquisition of Scottish Manufacturing Companies 1965–1980*, (Industry Department Scotland, ESU Research Paper 11, 1987.)

77. James Kellas, op cit., and Michael Fry, *Glasgow Herald*, 18 September 1986

78. C. Woolfson and J. Foster, *Track Record: the Story of the Caterpillar Occupation*, (London, 1988)

79. Alan Troup, *One Day Political Strikes in Britain 1969–1985*, Working Paper in Applied Social Studies, Paisley College, 1990; Alan Troup, 'One Day Political Strikes in Britain', PhD dissertation CNAA/Paisley College 1987. '

CHAPTER 8
Scottish Politics

C. Harvie

I

Generalising about Scottish politics is tricky. If you have already read John Foster's and David McCrone's chapters, you will have seen Scottish society either as 'proletarianised' through a growing support for the Labour Party, or becoming a 'principled' society of the type postulated by the social democrat David Marquand as the antithesis of the 'market individualism' of Thatcherism. At one level, the facts seem to bear Foster out. In 1990, with the collapse of East European Communism, nowhere did left dominance seem stronger than in some Scottish local authorities. Glasgow District in 1990 had only four Conservatives in a council of 100. But, in the same year, Scottish Labour seemed as anxious as 'reform Communism' in East Europe to terminate this hegemony, its acceptance in the Scottish Constitutional Convention of proportional representation favouring instead a pluralist order. Less similar to East Europe, however, was the cause in which this move was made: the partial independence of Scotland from a British state which had put the promotion of market forces and competitive individualism at the head of its agenda.

Did Scottish politics maintain a 'principled' society against *both* class politics *and* marketism? Or was the result much less consistent? In this chapter I will argue that Scots political history is too distinctive to confirm such systemic interpretations. 'Interpretation' has been *part* of the political culture, using the specific circumstances of a period to construct a 'frame' through which past history was viewed. In the 1930s the 'frame' was provided in by the decline of the Liberal and rise of the Labour parties; in the 1950s by the apparent rapid assimilation of Scotland to the 'British homogeneity' of the two party system; in the 1970s by a shift to a three or even four-party system; and in 1990 by a situation in which the future of 'British politics' of any sort looks, to say the least, debatable.

In such a subjective historical landscape 'facts' can be ambiguous, and myths — that of John McLean for instance — can walk. Parties frame political history, but in organisation, personnel and ideology they change, along with the social reality they reflect. Labour, in 1990 with

241

around 50 per cent of the support of the electorate in the opinion polls, holds only one seat outside central Scotland — Aberdeen South — which it did not hold (on a roughly similar percentage) in 1950. But in terms of policies, voters and members, and its elite of MPs, councillors and organisers, it is quite different. Over half the Scottish Labour MPs in 1945–51 were working class, scarcely a quarter today. Again, non-Labour Scotland seems broadly where it was in 1914; the radicals in the north and east, the Tories at bay in the suburbs, retirement areas and the South-West. But the SNP has altered the agenda of Scottish politics, while the Tories, uncharacteristically but perhaps fatally, are riven by ideological conflict. Yet the high profile of leading Scottish politicians, a new 'nationalist' agenda, and unprecedented dissent on constitutional issues — largely through opposition to the poll tax — has not changed the Scottish voter's appraisal of his or her political masters: 'Jock Tamson's bairns', are still no better than they ought to be.[1]

Before the mid-1960s the 'story' of Scottish politics seemed to consist of periods of almost geological solidity, punctuated by two 'revolutionary' upheavals — in 1826–32 and 1914–22 — sudden, history-less, and Westminster-derived. Tory 'management' vanished in the first, its Liberal successor in the second. In the absence of a legislature, the long calms emphasised normative relations between institutions, not party manoeuvre and personal ambition. But since 1966 conflict over Scotland itself has taken centre stage, and this has produced both a specific politics and a complex interpretative debate.

The 'long calms' appealed to the social scientists. James Kellas, in 1973, saw a 'system' which combined elected, administrative and pressure-group elements in a stable and mutually-sustaining balance. Although William Miller, in 1981, argued that the home rule issue pulled it apart, Kellas believed the system rode out the 1980s fairly well, restraining the Anglocentric extremism of Mrs Thatcher. But Michael Keating and Arthur Midwinter saw it breaking up through friction between the various tiers of local government, and growing English resentment of a Scots pork barrel which was, anyway, nearly empty. In the one historical overview of the 'story' since the beginning of the reform movement in the eighteenth century, the Tory home ruler Michael Fry regarded the *ethos* of Scottish politics as moralistic, didactic, and — after the fall of the Liberals in the 1920s — dead. The Constitutional Convention of 1989 was defending patronage, not principle.[2]

In 1990 Scottish politicians were, for the first time since the *Edinburgh*

Reviewers, contributing centrally to British affairs — on the Labour front bench, in the Convention, Charter 88 and the movement for a 'regionalised' Europe.[3] This development contained echoes of the 'Dangerfield' period before 1914, when Ernest Barker and Harold Laski expected 'home rule all round' to strengthen pluralism within British democracy. However, instead of that postulated outcome the class-structured behaviourism sketched (rather pessimistically) by Graham Wallas in *Human Nature in Politics* (1908) ruled the roost for almost half a century, without that Machiavellian awareness of political psychology that Wallas shared with John Galt.[4]

At a later point in time, Butler and Stokes' monument to political homogeneity, *Political Behaviour in Britain* (1964) dominated the intro-duction of political studies in Scottish universities, but was soon contradicted. Budge and Urwin's 1966 study of Scots voting peculiarities was quickly confirmed by the impact of the SNP.[5] The immediacy of political change, added to a remarkable growth in labour history, evicted the journalism or hagiography which had served as political history in the absence of a functioning *polis*. The effectiveness of party organisation had been unassessed; politicians discounted their historical importance, leaving few records even when, like Tom Johnston, they were practising historians![6] Many of the *lacunae* in the 'two-party' epoch have since been filled in, but the current 'nationalist' frame may produce its own distortions.[7] It masks a declining membership within all parties, and an embryonic 'new politics' — feminism, ecology, animal rights, moves for a 'people's' history and literature — which eschews traditional commitment, and might be activated by a major environmental threat.

II

Such interpretations at least nominate a cast of actors: politicians, parties, ideologies, the economy, the administrative structure, pressure-groups. Social-science approaches — Kellas or Keating — foreground the latter; but Fry on the right, and Tom Nairn on the left, have observed, and indeed promoted, a reversion to the 'ethical', power-struggle *ethos* of the nineteenth century, when the Liberals commanded over 50 per cent of the popular vote.

Scottish Liberalism did not handle the transition to welfare and interest-group politics well. In the 1900 election the Unionists even took most seats (38 to 34), partly out of enthusiasm for the Boer War and partly because the Liberals had offended such clients as the Irish and the fishing interest. The split over protection, however, proved the

Table 1. MPs Elected for Scottish Constituencies 1900–1987 (Showing Number of MPs and % of Vote)

	Unionist MPs	%	LU/NL1 MPs	%	Lib. MPs	%	Lab. MPs	%	Others MPs	%
1900	21		+ 17	(49.0)	34	(50.2)				
1906	8		+ 4	(38.2)	58	(56.4)	2	(2.3)		(3.1)
1910 (Jan)	8		+ 3	(39.6)	59	(54.2)	2	(5.1)		(1.1)
1910 (Dec)	7		+ 4	(42.6)	58	(53.6)	3	(3.6)		(0.2)
1918	32	(30.8)	19	(19.1)	15	(15.0)	7	(22.9)	1	(12.2)
1922	15	(25.1)	12	(17.7)	16	(21.5)	29	(32.2)	2	(3.5)
1923	16	(31.6)			23	(28.4)	34	(35.9)	1	(4.1)
1924	38	(40.8)			9	(16.5)	26	(41.1)	1	(1.6)
1929	22	(35.9)			14	(18.1)	36	(42.4)	1	(3.6)
1931	50	(49.5)	8	(4.8)	8	(8.6)	7	(32.6)		(4.5)
1935	37	(42.2)	7 +1	(7.6)	3	(6.7)	20+4	(41.8)	2	(1.7)
1945	25	(37.4)	5	(3.7)		(5.0)	37+3	(49.4)	4	(4.5)
1950	26	(37.2)	5	(7.6)	2	(6.6)	37	(46.2)	1	(2.4)
1951	29	(39.9)	6	(8.7)	1	(2.7)	35	(47.9)	1	(0.8)
1955	30	(41.5)	6	(8.6)	1	(1.9)	34	(46.7)		(1.3)
1959	25	(39.7)	6	(7.5)	1	(4.1)	38	(46.7)		(2.0)
1964	24	(37.3)		(3.3)	4	(7.6)	43	(48.7)		(3.1)
1966	20	(37.7)	-		5	(6.8)	46	(49.9)		(5.6)
1970	23	(38.0)			3	(5.5)	44	(44.5)	1	(12.0)
1974 (Feb)	21	(32.9)			3	(8.0)	40	(36.6)	7	(22.5)
1974 (Oct)	16	(24.7)			3	(8.3)	41	(36.3)	11	(30.7)
1979	22	(30.0)			3	(10.0)	44	(42.0)	2	(18.0)
1983	21	(28.4)			8	(24.5)	41	(35.1)	2	(12.1)
1987	10	(24.0)			9	(19.2)	50	(42.4)	3	(14.3)

(1 Liberal-Unionist to 1912; 'Coalition Liberal' 1918–22; 'National Liberal' 1931–64.

Note: The totals of MPs include two university MPs 1900–18 and three 1918–45. These seats were abolished in 1948. As they polled by proportional representation, party percentages cannot be established.)

'crucial destroyer' of their power. The Liberals got back in 1906 with 58 seats and stayed out in front in the two elections of 1910. Their losses in England were severe, but the Scottish Unionists were checked because promotion of Tariff Reform among the rank-and-file conflicted with the free-trade inclinations of the Scottish business elite. Party reorganisation produced some benefits by 1914, but such recovery as the Unionists enjoyed stemmed more from conflict between the Liberals and Labour.

Liberals liked to believe that the Scots legislated through consensus within 'the little parliament' of Scottish MPs. Yet they operated only fitfully as a pressure group.[8] Divided in 1886 over disestablishment and Irish home rule, they dallied with radicalism in the early 1890s, but then split over imperial policy, and let ideology lie, returning MPs who expressed (cheaply) the moralism of the country and troubled their

Table 2. *Ministries and Scottish Secretaries 1900–90*

1900–1905	Con	Marquess of Salisbury 1900–02	Lord Balfour of Burleigh 1900–03
		A J Balfour 1902–105	A Murray 1903–05
			Marquess of Linlithgow 1905
1905–1916	Lib	H Campbell-Bannerman 1906–08	Lord Pentland 1905-12
			T M Wood 1912–16
		H H Asquith 1908–16	H Tennant 1916
1916–1922	Coal	D Lloyd George	R Munro (Lib)
1922–1923	Con	A Bonar Law	Viscount Naror
		S Baldwin	
1924	Lab	R MacDonald	W Adamson
1924–1929	Con	S Baldwin	J Gilmour
1929–31	Lab	R MacDonald	W Adamson
1931–1935	Nat	R MacDonald	A Sinclair 1931–32
			G Collins 1932–35
1935–1940	Nat	S Baldwin	G Collins 1935–36
			W Elliot 1936–38
			J Colville 1938–40
1940–1945	Coal	W Churchill	E Brown 1940–41
			T Johnston 1941–45
1945	Con	W Churchill	Earl of Rosebery
1945–51	Lab	C Attlee	J Westwood 1945–47
			A Woodburn 1947–50
			H McNeil 1950–51
1951–64	Con	W Churchill 1951–55	J Stuart 1951–57
		A Eden 1955–56	J S Maclay 1957–62
		H Macmillan 1956–63	M Noble 1962–63
		A Douglas-Home 1963–64	
1964–70	Lab	H Wilson	W Ross
1970–74	Con	E Heath	G Campbell
1974–79	Lab	H Wilson 1974–76	W Ross
		J Callaghan 1976–79	B Millan
1979–	Con	M Thatcher 1979–90	G Younger 1979–86
		J Major 1990–	M Rifkind 1986–90
			I Lang 1990–

constituencies little — like James Bryce, MP for Aberdeen, 1885–1907.[9] Wallas criticised Bryce's elevated rationalism, but this was probably what his constituents wanted. After 1906, however, Liberal policy — land and temperance reform and a commitment to home rule — proved 'constructive', controversial, and popular, and the Scottish Secretary, Lord Pentland, was an original and unorthodox figure. Asquith disliked him and made him Governor of Madras in 1910 (Pentland took Patrick Geddes with him to India, where he inspired the young Nehru); his replacement, MacKinnon Wood, was unexciting.

This switch coincided with the onset of that multiple crisis — the government versus the Lords, militant trade unionism, suffragettes, Ulster Unionists and the Kaiser — which made Westminster the centre of political interest. Scots home rule inevitably seemed parochial, although the Irish issue ought to have made it more salient, but the England-residing cadre of MPs was now under attack from the Young Scots Society — obviously modelled on *Cymru Fydd* — an explicitly Liberal nationalist organisation.[10] Even after the affiliation of the Miners' Federation in 1909, Labour remained not much more than an interest-group, although the creation of a Royal Commission into Scottish housing, under pressure from the miners, doubtless nagged those Liberal councillors who were proud of their 'municipal socialism' with the thought of the vast problem of inadequate housing — and their own substantial interests in it.

The 1914–18 war killed off the individualist moralism of the Liberals, and any dialogue on constitutional change. The MPs were split when Lloyd George forced through his coalition in 1916; the Liberal rentiers, downed by an alliance of labour and industrialists in 1915–16 which imposed rent control, were knocked out by the report of the Commission on Housing in 1917, and the Reform Act of 1918, which almost trebled the electorate.[11] Iain Hutchison has attributed Liberal collapse (from 58 seats in 1910 to 28 in 1922 and 9 in 1924) to party conflict — Lloyd George's 1918 assault on the Asquithian 'Wee Frees' — the rapid rise of a Labour class consciousness, and Unionist co-option of many Liberal causes and client groups.[12] Yet Robert Munro, the Coalition Liberal Secretary, had maintained rent control, and reached a *concordat* with the Catholics over education: two basic planks of the welfarist/administrative devolution settlement.[13]

But the Liberals had not, like the Unionists, given their organisation an overhaul. Some local parties improved their position, but more were moribund, deserted by the local solicitors who had run things for decades. The undermining factor was local government. Labour's success and its programme of rent control and housing municipalisation, forced urban Liberals to fuse with Tories and many Independents into 'Progressive' or 'Moderate' alliances — much more rapidly than was the case in England. Despite 'municipal socialism' the roots of 'New Liberalism' did not go deep enough to outbid Labour at its own game.[14] Asquith's return for Paisley in 1920 helped little: he had little to offer to an economy toppling into recession. There was some recovery in 1923 — the glimmer of a three-party future — but MacDonald's motive in taking office with the first, minority Labour government was to evict the Liberals, and in the 1924 election he succeeded.

Thereafter the party was divided. Its Scottish leader, Archie Sinclair in remote Caithness, tended towards Lloyd George; Sir Godfrey Collins, the Glasgow publisher, moved from Asquith to the more conservative wing headed by Sir John Simon. Both combined to support the National government in 1931, but Sinclair resigned as Secretary of State over the adoption of protection. Collins succeeded him. Fry argues that he really remained a Liberal — notably by creating a Scottish Special Area Commissioner who extended the Scottish Office's remit into the economic field, but Walter Elliot, a pretty nominal Tory (and married into the Tennant clan) followed in the same furrow. The Independents and Collins' Nationals ultimately parted in 1935; some had already seceded to the Scottish Party in 1932–34.[15] The party retained more potential than its derisory vote (6.7 per cent in 1935, 5.0 per cent in 1945, 1.9 per cent in 1955) — as the support for John MacCormick's Covenant Movement in the late 1940s showed — but it only revived when the Unionists started slipping in the late 1950s.

III

Under a succession of able, and usually Scottish chairmen, the Unionists cashed in on First World War. They were the patriotic party of the 'Anglo-Scottish' Empire — ex-officers as agents, ex-servicemen in the British Legion, Orange Lodges discreetly tagging along — and fostered a kind of one-party-state ethos bridging businessmen, professionals and even collectivists: Walter Elliot, Noel Skelton, John Buchan.[16] This was, in its own terms, a 'principled society' — think of the work that William Weir put into the National Grid, or Tom Johnston's co-option into the Empire Marketing Board — and owed a lot to the fears of industrial capitalists about the problems caused by the economic downturn. Some, at least, were alert to possible remedies: mixtures, usually, of free trade and state-sponsored rationalisation and 'planning'. They drew on a dense network of family and financial relationships, and swallowed former Liberals to become an effective interest group, filling many senior government advisory posts and ensuring that Secretaries of State were chosen from among them, not out of any professional political elite.[17]

They were also unsuccessful. In the 1920s the City got its way in government economic policy, in the 1930s the new industries of the south east. In both cases Scots who stayed north lost out. Even the electoral triumph of 1931 deceived. The steel industry, having got what it wanted — protectionism — kept away from politics, while lawyer-and-gentry MPs were decoupled from business to an alarming and disabling extent. Tom Johnston, with only a minority following, was able thus to achieve a remarkable coup for social-democratic/corporate ideas in 1941–45.

The later recovery of the Unionist Party in the 1950s — to 36 seats and 50.1 per cent of the vote in 1955 — was equally misleading. Its policies were centrist (people actually believed in candidates calling themselves Conservative-Liberals) while old-style politics appeared to be doing as well as old-style industry. But management of both was complacent and slack. Churchill gargled with home rule rhetoric in 1950; he ignored Elliot, who could have provided strong and economically sensitive government. Macmillan sensed decay in the 1959 election results, and took a personal initiative to recover matters, but by then much of Scottish traditional industry — and industrial capitalism — was terminally sick.

IV

Against this combination of economic interest and policy heterodoxy, Labour was split. The 1918 Reform Act had strengthened it among urban workers, but despite the success of the Clydesiders in 1922, it was dominated by the country's 150,000 miners, and its largest group of MPs in 1924 were their agents, men of Lib-Lab tendencies, evangelical Christian and teetotal principles, nationalist or high Victorian culture, and little empathy with the cities.

Some of the 'parochialism' of John Wheatley and the Clydesiders may have stemmed from efforts to bridge this gap. Sociologically, the latter anticipated the 'public sector middle class' elite of Labour in the 1960s and 1970s, but the London leadership — then and later — had the edge on MPs whose basic loyalties were Scots.[18] Wheatley, exceptionally, used his London contacts; Maxton moved after the General Strike from home rule to the more 'British', and 'revolutionary', initiative of the Cook-Maxton manifesto of 1928. But this foundered on his own lack of application. Dominated in Scotland by dour, limited men of the Willie Graham and Willie Adamson kind, the second Labour government staggered towards crisis. Although the government attempted to cope with mounting unemployment by welfare measures and some public works, the reflationary ideas of Tom Johnston and Allan Young were spurned. In the 1931 'Doctor's Mandate' election, Labour's poll fell back only to its 1922 level, but the switch of former

Liberals to 'National' candidates cut it down to seven MPs. By 1932 there were only three. At ease neither in London nor in Glasgow (where Patrick Dollan kept the ILP orthodox), Maxton allowed his charisma to lead the ILP into the wilderness.

Labour's parliamentary recovery was slow, but its advance in local politics rapid. This meant that housing, in particular, became a double-edged issue for Labour. It aided municipal advance during and after the 1914–18 war, particularly after the Wheatley Act of 1924, but it also swamped MPs in the *minutiae* of local authority business, particularly after Elliot's abolition of parish councils in 1929. The stress of a life divided between Scotland and London either cut down ambition to a 'sweetie wife' level ('wee hard men' occurred more in the unions or local government) — or took its toll in ill-health and premature death. Even with unemployment never under 15 per cent, Labour had not the competence to get its most effective performer, Tom Johnston, into the Commons until 1935, when Adamson was evicted from West Fife by the Communist Willie Gallacher. Despite much noisy prompting from intellectual and 'popular front' ginger groups, the Scottish Council took few policy initiatives. The foundations of Labour's post-war industrial policy, of London-centred industrial direction, were briskly laid down by Hugh Dalton's Commission on the Distressed Areas in 1937. An attempt by the Council in 1941 to revive the party's traditional home rule commitment was as ruthlessly squashed at Transport House by Emmanuel Shinwell.[19]

Labour made its major pre-war advance in south-east England, while left activists in Scotland split three ways. The self-immolation of the ILP was accompanied by the rise both of the Communist party and (in a more diffuse way) of political nationalism. Despite the long shadow of Stalinism, the 'Popular Front' after 1935 moved the CPGB out from its 'Little Moscows' in the Fife Coalfield and the Vale of Leven, and won it lasting credibility through the commitment of its members to the cause of Republican Spain.[20] The Scottish Communists were a distinguished and dedicated group, but their millenarianism had little time for the nation — even when personified in its greatest poet. (Hugh MacDiarmid was expelled for 'nationalist deviation' in 1938.)

The first of the National Party of Scotland's election attempts was frustrated by the crisis of 1931. Its leader, John MacCormick, then tried to re-animate the latent Liberal vote by an alliance in 1934 with the Scottish party, a bruising business which led to mass-desertions.[21] Yet nationalism of a generalised, cross-party sort helped evolve the economic and planning initiatives which underpinned more spectacular wartime developments. Something close to an autonomous agency for Scottish economic development had been formulated by Scottish Economic Committee, and Tom Johnston would draw on the ideas and personalities it encouraged. He was also not above waving the bogey of 'a sort of Sinn Fein movement' in front of cabinet colleagues, when he wanted to get his way. The SNP obliged by winning its first, and for a long time last, seat in Motherwell in 1945.

V

Johnston's *demarches* were also aided by the northward migration of administration. Even before 1914 the growth of the Scottish Office was making executive control from Dover House in Whitehall irksome. Post-war transfers of further powers over education, public health and housing — and the conversion of the semi-autonomous boards into civil service departments under Sir John Gilmour in 1926 — ensured that most of the Office would move north. A new elite of civil servants, on the whole recruited from Scottish universities and informed by the Hegelian reformism of the 1890s and 1900s, increased their grip with the construction after 1930 of St Andrew's House in Edinburgh as a 'Scottish Whitehall'.[22] The beginnings of economic intervention, 1934–39, and the imposition of a corporate structure under the Secretary of State after the Gilmour Committee's report in 1938, prepared the new system for its wartime *tour de force*.[23]

The maturity of the Scottish Office coincides neatly with T H Marshall's definition of 'social citizenship' in 1932. From its foundation in 1885 it acted as a handbrake on the engine of parliamentary sovereignty, securing to successive groups of Scots — crofters, urban tenants, Catholics — a range of welfare rather than participatory rights.[24] It also manoeuvred, much more tactfully than Whitehall operators ever could, in the internal politics of tne Scottish 'estates' — interest groups like farmers, businessmen, local government and education. The entry into the economic sphere in the 1930s was a case in point: the Scottish Office shared the concern of leading businessmen like Sir James Lithgow to provide employment for labour 'liberated' by rationalisation in the heavy industries. The result was the commitment to 'diversification'.

But the stylish and internationally-recognised urban consciousness which pervaded Patrick Geddes' Scotland seemed to evaporate in the inter-war years. This could be put down to a limitation of funds for infrastructural investment because of economic decline and the priority granted the appalling problem of overcrowded housing (over five times worse than England) which the earlier 'progressives' had suppressed.[25] Iain Levitt and Andrew MacPherson, surveying social policy and education, also detect an 'official' paradigm of community derived not from the city but from the countryside and the medium sized market town. It was perhaps appropriate that Johnston's greatest achievement was to bring electric power to the Highlands, for conservation reasons the only Scottish issue to occupy the Cabinet much before 1939.[26]

State action in the inter-war years ended the legal peculiarities which made working-class urban settlement unstable. It began to integrate — through the Labour party in particular — the large Irish minority in the cities.[27] Anti-Irish sentiments were common among the Scottish elite, but the political protestantism of the 1930s, Scotland's contribution to the radical right, in fact aided Labour's capture of Glasgow in 1934.[28] Some Labour and Liberal politicians regarded Stormont as a promising experiment and it had some influence on MacCormick's Covenant movement.[29] But the informal *concordat* maintained by the Scottish Office, the Labour Party and the Catholic Church proved the real success. By the 1960s, when Catholics achieved political power and status, home rule was losing its sectarian linkages and becoming the logical terminus of administrative devolution. The pro-devolution official in charge of economic policy in the Scottish Office, John MacGuinness, was the first Catholic head-of-department.

VI

Scottish politicians rarely peered beyond immediate pragmatism to articulate any longer-term philosophy. Christopher Smout, who sees one, is inconsistent about it. He complains that Labour rejected 'self-government' along Scandinavian lines for a bureaucratic welfarism, but he has also suggested that the energetic individualism of the Scots — as trade unionists, for example — conflicted with the 'resignation' necessary to co-ordinate involvement in the state.[30] Neither position yields pragmatism its due. Rent control and the religious settlement in education — usually associated with Labour — were the work of the post-1915 wartime coalition; the incorporation of the unions into government consultation (which started in Scotland in 1935; in England not until 1940) was the result of Sir Godfrey Collins' Scottish Economic Committee.[31]

'Enlightened bureaucracy' had some roots in Hegelianism and the administrative skill of R B Haldane. Walter Elliot's *Toryism and the Twentieth Century* (1928) extended this to argue for authority in a time of political and philosophical revolution, using Bergson and Einstein to refute the mechanical causation of orthodox Marxism, and pleading for the traditional elite to fuse with a technocracy of applied and social scientists and deploy the national and international planning mechanisms evolved during the war.[32] This ethos was also found in John Grierson's documentary movement and among the scientist-Marxists of the 1930s and 1940s, notably J B S Haldane and Hyman Levy, who boosted the popularity of the Communist Utopia. Statism, quite different to the small-scale co-operation of Plaid Cymru, also influenced the SNP. J A A Porteous, Elliot's appointment to the Scottish Economic Committee, and later economics expert of the SNP, took a Keynesian/corporatist line, as did J A Bowie, in *The Future of Scotland* (1939).[33] More popular than Keynes, however, was Social Credit, which enthused *literati* like Edwin Muir and Hugh MacDiarmid, Commonwealth territories with a strong Scottish tradition — Manitoba, British Columbia and New Zealand, and two central Labour figures: Arthur Woodburn and Tom Johnston.[34] They regarded C H Douglas's programme — otherwise strongly individualistic, pro-small-business and rather anti-semitic — as a form of bank nationalisation, persuasive when Scotland's substantial financial sector rarely showed any interest in national economic development.

Scottish Catholic socialism was not very cerebral, but John Wheatley had to take on the casuistic ability of Jesuit apologists, and his vision of the socialist city state seems to owe something to the localist ideals of many European Catholics in the late 19th century, given vivid life in G K Chesterton's *The Napoleon of Notting Hill* (1907), and, through Saunders Lewis, part of the early ideology of Plaid Cymru. Chestertonian influence continued in Catholic circles until the 1960s, the Distributist Club at Glasgow University being the equivalent of Labour clubs anywhere else. There was little Chestertonian about the use of public housing and education as a means of socialising Catholics within the Scots community; but by the 1980s it was evident that the *idea* of community, common to Catholic and secularised Protestant, was different from the competitive individualism perceived elsewhere.[35]

VII

At the end of World War II there was a remarkable degree of consensus about welfare goals — particularly evident in religious circles — but much less unity on economic and constitutional issues. Labour retained a remarkably high degree of support throughout its term of office, although response to its legislative programme was mixed; enthusiasm for the National Health Service (1948), indifference to nationalisation, mingled with worry over centralisation. The old heavy industries, benefitting from the elimination for a few years of German and Japanese competition, preserved the labour relations and, within the working class the social gradations, of the Edwardian period.[36] Committed to building a mass party, Labour condemned the emotional and largely middle-class Covenant movement.[37] Its own politics still bore utopian and sectarian traces, furthered by the role of Communists in the trade unions and, after the split of 1956, in the party itself.

The eclipse of deferential Conservatism went faster than the 'secularisation' of the old working class.[38] As religion and barriers between the skilled and the unskilled declined, so too did Unionist affiliations in areas like Glasgow Craigton and Leith.[39] When Scotland failed to share in the boom of the late fifties, she started to withdraw from the 'British homogeneity' pattern. Did she also, as John Foster has argued, become more 'proletarianised'? After the late 1940s, Labour's grassroots withered, too. The local socialist movement in country districts — railwaymen and postmen, farm and textile workers, teachers and civil servants — had expected a breakthrough around 1950, but its votes then peaked and fell. Such groups themselves declined, and their supporters shifted back to the Liberals.[40] Labour's utopian and trade union identities had been sacrificed to a pragmatic 'modernisation' ethos, and urban social change also put it under pressure. Heavy industry closures, the decanting of city-dwellers into peripheral housing estates and the five new towns, and local government changes produced instability within the working class, soon visible in the impact of the Scottish National Party.

Why the SNP, and why not Liberalism or a right-wing Toryism? The Liberals could have offered a 'Scottish' deal to the SNP, but maintained a 'British' identity in the hope of a breakthrough in the south.[41] Slow economic growth in Scotland ruled out an immigration issue, and while the Scots *may* be more tolerant — due to the large immigrant element (Highland, Irish, Italian, Polish) in the existing population — a Powellite expression of 'British' identity might still have been possible, and was hinted at in the 'Save the Argylls' campaign. The very simplicity of the SNP's approach seemed to help it. It had been for almost two decades in the grip of the fundamentalists who had ejected John MacCormick in 1942, and some elements of its radical and literary progenitors remained, boosted by an intake from CND and co-operative industrial projects. Its chairman for most of the 1960s and 1970s, William Wolfe, occupied a position similar to that of Keir Hardie, as 'conscience' of the ILP, before World War I, but with an un-Hardie-like gift for organisation and publicity.[42]

Labour's long tenure of municipal power, decaying party organisation, and (when in government) centralised authoritarianism, gave the SNP its chance. The regime of William Ross, 1964–70, meant gains in regional assistance, housing development, educational modernisation, and the bold and successful scheme for a Highlands and Islands Development Board. But the personnel of the 'quangocracy' of non-elected bodies were distinctly mixed, and when Labour had to curb ambitious planning schemes after the balance of payments crisis in 1967, protest at the Pollok and Hamilton by-elections, and at municipal elections in 1967 and 1968, went to the SNP, whose vote in May 1968 peaked at over 33 per cent.

SNP voters were largely people who would not have voted at all, in such elections, although they contained more refugees from Labour than from the Unionists. But who *joined* the party — some guesses put its strength at around 100,000 in 1968 — and stood as its candidates in its local election campaigns? Its candidates — small business people, it seemed — became an embarrassment, when attacked for naivety by veterans from the other parties. Where did they end up? As membership had already fallen fairly steeply when the party revived in the early 1970s, they seemed to fall out, and the party changed to become a rather more nationalistic section of the public sector middle class.[43]

VIII

The rise of the SNP implied a revolution, since a new central issue altered the relationships of the main parties; William Miller's *The End of British Politics* (1981) showed Scotland chronically out of synchronisation with the rest of the UK.[44] A politics of transaction and manoeuvre, intitially inept, later carried out with increasing *panache* and purpose, had not yet evicted the hitherto dominant two-party competition, but meant that it only carried on by adopting a quite different agenda.

The Conservatives tried to regain their 1950s dominance by re-packaging 'decentralisation' as the legislative devolution proposed by its Constitutional Committee under Sir Alec Douglas-Home. This reported in March 1970, in advance of the Royal Commission on the Constitution which Harold Wilson, panicked by Hamilton, had set up in 1968. But once in government, they took advantage of the fall in the SNP vote to replace devolution with an ambitious two-tier reorganisation of local government. Even before this was inaugurated in 1974, the Kilbrandon

Report coincided with a four-fold increase in the price of oil. The SNP revived through its skilful exploitation of the 'Scottish Oil' theme, and the economic crisis and two elections of 1974 took its parliamentary vote to over 30 per cent, and eleven MPs. With a tiny Labour majority, the prospect of a constitutional crisis loomed up, should it capture over half the Scottish seats.

From this point the two main parties were affected both by the loss of confidence in British 'convention' and (in a Scottish context) by an unprecedented politics of manoeuvre. Frightened of being whitewashed by the SNP in the second election of 1974, Labour whipped its reluctant Scottish Council into supporting devolution. This was not enough for an articulate 'national left' minority which, headed by Jim Sillars, founded the new Scottish Labour Party. Its career was as disastrous as the ILP's after its disaffiliation in 1932 — but much shorter — and it left the devolutionary left sorely weakened. James Callaghan replaced Ross as Secretary of State with Bruce Millan, who was fatally uncharismatic, and Labour's adherence to the 'Westminster system' for electing the Assembly cost it Liberal support.

Under Mrs Thatcher the Tories retreated from devolution and, at least in the short term, acted with lack of scruple and great skill. They let Labour, now devolutionist but not enthusiastic about it, outmanoeuvre the SNP — whose shift to a more devolutionary stance did them little electoral good — and then exploited Labour's internal divisions. As the referendum on the act approached, Lord Home announced that the Tories had 'something better' on offer. Given nationalist misgivings, trade union misbehaviour, government unpopularity and organisational ineptitude on the 'Yes' side, the wonder is that a majority of any sort was found for the bill on 1 March 1979.[45]

By mounting a vote of no-confidence in the Callaghan government the SNP virtually wrote itself out of parliament. The Conservatives enjoyed a boomlet of support, and even took five out of the eight Scottish seats in the first elections to the European parliament. George Younger, a shrewd and affable dynast, disciplined some rebellious Labour councils but did what he could to temper the Thatcherite wind, without much success, as the collapse of manufacturing capacity in 1979–81 — and the election of 1983 — showed. Only marginally affected by the secession of the Social Democrats in 1981, Labour held on to its vote, while the centre parties inflicted more damage on the Conservatives, who also made up very little ground in local elections.

When Younger unexpectedly took over the defence ministry in 1986 he was succeeded by Malcolm Rifkind, hitherto accounted a liberal and devolutionist, who instead set out to combat what Conservative propaganda saw as Scotland's culture of dependency. This aggression had no appeal to the Scottish voters, and despite a pre-election boom the Conservatives suffered in 1987 their worst reverse in terms of seats since 1906. Rifkind, now overlooked by a Thatcher trusty in the shape of Michael Forsyth, had to proceed with a right wing agenda. The deeply-resented poll tax was followed by the replacement of the Scottish Development Agency by the business-oriented Scottish Enterprise, the privatisation of bus services, the steel industry and the two electricity undertakings (although not the nuclear stations that provided more than 60 per cent of Scottish power). The effect of these measures, combined with a rapidly-decaying economic situation, was to marginalise Rifkind's party to the point where its extinction in the next election seemed a practical possibility.

IX

Conservative decline was not the result of two-party competition. Scottish attitudes to Britain changed measurably during the 'oil boom' decade 1975–85. Support for independence, in the 1970s stable at around 20 per cent, rose after 1980 to around 35 per cent. In David McCrone's conspectus, Scotland had traditionally provided the 'lieutenant class' for imperial expansion, which had also performed corporate administrative functions in Scotland itself. As an independent Scots capitalism declined — very sharply in 1984–85 — it tended to align itself with a non-party nationalism which now regarded itself as being exploited by multinational capital, and — over devolution — betrayed by its political partner. Emotionally, this expressed itself in indifference to the 'Falklands fever' of 1982, while right-wing centralisation changed Labour local government hostility to devolution into the close alignment of the Convention of Scottish Local Authorities with the movement for a cross-party Scottish Constitutional Convention. Labour's attitude to the Convention remained sceptical, even after the 1987 election made the conduct of government business possible only through the deployment of English Tory MPs — the 'Doomsday scenario' anticipated by the periodical *Radical Scotland*. Its conversion was encouraged by a further SNP revival: the Govan by election of November 1988 which returned Jim Sillars to Westminster.[46]

Scottish political discourse meanwhile gave these developments an unprecedented coherence. John Mackintosh's *The Decentralisation of Power* of 1968 set out the case for home rule in terms of the management of a British mixed economy, but the debate which then ensued saw a re-emphasis of the European locus of Scottish politics in the work of Tom Nairn, and an increasingly corrosive critique of the institutions of social democracy and the British state.[47] How much did this affect the ordinary voter? More than might be thought, as insistent arguments rapidly penetrated the 'estates' of education, social work, religion and the media. The onus of proof had been put on the defenders of the *status quo*, partly because of the weakness of Scottish industrial capitalism, and because the business of the culture-national or regional unit in late-capitalist Europe is increasingly to do with education, communication and information.

Throughout Scottish society a sense of identity separate from the rest of the United Kingdom has grown, for obvious enough reasons among the disadvantaged, but also among more fortunate groups, to whom 'society' has tended to matter more than the privatised 'life-style' of the English South-East. In fact the the more that the latter seems eccentric in Europe, the more determined are the moves — not only by the state-sector element of the Scottish middle-class — to reconstruct the country's economy as an European region, in the teeth of the antithetical policies of the financial and political metropolis.

The culture of political nationalism in Scotland, by now perhaps more sophisticated than in any other 'British nation' counterpart, has moved beyond the defence of former distinctiveness to a critique of the 'backward' British state — ironically when, for the first time since the 1920s, Scots occupy leading positions in the Labour party. Should they assume power in the early 1990s, a broad measure of autonomy will be inevitable. Whether the Union will persist will depend largely on their ability to clear up the economic debris of the Thatcher experiment. If they fail in this — and the prospects are not auspicious — its final break-up could be swift.[48]

NOTES

1. See the attitudes of voters to politicians in the System 3 Poll carried out in association with the BBC's 'Grasping the Thistle' programme, February 1987, in Ken Cargill, ed., *Scotland 2000*, (BBC 1987.) appendix. p. ii, and my essay on pp. 1–35.

2. James Kellas, *The Scottish Political System*, (Cambridge 1973, revised edition 1989), pp. 17ff.; William L. Miller, *The End of British Politics: Scots and English Political Behaviour in the Seventies*, (Oxford 1981), p. 15, 258ff.; Michael Keating and Arthur Midwinter, *The Government of Scotland*, (Edinburgh 1983), pp. 107–109; Michael Fry, *Patronage and Principle*, (Aberdeen, 1987.)

3. See Owen Dudley Edwards, ed., *A Claim of Right for Scotland*, Polygon 1989, and the Scottish content of the *Charter 88* manifesto published in the *Independent*, 17 December 1988; Tom Nairn, *The Enchanted Glass: Britain and its Monarchy*, (Radius 1988); David Martin, *Bringing Commonsense to the Common Market*, (Fabian Society, 1986); Christopher Harvie, *Europe and the Scottish Nation*, (Scottish Centre for Economic and Social Research, 1989.)

4. Ernest Barker, *Political Thought in Britain from Spencer to the Present Day*, (Williams and Norgate 1915) pp. 181–2; Harold Laski, *Studies in the Problem of Sovereignty*, (Yale University Press 1916), pp. 65, 208; for a study of, *inter alia*, the 'Machiavellian' tradition in British political culture see Christopher Harvie, *The Centre of Things: Political Fiction from Disraeli to the Present Day*, (London, forthcoming.)

5. Ian Budge and D. W. Urwin, *Scottish Political Behaviour*, (London, 1966,) esp. pp. 112–138.

6. A good example of the higher journalism was James Margach (of the *Sunday Times*), *The Anatomy of Power: an Enquiry into the Personality of Leadership*, (London 1979). I recollect the late Lord Ross of Marnock gleefully saying in 1981 that he'd just burned a garage-full of papers!

7. Although Gerald Warner's *The Scottish Tory Party*, (London 1988) is a disgrace.

8. Charles Cowan, *Reminiscences*, privately printed 1878, p. 263.

9. H. A. L. Fisher, *James Bryce*, (London 1927), vol 1, p. 201; Aberdeen political culture is covered, incidentally but persuasively, in William Donaldson, *Popular Literature in Victorian Scotland*, (Aberdeen, 1986.)

10. Iain Hutchison, *A Political History of Scotland, 1832–1923*, (Edinburgh 1986), pp. 233ff.; H. J. Hanham, *Scottish Nationalism*, (London 1969), p. 95.

11. See Joe Melling, *Rent Strikes*, (Edinburgh 1983), pp. 104ff.

12. Hutchison, op. cit., pp. 309–328.

13. See Gordon Brown, 'Labour Politics in Scotland, 1906–26', Edinburgh Ph.D, 1981, pp. 242ff.

14. Christopher Cook, *The Age of Alignment*, (London 1975), pp. 83ff.

15. See Fry, op. cit., pp. 178–9; Roy Douglas, *A History of the Liberal Party*, (London 1971) pp. 228ff.

16. See Colin Coote, *A Companion of Honour: the Life of Walter Elliot*, (Glassgow 1965) 77ff.

17. Tom Burns, *The Real Rulers of Scotland*, London Scots' Self-Government Committee 1938, *and* Allen Hutt, *The Condition of the Working Class*, (1933) are very informative on political-industrial linkages.

18. Largely thanks to the Scottish Labour History Society and Ian MacDougall, whose *Labour Records in Scotland*, 1978, is seminal, the bibliography here is potentially limitless. Ian Donnachie, Christopher Harvie and Iain S. Wood, *Forward: 100 Years of Labour Politics in Scotland*, (Edinburgh 1989) can serve as an introduction; William Knox, *Scottish Labour Leaders 1918–1939*, (Edinburgh 1984) has besides its biographies useful essays on the sociology of the Labour elite, and there have recently been a succession of scholarly biographies: Graham Walker, *Thomas Johnston*, (Manchester 1988); Gordon Brown, *James Maxton*, (Edinburgh 1987); Ian S. Wood, *John Wheatley*, (Manchester, 1989.)

19. See Christopher Harvie, 'Scottish Labour and World War II' in *The Historical Journal*, vol 32, 1983.

20. Stuart MacKenzie, *Little Moscows*, (London 1980); Ian MacDougall, ed., *Militant Miners*, (Edinburgh, 1981), and *Voices from the Spanish Civil War*, (Edinburgh 1989.)

21. Jack Brand, *The National Movement in Scotland*, (London 1978,) pp. 24ff.

22. For the Scottish Office see John S. Gibson, *The Thistle and the Rose*, HMSO 1985, esp. ch. 3; and George Pottinger, *The Secretaries of State for Scotland*, (Edinburgh 1979,) pp. 33–99. James Mitchell's forthcoming *The Evolution of the Scottish Office, 1885–1939*, (Edinburgh), should prove definitive.

23. For the Scottish Office and economic affairs in the 1930s and 1940s see R. H. Campbell, 'The Scottish Office and the Special Areas in the 1930s' in *The Historical Journal*, vol 22, No. 1, 1979, pp. 167–84; and C. T. Harvie, 'Scottish Government: the Age of Tom Johnston' in *Bulletin of Scottish Politics*, vol 2, 1981, pp. 1–19.

24. See Christopher Harvie, 'Dicey's Last Stand, or Thoughts on the Union between Law and Opinion' in Colin Crouch and David Marquand, eds., *The New Centralism*, Political Quarterly/Blackwell, 1989, esp. pp. 48ff.

25. See Harvie, *No Gods*, pp. 70–3.

26. Andrew MacPherson 'An Angle on the Geist' in Walter Humes and Andrew Paterson, *Culture and Education in Scotland*, (Edinburgh 1983) pp. 236–7.

27. See David Englander, *Landlord and Tenant in Urban Britain*, (Oxford 1982.)

28. Tom Gallagher, *The Uneasy Peace: Religious Conflict in Modern Scotland*, (Manchester, 1987), ch. 4; *Edinburgh Divided*, (Polygon 1987) chs. 3–8; Steve Bruce, *No Pope of Rome*, (Oxford, 1986); and the various essays in Tom Gallagher and Graham Walker, eds., *Sermons and Battle-Hymns: Protestantism in Modern Scotland*, (Edinburgh 1990)

29. Cabinet Papers (Public Record Office, Kew): 11 May 1950, pp. 7–8.

30. Christopher Smout, *A Century of the Scottish People*, (Glasgow, 1985.) pp. 274–5; 'The Scottish Identity' in Robert Underwood, ed., *The Future of Scotland*, (London 1977) p. 19.

31. I survey such consultative bodies in 'Nationalism and the Politics of Culture in Scotland' in *Anglistik und Englischunterricht*, vol 38/9, Heidelberg, 1990.

32. Walter Elliot, *Toryism and the Twentieth Century*, (London 1927) pp. 82ff.

33. See Eric Ashby, *Haldane on Education*, (London 1975) and Gary Werskey, *The Visible College*, (London 1977). For economic thought in the 1930s see J. A. A. Porteous, *The New Unionism*, (London 1935,) and J. A. Bowie, *The Future of Scotland*, (London 1939.)

34. Walker, *Johnston*, p. 122; Arthur Woodburn, unpublished autobiography in Woodburn Ms. (NLS Acc 7646. Box 4), p. 102.

35. Gallagher, *Uneasy Peace*, Ch. 7; some fitful light is cast on this by Compton Mackenzie in his *Memoirs: Octave Six and Octave Seven*, (London, 1967, 68) and see P. J. Dollan, *A Tale of Two Cities*, (Aird and Coghill 1940) pp. 43–62.

36. See the essays in Richard Saville, ed., *The Economic Development of Modern Scotland, 1950–1980*, (Edinburgh 1985.)

37. Harvie, 'Labour in the Forties' in Donnachie, Harvie and Wood, coll. cit.; the Covenant movement still lacks its historian; John MacCormick's *The Flag in the Wind*, (London 1955,) is naturally partisan. See Woodburn's report in Cabinet Minutes, No. 72 (1949), 15 December.

38. See, for example, Tom Brennan on the Govan Labour Party in *Reshaping a City*, (Grant 1959,) pp. 111–117.

39. Budge and Urwin, op. cit, pp. 76ff.; Gallagher, *Uneasy Peace*, ch. 7.

40. Frank Bealey and John Sewel, *The Politics of Independence*, (Aberdeen 1981,) shows such tendencies at work in the north-east. The minutes of Roxburgh, Selkirk and Peebles Labour Party, in the National Library, also bear this out.

41. See David Steel, *Against Goliath*, (London 1989,); and Graham Watson., 'Scottish Liberals and a Nationalist Alliance', unpublished paper 1988.

42. Hanham, op. cit., pp. 204ff; C. T. Harvie, *Scotland and Nationalism* (London 1977,) pp. 238ff.

43. These debates are summarised in John Bochel and David Denver, 'The Decline of the SNP: an Alternative View' in *Political Studies*, Sept. 1972, vol 20., pp. 311ff.

44. Miller, op. cit., pp. 287ff.

45. Michael Keating and David Bleiman, *Labour and Scottish Nationalism*, (London 1979), pp. 150–188; Raymond Levy, *Scottish Nationalism at the Crossroads*, (Edinburgh 1989) chs. 4, 5; John Bochel, David Denver and Allan Macartney, *The Referendum Experience*, (Aberdeen, 1981).

46. See James Naughtie, 'Labour since 1979' in Donnachie, Harvie and Wood, coll. cit.; and for the background to the Convention, Owen Dudley Edwards, ed., *A Claim of Right for Scotland* (Edinburgh 1989) A basic source for contemporary politics is the *Yearbook of Scottish Politics*, published annually since 1976, by the politics department of Edinburgh University.

47. The Nairn corpus consists of the 'hostile' 'Three Dreams of Scottish Nationalism', in Karl Miller, ed., *Memoirs of a Modern Scotland* (London 1969) followed by *The Break-up of Britain*, (London 1977,) and *The Enchanted Glass* (Radius 1988.)

48. This chapter was written before the downfall of Mrs Thatcher and her replacement by Mr Major in November 1990.

CHAPTER 9

Patterns of Culture

T. C. Smout

Was Scotland less Scottish by 1980 than it had been in 1914? One of the themes of Scottish History since the Union of Parliaments of 1707, indeed since the Union of Crowns of 1603, has been the erosion of the distinctive culture and identity of an ancient nation. It was lamented in the poetry of Fergusson and Burns in the eighteenth century, and deplored by Henry Cockburn in a well known passage in his *Journal* in 1853:

> The prolongation of Scotch peculiarities, especially of our language and habits I do earnestly desire. An exact knowledge and feeling of what these have been since 1707 till now would be more curious five hundred years hence than a similar knowledge and feeling of the old Greeks. But the features and expression of a people cannot be perpetuated by legislative engraving. Nothing can prevent the gradual disappearance of local manners under the absorption and assimilation of a far larger, richer and more powerful kindred adjoining kingdom.[1]

There is no reason to suppose the pace at which Scottish peculiarities became washed out of Scottish life slowed between then and the First World War. The coming of the penny post, the telegraph and the telephone created an immediacy of communication between England and Scotland: combined with modern transport, the railway which had reached into the corners of the Highlands by 1900, and the lorry and the automobile which at that point were beginning to create a demand for tar-macadamed roads, the gap between the ends of the island shrank dramatically. The English for the first time became familiar visitors, as romantic tourists in Edinburgh and the Borders, and as tourists and especially as sportsmen in the Highlands. The coming of the board schools in 1872 was a force both for reducing regional distinctions within Scotland, and for Anglicisation: the former is illustrated not merely by the discouragement of Gaelic in the Highlands but of Doric accents in the north east in classroom and playground, the latter by the disregard of Scottish traditions of 'secondary' education in the 1872 Education Act in the interests of a spurious uniformity with the English act of 1870. By the outbreak of the First World War a vast amount of the cultural texture of Scottishness in language and custom which had still been evident in 1750 and 1830 had been eroded and replaced by

261

something blander and more British. If much remained, for example the civic pride of Glasgow expressed in its great international exhibition at Kelvingrove Park of 1901 and its Edwardian comics of the music hall, or the universal vogue for kailyard novels and popular journalism in the vernacular, it was too often of the kind that Hugh MacDiarmid in the 1920s and 1930s was to scarify as the vulgar relics and imitation of a vanished national culture.

It is tempting to assume that the process has continued at the same pace ever since, and that Scotland by 1980 is still less culturally identifiable than the Scotland of 1914. Such an assumption, however, needs to be considered rather than taken for granted. For one thing, a nationalist party has emerged, seeking complete independence from England, and capable at its peaks of popularity in the 1970s and 1980s of such striking successes in bye-elections, local elections and opinion poll ratings as to strike terror into conventional Labour, Liberal and Conservative politicians: by the general election of 1987, the only political party that did not campaign on a platform of a Scottish assembly with devolved powers was the Conservatives, who obtained 24 per cent of the vote and gained ten seats out of 72. Such developments are, in political terms, a much more striking assertion of Scotland's consciousness of being different from England than any equivalent in previous periods since 1750.

The importance of not being English is held to as doggedly as ever in many other parts of Scottish life. In football there are still, as there were in 1914, separate English and Scottish leagues, and no shortage of the Lion Rampant waving in the hands of the crowd at Hampden Park and Murrayfield. In most international sports, to the puzzlement of foreigners, Scotland continues to be represented separately from England. In religion, the ecumenical discussions to reconcile the Church of Scotland with the Church of England under a new episcopacy in the 1950s ended in breakdown. The persistence of written Scots embraces both the revival of serious poetry under Hugh MacDiarmid and his many successors and the couthy columns of the *Sunday Post*. When radio and television arrived, after the first and second world wars respectively, they brought in their train what evolved into Radio Scotland and STV, not a British blanket. The persistence of a Scottish Press — *The Scotsman, Glasgow Herald, Daily Record, Aberdeen Press and Journal, Dundee Courier* and so on — has long been an irritant and a challenge to the barons first of Fleet Street and then of Wapping. Their response has been to buy up Scottish papers, beginning with Lord Thomson's purchase of the *Scotsman*, so that of the larger groups now only the D. C. Thomson empire in Dundee remains free of external ownership: but the new owners found it necessary at least to allow a continued Scottish identity for their papers. The 1930s produced both a National Trust for Scotland and a Scottish Youth Hostels Association as deliberate assertions of patriotic identity in the new outdoors and heritage movement. Has the tide of cultural erosion stopped, or even turned?

Against a proposition that Anglicisation is on the retreat, however, a host of counter-arguments present themselves from everyday observation. The crowds shopping in Glasgow and Manchester look much the same, wear much the same, buy much the same consumer goods, and since the 1960s have increasingly shopped in chain stores or superstores of the same name and management. An investigation of Scottish expenditure patterns, 1961–1971 found that Scots spent proportionately more than others in the UK on alcohol and especially on tobacco, much less on housing (due to council house policies then pursued in Scotland) and less on chemists goods and recreational goods. They spent more on travel, or at least on public transport, but less on automobiles. The numbers of cars per thousand of population grew in Scotland from 86 in 1961 to 171 in 1971, while in the UK as a whole it grew from 116 to 223 in the same period. Most of what the survey revealed appeared to be the consequences of marginally less spending power in Scotland, rather than different cultural choices.[2] Odder, perhaps, was the Scottish liking for the cinema: in 1951 the entire Scottish population visited films, on average, 36 times a year (compared to only 28 visits in the UK as a whole). Perhaps a colder and wetter climate, combined with smaller houses with fewer places to sit alone and hold hands at home, is the explanation. In any case, by 1971 there were only a third of the cinemas left, and attendances had fallen to 3.7 a year (3.2 in the UK as a whole): TV had eclipsed the big screen, and though there has been some revival of popularity by the cinema in the last decade, this has been on a relatively minor scale.[3]

Even in areas where the Scots had a tradition of being distinctive, things have often changed notably. Is there any difference in the observation of the Sabbath in Scotland and England, except where 'wee free' Presbyterianism still commands the faithful in the Outer Isles? The sabbatarianism of the Scottish towns, albeit declining, was still very evident in 1914 and was not dead even in 1950, but the only distinction now likely to be noticed by the visitor is that, thanks to differences in the law governing Sunday opening hours, shops are actually more likely to be open in Scotland than in England. Much is made of the continuing differences in Scottish traditions of the law and education, but it is notorious that in the universities English professors and lecturers are in the majority, and especially in Edinburgh and St Andrews there have been since the 1950s high percentages of English students: such was not the case on the eve of the First World War. Do Scottish businesses maintain an independence from England of a sort that would not only allow Scots greater control over their own economy, but provide for their managers a career structure spent within Scotland? All the evidence points to this being substantially the case in 1914, and to a steady fall in the percentage of Scots-owned firms since, following the collapse of home-owned heavy industry and its replacement by firms with head office in London, or more recently in America and Japan.[4] One might further ask whether even such media institutions as Radio Scotland or the *Scotsman* are distinctive, Scottish and national in their output, rather than merely local like Radio Yorkshire and the *Yorkshire Post*. With external ownership of the press have gone varying degrees of external interference in editorial policy; the *Scotsman* and the *Glasgow Herald* appear to have enjoyed more freedom for their editors than some of the more 'popular' titles, but none of the papers, however owned or managed, gives the kind of prominence to Scottish cultural or literary affairs that is given for example to the Irish intellectual scene by the *Irish Times*.

The straws of evidence, in fact, point in two ways at once — some towards the determination of a twentieth-century society to hang on to the trappings of Scottish identity, others to the submergence of that society into a bigger homogeneous whole. One way to explain the paradox is to see Scotland as tugged, like every other advanced country, into the slipstream of an overwhelming international capitalist civilization that takes its lead in popular culture from America (with secondary British input) and in high culture from an eclectic mix of London, Paris, Frankfurt, Rome, New York and California. Like many other small European countries, Scotland is essentially powerless and peripheral in this slipstream, provinces of a civilisation that since the 1960s has been mediated through television, and one where fashions are set and initiatives taken elsewhere. In 1951 there were 200 television licences in Scotland, by 1958, 600,000, by 1961 just over a million, by 1971 a near saturation 1,468,000. The Danes in Copenhagen and the Irish in Dublin are in the same situation as Scots in Glasgow and Edinburgh, the young uniformly drawn to Elvis Presley in the 1950s, the Beetles in the 1960s, hard rock in the 1970s, Macdonalds and video games in the 1980s. When Scots do make a reputation in this international culture, like Cary Grant or Sean Connery in film, or the Bay City Rollers and the Sex Pistols in pop music, nothing identifiably Scottish remains in their performance. There are of course still entertainers, the Billy Connollys, as there were once the Will Fyfes and the Harry Lauders, whose following in Scotland is deep: but beyond Scotland, save among expatriates, they have limited appeal, and even among Scots they hardly dominate popular culture.

In the second half of the twentieth century, the persistent demand to maintain a Scottish label — the 'nationalism' in cultural bodies — does not on close inspection often seem to express determination to reject this world of one powerful culture in pursuit of greater emphasis on Scottish peculiarities. There are of course flourishing folk song clubs and societies, and no shortage of listeners for Scottish dance and music on the radio. Since 1892 An Commun Gaidhealach has been devoted to the preservation and revival on Gaelic, and in northern country areas meetings for Highland Games are more than tourist occasions. The Saltire Society, founded in 1936, aims to encourage the serious Scottish cultural traditions of the Lowlands and Highlands alike. There are courses in Scottish history and literature at most of the universities, and some attempt to insist on their place in the curricula of the schools. But such are not by any means characteristic of Scottish cultural life at any level. Much more typical are for example, the Scottish Football Association and the Scottish Amateur Athletic Association, devoted to playing international sport under a Scottish label, or the Scottish National Orchestra and Scottish Opera, devoted to performing international classical music under a Scottish label.

Such labelling is universal in European countries, and important. In Scotland (as in Denmark or Ireland) it stakes a claim for the country to be identifiable as part of the shared modern international culture. Without identification, society feels rootless and offended: in Scotland's case the alternative is to be unthinkingly associated with England, a state of affairs about which Scotland even after nearly three centuries of Parliamentary Union, remains as dissatisfied as Ireland would be, or as Denmark would be in association with Germany. There is a genuine and apparently irreducible core sense of being a nation simply in the use of the label, irrespective of the other aims of the organisation. On the other hand, without the shared modern culture, Scotland would not be a country of our time at all, but would appear even to herself as an isolated, anachronistic backwater. All modern European nations allow a slot for the traditional, expressed perhaps in the preservation of ancient monuments, 'heritage' museums and the encouragement of traditional music: none allocates more than a fairly minor role for this in social life. It is worth noting, though, that in the later 1980s more people paid in Scotland to visit museums, old castle, stately homes and similar places than went to football matches, the cinema and public arts performances put together.[5] The fact that England and Scotland have a shared language as well as a shared state has obscured the fact that in many other ways Scotland behaves in the twentieth century like other European nations.

In theoretical discussions about the character of Scottish nationalism over the years this has tended to be overlooked. Much anxious consideration has been afforded to the question of what Tom Nairn has called 'cultural sub-nationalism', that is to say to the attachment of Scots to such trivial symbols of distinction as tartans, kilts, shortbread and Granny's hieland hame.[6] It began in the 1930s with Hugh MacDiarmid's attack on the kailyard writers like Ian Maclaran and James Barrie, who wrote sentimental novels of rural and small town life with watery Scotch dialogue. For MacDiarmid, fighting for his own muscular political and lyrical poetry in Scots, a Scottish literary Renaissance depended on the prior demolition of such enervating parodies of reality. The Renaissance indeed followed: MacDiarmid and Edwin Muir were joined by Sorley Maclean in Gaelic poetry, by Lewis Grassic Gibbon and Neil Gunn as novelists, and by writers in Scots, English and Gaelic since the war like Ian Crichton Smith, Norman MacCaig, and Robert Garioch. The period since 1914 has been very distinguished in literature, but this had made little impact on popular consciousness, which would indeed identify the television series 'Dr Finlay's Casebook' as more quintessentially Scottish than MacDiarmid's great poems in 'a Drunk Man looks at the Thistle'. For Nairn, this is a fatal weakness in the national psyche, leading to a lack of political seriousness and a deformed sense of what constitutes the real Scotland. Barbara and Murray Grigor pursued these ideas in 1981 in their exhibition of 'Scotch Myths' in the Edinburgh Festival, a wonderful assemblage of tartan monstrosity and Scottish *kitsch*. Others on the left found the perpetuation of tartanry by the media sinister, the distillation of two centuries of British hegemonic rule trapping the Scots into a sense of their own inferiority in the face of Anglocentric culture.[7] David McCrone has cogently argued that much of this is far too solemn and over intellectualised. There is no advanced country in the modern western world that takes its own high literary culture as an important course of nationalist energy any more: 'in modern pluralistic societies no single "national" culture is to be found'.[8] Still less, of course, is there any evidence that those who watched 'Dr Finlay's Casebook' or wore tartan bonnets at football matches were ever profoundly affected in their political attitudes one way or the other.[9] Tartan, after all, is a label, and labels have their own simple and important purposes as means to identify.

To describe Scottish culture as conforming to a European norm, however true that may be, nevertheless conceals many changes, strains and distinctions in its recent history. It is, for example, emphatically an urban culture. In the course of the twentieth century the decline of the countryside has been related to the loss of much that was honoured in rural life, obliterated by the steam-roller of town values. James Littlejohn, studying the Borders in his classic of rural sociology, *Westrigg*, of 1963, maintained that depopulation of remote areas was by no means merely a matter of differing economic opportunity in country and town.[10] It was closely linked with the failure of country people to maintain their own belief in the validity of a rural way of life. In the localities he studied, shepherds and their families in isolated cottages first moved nearer the road and then to the villages, often apparently at the request of the wives, because they could not stand the loneliness: villagers moved to the country town to escape the lack of 'life' in the glen; the inhabitants of the country town chose Glasgow or Edinburgh because they, too, did not wish to be buried in the country. The younger generation were unhappy to be so far from the shops, the pubs, the dancehalls, the cinemas, a nexus of enjoyment and sociability portrayed first on the radio and in the press, later even more compellingly on television. Their elders in turn felt betrayed by children who would not share a complex inheritance of local values and customs that had given life meaning to generations past. Talk of a 'generation gap' was common everywhere in the 1950s and 1960s, nowhere more so than in such small towns and villages.

Nevertheless, depopulation was not only due to the preferences of the rural workers: the quality of rural life declined as the number of people in the villages fell and not everyone left of their own accord. The Border shepherd Andrew Purves has contrasted the former sociability of a large farm like Fogorig, near Duns in Berwickshire, where in 1927 twenty-eight regular workers were on the pay roll and a total population of about sixty on the farm — 'there was life, laughter and bustle in those days on the farms' — with the modern situation where 'the countryside is dead and the farm towns virtually deserted; the people who are left have become partly urbanised, having largely discarded the social and

21. Workers at Fife Radio and Television Company, Westgate, Crail, 1952. Cowie Photographic Collection, University of St Andrews.

22. Stooking near St Andrews, August 1936. Cowie Photographic Collection, University of St Andrews.

cultural links with their environment'.[11] For him, a watershed appeared in the late 1950s and 1960s, when 'the Lowland Clearances really got under way': arable workers were paid off because machines rendered them redundant, shepherds were sacked because barley paid better than sheep, and in some places whole farms were cleared for afforestation. The decline of population in the countryside has of course been a long drawn-out phenomenon, beginning in the nineteenth century, and continuing throughout the twentieth: as in all migrations the push and pull factors are hard to disentangle.

Other writers noted a new uniformity even within the countryside. One side effect of modern transport, (at first above all the daily rural bus services), modern education and the modern media was to diminish distinctions of character between small communities in the same region. The editor of the Fife volume of the *Third Statistical Account* put it well in 1952:

> Many variations will be seen, for there are still great contrasts between such communities as, say, Cowdenbeath and Crail, or even neighbours like Inverkeithing and Aberdour. Yet perhaps the most striking thing is how alike they have become in much that is fundamental. For an increasing number of people, the houses in which they live, the broad conditions under which they work, the educational system by which they are taught, and the type of entertainment they seek, have become very similar. As a result, there has been a standardisation of dress, of speech, of manners and of the whole attitude to life. Increased travel has worked in the same direction. . . . With this standardisation, opportunities and creature comforts have both become more plentiful, but whether happiness has increased is a point on which few people would care to make a firm pronouncement'.[12]

In localities where the cultural fortress of the older generation was distinctive and strong, the defence of tradition could be fierce and the contrast with modern life piquant. By the third quarter of the twentieth century, Gaelic speech had become largely restricted to the Hebrides. Total numbers of Gaelic speakers declined from 6.85 per cent of the Scottish population in 1891 (254,000, of whom about one sixth spoke only Gaelic) to 1.66 of the population in 1961 (81,000, of whom less than a thousand spoke only Gaelic). The reasons for the decline of Gaelic are complex, connected both with the pressures of the 1872 Education Act and its successors and an understandable demand from parents in Gaelic-speaking families that the children must be taught fluent English if they were to 'get on in life'. In the postwar period, the largest concentration of Gaelic speakers was living on the Isle of Lewis which also enjoyed (if that is the right word) an exceptionally strong tradition of Calvinist fundamentalism. By the 1980s, however, there was no sign of either the language or the religion being extinguished here: the former had become, for the first time, the official language of local government in the Western Isles following the reorganisation of local government in the 1970s, and the latter had, as late as 1989, compelled MacBrayne's to withdraw their threat (or offer) of Sunday ferries. On the other hand, in the twentieth century many concessions had been made: dancehalls, for example, arrived in the teeth of kirk opposition, and cinemas. No-one was able to prevent the youth of Stornoway in the 1980s following the latest rock bands on their stereo equipment or eating pizza like the youth of Glasgow. There was uneasy co-existence between the values of yesterday and tomorrow.

It is also possible to consider culture distinctions in Scotland (as all over Britain) as determined by class and gender. So much of Scottish life is still, as it has long been, determined by social class. A middle-class family was likely to live in their own house, a working-class family in the early decades of our period in rented accommodation, later in a council house. The middle class at least in the larger towns was likely to send their children to grant-aided or independent schools, the working class to public sector schools. The middle-class man at work was likely to eat in the management canteen apart from the worker. It is therefore not surprising to find that leisure and recreation patterns were also largely correlated with class.

In sport, the working class have traditionally provided almost all the spectators at football matches, the middle class those at Rugby matches, except perhaps in the Borders. Expense as well as prestige made deer stalking, salmon fishing and grouse shooting exclusive preserves of the upper class; the farm labourer might have his ferret for rabbits, and the miner his whippet for hares. Cock-fighting, common in all areas and among most classes in the early nineteenth century, was still surviving illegally in Fife mining communities in the 1930s, despite RSPCA awards of £500 for information leading to the arrest of offenders.[13] Dog racing and probably most gambling (apart from that which is also the diversion of the very rich) have also always been amusements of the working class; attending concerts, the theatre (except Pantomime), and art galleries is middle class. Draughts was a working-class game: in the interwar period a world champion was a Fife miner from Kelty. Other diversions are largely gender specific. When a new use began to be found for the hundreds of redundant cinemas driven out of business by television in the 1960s, most of those who attended the bingo halls which occupied the premises were working-class women of middle age or older: but few Scots women of any age have ever been to a football match or the dog races.

Such things are not, however, fixed for all time. Before the first world war, though there was a substantial problem of female drunkenness, the public house was nevertheless not a place where a 'respectable' woman would be seen. In the interwar years, observers concluded that pubs were a safe haven for men: Edwin Muir and Hugh MacDiarmid did not agree on much, but the first described the males of Edinburgh fleeing to the bar away from the sexual encounters of the streets, 'to wrap themselves in the safe cloak of alcohol', and the second praised the drinking dens of Glasgow as female-free refuges.[14] By the 1950s, however, boozing apartheid was on its way out, as more and more women gained a toehold in the lounge bar and eased their way into the public bar when the distinction between these two areas declined. It vanished after the Clayson Committee, the subsequent liberalisation of the licencing laws and, in the 1970s and 1980s, the advent of bar meals and smart décor. The pub eventually became a place of relaxation almost irrespective of sex, age and class, one of the few truly democratic social institutions in Scottish life.

Drinking patterns themselves, however, retained some quite striking class and gender characteristics. In a survey of 1972, Susan Dight demonstrated that 86 per cent of all that was drunk in Scotland in a typical week was consumed by men, and only 14 per cent by women. The younger the person, the more likely they were to be regular drinkers. In households headed by a professional, 76 per cent of the men and 74 per cent of the women were regular drinkers, but in households headed by semi-skilled or manual workers, 73 per cent of the men but only 28 per cent of the women were regular drinkers. In other words, social position made little difference to the number of males who drank regularly, but it had a considerable effect on the number of wives who drank. Furthermore, among regular drinkers in all social classes men drank much larger amounts of alcohol than women (by a factor of three or four), but regular drinkers among men at the foot of the class ladder drank nearly half as much again as those at the top. The young unskilled worker downing several pints a night in the male camaraderie of the pub was still perfectly identifiable.[15]

Some other aspects of recreation have also changed in an interesting way since 1900. In the Edwardian cities there was a much livelier tradition of working class performance of serious music than there is today, based on the enthusiasm of temperance societies and some of the ILP and socialist groups, reaching its apogee with the formation in

1906 of Hugh Roberton's Orpheus Choir in Glasgow, which attained a world reputation for choral performances in the interwar years. That died away with the tradition of self-help sociable amusement that gave it birth, and the choir was itself wound up shortly before Roberton's death in 1952. When the Edinburgh International Festival was founded in 1947 by Rudolf Bing, it transformed the capital into a major centre for the performing arts at least for three weeks every year, but the working class neither made the music nor attended the performances. In the early years of the festival Yehudi Menuhin in a missionary spirit took his violin to the council estates, but, as with most missionaries, his message fell on singularly deaf ears. Glasgow's Mayfest three decades later had a more popular character in every sense, but hardly recreated the Orpheus tradition.

Popular recreation in Glasgow in the first half of this century has been the subject of some dispute among historians. Douglas Allen speaks of a 'socialist counter-culture' in the city which could take the devotee 'from the cradle to the grave', beginning with the induction of basic socialist principles through the Socialist Sunday Schools, with further study of socialism through Clarion and ILP branches, then providing sporting activity on Clarion cycle outings and swimming with the Socialist Amateur Swimming Club, shopping at the Co-op, exercising artistic talent through the Scottish Socialist Art Circle, or one of a variety of socialist choirs, and taking part in an annual Socialist drama festival.[16] Elspeth King, while denying none of the vigour of the socialist organisations, stresses that they were only one group among others, the temperance and evangelical societies making at least an equal contribution prior to the First World War, and, for that matter, private enterprise and municipal provision also catering for popular taste in the music halls, the cinemas, the fairs and the parks. Few people belonged only to one cultural circle exclusively: most enjoyed different entertainments provided by different groups and organisations.[17]

In any case, the world of socialist entertainment itself largely mimicked the world of bourgeois entertainment in its form and values. An interesting exception to this emerged in the later 1930s in a type of drama known as 'agit-prop' and 'agit-realism', which affected in particular the Kino Film Group in Glasgow, and the Glasgow Workers' Theatre Group, both involved in depicting the class struggle in the Spanish Civil War.[18] In the 1970s, the rise to national reputation of John MacGrath's 7:84 theatre group, with its productions of the Scottish and British class war in 'the Cheviot, the Stag and the Black Black Oil', and 'The Little Red Hen' was even more remarkable. The aim of these productions was to drive home the ideological message of anti-fascism and of revolutionary socialism. They were undeniably popular, the 7:84 group, for instance, playing to packed houses throughout the crofting communities of the west coast. Whether they raised socialist consciousness is another matter.

Certainly in the second half of the twentieth century it becomes even less appropriate to speak of a working-class culture separate from a middle-class culture, and clearly not of an enveloping socialist counter-culture. In any period, correlations of patterns of recreation with class are often merely correlations with disposable income and spare time. In other words, you enjoy what you can afford when you have the chance. With a general rise in the standard of living, increasingly evident after 1950, the exclusive cultural preserve of one social group could in a remarkably short space start to become the general property of others.

Holidays are a case in point. In Victorian and Edwardian times the Firth of Clyde was the playground of all classes, but not to an equal degree.[19] The rich could take a family villa for months in the summer at Rothesay or Dunoon, the father working in Glasgow and travelling by steamer to be with them at weekends or vacations. The working class family remained largely confined to the tenements of Maryhill or Govan, but went together 'doon the watter' on the steamers on bank holidays, briefly and sometimes riotously disembarking at the piers: hence 'steaming drunk'. In the Highlands, the hills were left to the wealthy shooters and anglers in the sporting lodges, the glens to middle-class romantic tourists packing the big new hydro hotels: Fife miners might manage to Pitlochry by excursion train on the annual outing. A few generations later, cheap boarding houses were providing for short working class and lower middle class holidays away from home, for example at Dunbar or by the cold beaches of Portobello and east Fife. In the countryside, rambling began as early as the 1850s, and cycling was a craze by the 1890s, but in the 1930s the Scottish Youth Hostel Association and various rambling clubs in the West of Scotland were introducing the youth of all classes to Argyll and Lochlomondside to an extent undreamed of before, fuelling renewed political demands for an Access to the Mountains Bill, and also for National Parks envisaged as wild places where the population could roam at will.[20] Rural interests fought off these campaigns, but the Forestry Commission took the lead in making land available to the public by providing National Forest Parks with facilities for camping and walking, the first at Cowal in 1936, with three more by 1954.[21]

After the Second World War, the advent almost universally of two or three weeks holiday with pay, combined with rising incomes, better roads, more cars and cheap package air holidays, transformed popular leisure again. Even the remotest parts of the Highlands came within reach of the ordinary tourist, but by the 1960s in the youth hostels the numbers of young Scots began to fall, though the numbers of young foreigners on holiday in Scotland increased. Traditional Scottish resorts were becoming deserted as travel abroad became commonplace: 'why don't they come back to Dunoon', sang Billy Connolly with soulful irony. The young skilled working class from the 1960s and 1970s made for Benidorm and Majorca, while the middle class reached with their extra pounds to get marginally further away to Greece, even to Turkey. Scots joined the throng on the beaches with Germans, Scandinavians, Dutch, French and English in an international cultural habit as compulsive as pop, of trying to turn almost all of their bodies brown in a fortnight.

Many outdoor recreations have seen a similar process of filtering down the class scale. Mountain climbing from its inception as a serious hobby in the 1880s was exclusively a middle and upper class pursuit, part of the new fad for physical sports crossed with a dash of traditional romantic tourism. So was skiing, from its introduction in the decade before the First World War, though here the thrill of speed decisively eclipsed the admiration for nature. By the 1930s when access to the hills came within reach of so many more, the unemployed of Glasgow began to climb the Munroes. The first ski developments contemplated at Aviemuir in the 1950s have been called 'an altruistic private venture designed to tempt the youth of Scotland's crowded industrial towns, Glasgow in particular, to learn to appreciate the open air and an exhilarating sport'.[22] When the chairlifts were ultimately opened they were an instantaneous success — 80,000 used them in the first nine months of their operation in 1962. Now all forms of hill walking, climbing, skiing and watersports are popular with most social groups, with consequently immense pressure on areas like Speyside at week-ends: it should be added that many parts of these sports are so circumscribed by access to disposable income that only the young and best paid among the workers are likely to be able to play much part.

Bird-watching provides a particularly arresting example of changing social composition in an outdoor activity. When the Royal Society for the Protection of Birds was founded in 1889, it was largely the preserve, both in its organisation and its membership, of well-heeled English ladies; a Scottish equivalent, the Scottish Society for the Protection of Wild Birds appeared in the 1920s, with a similar structure. To both bodies, the working-class appeared mainly as a menace, full of bird-trappers and youthful birds' nesters. The RSPB became transformed into a popular middle-class body around the middle of the century, opened a Scottish headquarters in 1954, and embarked on an extraordinary increase in membership that made it one of the most successful voluntary societies of our age.[23] By 1987 it had 440,000 UK members, including some 18,000 in Scotland, more than the membership of any political party (but compare the National Trust for Scotland, with about 110,000). By the start of the decade, more and more Scottish working class bird-watchers were coming to raise their binoculars alongside the middle class ones, though in the former there were many males and few females, in the latter more equality of numbers between the sexes. Scotland, however, remains distinctly less green than England, as measured, for example, by votes for the Green Party in the 1989 European elections, RSPB and Wildlife Trust members per head of population, and uptake of Nature Conservancy Council grants to schools.

It has often been suggested that one of the cultural transformations of our century has been the rise of 'privatism' — in less ugly language, the replacement of a way of life that stressed mutual interdependence and sociability with one that emphasises the individual, the nuclear family and privacy.[24]

There is no doubt that for many people, over a long period, there has been such a change. The workplace is often cited as an example. In a traditional agrarian society work in many cases was sociable: the farming year included haymaking and harvesting which were occasions for the whole community to work together in the fields, and gathering peats, rounding up animals, hoeing crops and carting also involved working together: meals were taken together in the farm house, often with the farmer. Almost all of life was taken up with labour, and on the one rest day in the week the only approved activity, that of going to the kirk, was also a communal one. In the one-room house where the parents and their children lived there was some privacy on the level of the family, but hardly any on that of the individual.

Early industry was scarcely less communal, though the distance from the employer increasingly widened, and the sheer pressure of factory employment made it less sociable than the work-place culture of the farm. In a great factory, such as those in the jute trade of Dundee or the cotton trade of the West of Scotland, a thousand or more hands might be employed, but working from dawn to dusk, at unremitting speed amid noisy machinery: interaction between the workers on the job would be more limited here than in those parts of the industrial scene that still retained much of the organisation of pre-industrial times, like a building site or a shipyard. Miners, of course, developed a particularly strong workplace culture, that spread and enveloped the whole of a community in an ethic of solidarity. Their feelings of distinctiveness went back to the eighteenth-century days of serfdom, and class consciousness arose easily in an environment where the men worked together below ground in a beastly and dangerous environment while the bosses organised production above ground in comfortable boardrooms. A community like Lumphinnans in Fife became a 'Little Moscow' in the 1920s and 1930s, reacting to the strikes and lock-outs of the declining interwar coalfields with a fierce militancy, left wing candidates being elected to take over the parish council and the local education authority, even the Old Folk's Treat Committee, the Children's Gala Committee, the committee of the new Welfare Institute and the ex-servicemen's association.[25]

Strong cultures of this sort could develop in many trades; the dockers were similar in the earlier twentieth century, despite a broken pattern of hiring, and in many skilled trades a pride in association was reflected in voluntary associations ranging from unions and friendly societies to gardening and rambling clubs. They tended, though, to concern men more than women: a survey of Lanarkshire miners in the Second World War showed that the cinema, football matches, the pub union meetings, the welfare institute and the library all attracted participation from 25 per cent or more of the respondents, but for women it was only shopping, the cinema and the church. They might or might not be associated with political activism: Alexandria in the Vale of Leven was another 'Little Moscow' in a textile printing centre, but this was exceptional.[26]

As the twentieth century proceeded, many things changed. Some jobs certainly became much more isolated: few are more solitary than modern farm workers ploughing a field or using a combine harvester. Most remained the same — as in the building trades — or showed a mixture of old and new styles: in the 1980s the very modern paper-mill of Tullis Russell at Glenrothes had the production line managed by computers and a few highly trained technicians, but quality control maintained by a squad of girls sifting the paper by hand at speed in an entirely Victorian way. As older industries collapsed — coal-mining, ship-building, steel — or became 'deskilled', as in much of engineering — what was distinctive and sociable about their workplace culture and that of the communities around them, collapsed as well. The gap was filled by the homogenising forces of modern popular culture of which we have already spoken. Nevertheless, for most people it is still true that the work-place, whether it is a factory or an office, remains a theatre of sociability, in contrast to the home as a theatre of privacy. Perhaps the main change has been that there is much less often a carry-over of workplace cultures to the local community itself.

Outside the workplace, change came about through a combination of more free time, larger houses and more disposable income. Free time and money created the opportunity (but not the necessity) for more privacy and individual relaxation: on a free Saturday an affluent man by the 1960s might go to the football match with his friends or take his wife and children for a drive in the country (if he had a car), but at least there was a choice.

The replacement of houses of one and two rooms with those with three, four and five, which came about largely as a result of the council house programme especially after the Second World War, reduced the pressure to get out of the home and into the pub, or the union meeting. In Edwardian Scotland, commentators had claimed that men were driven into the public houses in the evening by the claustrophobia of a two-room flat occupied by a harassed wife and crying children, and many observed the vigour of Scottish street life: the many children's street games, the women spending much time together sitting in the stair ways or standing on the kerbs, the crowds walking together to see and to be seen. First the coming of the radio in the 1920s, then, especially the coming of television in the 1960s, along with wider car ownership killed all that. With a larger house a family is likely to spend more time inside it: the 1977 General Household Survey showed that 53 per cent of the adult population of Great Britain listed DIY among their leisure activities.[27] There was, in the previous decade, a switch from going out to the cinema and the dance hall to staying in, watching films, sport and top-of-the-pops on television.

For women, life should in theory have offered more time for being sociable, as a lot of the sheer slog went out of daily chores associated with childcare and housework. Washing, which as late as 1950 had occupied at least one day a week in hard labour, was relieved by washing machines; cooking was made easier by gas or electricity (as late as 1945 over half British households used coal for cooking, with all the attendant labour and dirt of the stove and hauling the fuel up); cleaning was greatly eased not only by vacuum cleaners but by clean air legislation. 'Auld Reekie', with the attendant tedium of coal dust, smoke, grimy clothing, became a legend instead of an unpleasant reality. However, some of the communality also went out of working-class women's life as the sociability of the common washing green and the 'steamies' —

the public laundries — disappeared. A middle class woman at the start of the period, in charge of a household of four or five children and several servants, had been a manager of labour and resources in her own home; by the end, she was in danger of being reduced, by the decline of domestic service and the rise of 'labour saving devices', to a general labourer working on her own.

It is, nevertheless, possible to exaggerate the extent to which social culture has declined. The pub, that age-old gathering ground of Scottish people, has survived, altered, more comfortable, more family-centred (or at least couple-centred) but at least as popular as ever. Eating out in public is more popular than it was in the past. Outdoor sporting clubs proliferate for the young and fit, and various hobby activities enjoyed in company, from evening classes to aerobics, amuse the older and less fit. The middle class have usually appeared to be less sociable than the working class, perhaps because they are more competitive, perhaps because larger incomes gives them the choice of greater privacy: on the other hand they are generally the bulk of the membership of active voluntary societies today. Even in working class circles one is now unlikely to find the world of Tom Bell's autobiography, describing a Glasgow of around 1900 where neighbours loaned wash tubs and wringers to one another, or men their suits to friends for a wedding or a funeral.[28] But there is still a warmth in relationships between families and friends, ritually celebrated at Hogmanay but also present on ordinary occasions of need and festivity. Despite the television, the video game and the net curtains, people are still ready to emerge from their dens of privacy to visit acquaintances, play in a crowd and make common cause. We are still, and for ever, one of Nature's social animals.

Is Scotland then less Scottish than it was? We have emphasised in this account many things that made the Scots alter old habits, modify old loyalties, follow new fashions, enjoy new cultural opportunities. Scotland, England and every other country are travelling down the same river of time which at this point tends to draw together and dilute national characteristics. As we move we change, and all are apparently becoming more alike, tending to conform to an international cultural norm. Change itself is inevitable, and to hope for a distinctiveness that is based only on preservation of Scottish things as they used to be is quite fruitless. On the other hand, conforming itself is only a tendency, and there is no very clear reason to maintain that Scotland is losing her cultural peculiarities faster than, say, Ireland, England or Sweden. In many ways Scottish institutions have proved very adaptable

23. Sports day at West Wemyss, 1938. Cowie Photographic Collection, University of St Andrews.

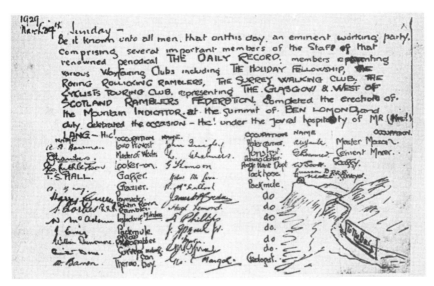

24. The *Daily Record* staff at leisure, 1929. Cowie Photographic Collection, University of St Andrews.

and durable in a British state that has only grudgingly decentralised any power: Scottish education, law, the churches, the Scottish trades union movement, none of these shows signs of totally giving way, becoming moribund, or absorbed in English institutions. Scottish party political life is still distinctive. The Gaelic movement is more lively than it was, even though it is regional rather than national. Devolution as a political programme becomes again more popular, not less.

So the story in 1990 is of a society which, in cultural terms, has survived nearly three centuries of Union in fairly good heart. Lord Cockburn's earnest desires are fulfilled to a degree he might not have expected, and if all is not as that great Whig would have wished, perhaps not everything would fill him with despair either. Scotland has still resonance and meaning as a room in the common European home, not just as a tartan rug on the English floor.

NOTES

1. Henry Cockburn, *Journal, 1831–1854* (Edinburgh, 1874), vol II, pp. 301–302.

2. H. M. Begg, C. M. Lythe, R. Sorley, *Expenditure in Scotland, 1961–1971* (Edinburgh, 1975).

3. *Scottish Abstract of Statistics* (HMSO, 1972).

4. John Scott and Michael Hughes, *The Anatomy of Scottish capital* (London, 1980).

5. *Scotland's Heritage: the Work of the Scottish Office and the National Library, National Galleries and National Museums of Scotland* (HMSO, 1989), p. 5.

6. Tom Narin, *The Break-up of Britain* (London, 1977).

7. Colin McArthur (ed.), *Scotch Reels, Scotland in Cinema and Television* (London, 1982).

8. David McCrone, 'Representing Scotland: culture and nationalism', in D. McCrone, S. Kendrick and P. Straw (eds.), *The Making of Scotland: Nation, Culture and Social Change* (Edinburgh, 1989), pp. 161–174.

9. Craig Beveridge and Ronald Turnbull, *The Eclipse of Scottish Culture* (Edinburgh, 1989), p. 14.

10. James Littlejohn, *Westrigg: the Sociology of a Cheviot Parish* (London, 1963).

11. Andrew Purves, 'A shepherd remembers', *Journal of the Scottish Labour History Society*, no. 15 (1981), pp. 26–33.

12. Alexander Smith, *The Third Statistical Account of Scotland*, vol 2 (Fife), p. 83.

13. George Beattie, 'The Scottish miner and his game cock'. *Scots Magazine*, vol 27 (1937), pp. 213–217.

14. Edwin Muir, *Scottish Journey* (Edinburgh, 1979 edn.), p. 19; Hugh Macdiarmid, 'The dour drinkers of Glasgow', in *The Uncanny Scot* (London, 1968).

15. Susan E. Dight, *Scottish Drinking Habits* (HMSO, 1976).

16. Douglas Allen, '"Culture" and the Scottish Labour movement', *Journal of the Scottish Labour History Society*, no. 14 (1980), pp. 30–39.

17. Elspeth King, 'Popular culture in Glasgow', in R. A. Cage (ed.), *The Working Class in Glasgow, 1750–1914* (London, 1987), pp. 142–187.

18. Allen, '"Culture"', pp. 32–34.

19. King, 'Popular culture', pp. 167–169.

20. John Sheail, *Rural Conversation in Inter-War Britain* (Oxford, 1981);

21. Gordon Cherry, *National Parks and Recreation in the Countryside: Environmental Planning 1939–1969*, vol 2 (HMSO, 1975), pp. 67–80, 141–152.

22. Dudley Stamp, *Nature Conservation in Britain* (London, 1969), p. 171.

23. Tony Samstag, *For Love of Birds. The Story of the Royal Society for the Protection of Birds, 1889–1988* (RSPB, 1988).

24. Steve Kendrick, 'Scotland, social change and politics', in McCrone, Kendrick and Straw (eds.), *The Making of Scotland*, pp. 83–86.

25. Stuart Macintyre, *Little Moscows: Communism and Working-class Militancy in Inter-war Britain* (London, 1980), p. 60.

26. *Ibid.*, pp. 79–108, 139.

27. Gordon Cherry, *Leisure and the Home* (Birmingham, 1982).

28. Tom Bell, *Pioneering Days* (London, 1941), p. 17.

Index